Courting the Virgin Queen

Courting the Virgin Queen

Queen Elizabeth I and Her Suitors

Carol Ann Lloyd

PEN & SWORD
HISTORY

First published in Great Britain in 2024 by
Pen & Sword History
An imprint of Pen & Sword Books Limited
Yorkshire – Philadelphia

ISBN 978 1 39904 342 7

A CIP catalogue record for this book is available from the British Library

Typeset by Mac Style
Printed in the UK by CPI Group (UK) Ltd, Croydon, CR0 4YY.

MIX
Paper | Supporting responsible forestry
FSC® C013604

Pen & Sword Books Limited incorporates the imprints of After the Battle, Atlas, Archaeology, Aviation, Discovery, Family History, Fiction, History, Maritime, Military, Military Classics, Politics, Select, Transport, True Crime, Air World, Frontline Publishing, Leo Cooper, Remember When, Seaforth Publishing, The Praetorian Press, Wharncliffe Local History, Wharncliffe Transport, Wharncliffe True Crime and White Owl.

For a complete list of Pen & Sword titles please contact

PEN & SWORD BOOKS LIMITED
47 Church Street, Barnsley, South Yorkshire, S70 2AS, England
E-mail: enquiries@pen-and-sword.co.uk
Website: www.pen-and-sword.co.uk
or
PEN AND SWORD BOOKS
1950 Lawrence Rd, Havertown, PA 19083, USA
E-mail: uspen-and-sword@casematepublishers.com
Website: www.penandswordbooks.com

To my mother, Karen Marie Nelson Lloyd, a fiery redhead
who lived life on her own terms and taught me to do the same.

Contents

Acknowledgements

It would not have been possible to write this book without the support and affection of many people.

I so appreciate all the kind and helpful staff at the National Archives UK and the British Library. I was able to read and work with documents that I have long dreamed of spending time with in person. Each trip was a remarkable experience, and I am so grateful for all the support.

I'm also fortunate enough to have been able to spend time speaking with many of the leading historians of the Tudor period. I thank them for taking time to meet with me and to join me on my podcast. I appreciate and admire the marvellous research they have conducted and shared with the people.

I want to thank all the folks at Pen and Sword Books who have made this journey such an exciting adventure. Many thanks to Sarah-Beth Watkins, who first helped me create the vision of this book and has supported me all along the way. I also thank Cecily Blench, Laura Hirst, Lucy May and the other editors and team members who have so generously helped with this project.

I also thank my friends and family who have been my foundation and inspiration at every step. My colleague and friend Lindsey Lindstrom has continued to be my podcast partner, my first and most reliable reader and reviewer, and my cheerleader. I also thank my family, who are my heart and the best part of my life. I thank my mother, who always believed in me and whose spirit and support I feel every day. I thank my brother and his family, who always remind me that I am loved and who never miss a chance to make me laugh. I thank my husband Marv, who managed to look past the piles of books and papers that filled tables and couches and the floor, to find me and keep me on track. His support of research trips and nights spent writing was the foundation of my being able to complete this project. I also thank my daughter Chelsea and her husband Lance for their support and love. And finally, I am thankful for my three little granddaughters, Elise, Olivia, and Claire. I write about the past to help them imagine their future.

Introduction

Elizabeth Tudor was in 1533 born as a princess and heir to the throne of her father, Henry VIII. Before she turned 3 years old, she had been declared illegitimate and banished from the succession and from her father's court after he had her mother, Anne Boleyn, executed. Ultimately, she was returned to last place in the succession in the time of her fourth stepmother and her father's final wife, Katherine Parr. Elizabeth grew up in and out of favour in the reigns of her father, her half-brother, and her half-sister. All three of them reinforced Elizabeth's illegitimacy, making her life and her road to the throne increasingly difficult.

Elizabeth's first suitor arrived when she was still an infant, when she was considered as a possible bride for the son of the French king. From that point, other matches were considered for her. That's not surprising – as the daughter of a king, she would be expected to be married into a royal house to make an alliance for her family.

Against all odds, Elizabeth came to the throne in November 1558. Surprisingly, she was still unmarried. Her marriage one of the first topics taken up in her first parliament, and her marriage continued to be centre stage for her privy council and parliament as well as international discussions.

The story of Elizabeth's suitors incorporates the life of a young woman who had plenty of reasons to avoid marriage, a queen who faced threats to her reign on every side, and a woman who could never trust that she was appreciated for herself and not just for her crown. She navigated her place in the world, holding onto her crown while dancing through relationships that entertained her and, as far as she could manage, served the country.

There are many reasons that Elizabeth didn't marry. We can never know the feelings of her heart or her intent for the future. She frequently said she preferred the single life, and she frequently said she would marry. She positioned herself as wife to and mother of her kingdom, and she assured her council and parliament she would become a wife to a husband and mother of an heir. She well understood the values and the dangers of marrying and the values and dangers of remaining single.

At the end of her reign, Elizabeth died as the only English monarch who ruled as an adult and never married. At the start of her reign, Elizabeth is reported to have said that she would prefer to come to the end of her reign having 'lived and died a virgin'. She evolved from being a young, attractive, and eligible virgin, the most sought-after bachelorette of Europe, to becoming the unassailable Virgin Queen, symbolising the independence of her nation. The story of that evolution involves Elizabeth, the men who served at her court, the foreign leaders who considered her a valuable tool for an alliance, the English courtiers who thought she would make a profitable wife, a foreign ruler who wanted her as a daughter-in-law, a relative who wanted her kingdom, and the one love that remained until the end of her days.

This is the story of courting the Virgin Queen.

Part I

The Young Queen and the Changing World

Chapter 1

Now but 'My Lady Elizabeth'

There goeth rumours abroad which be greatly both against mine honour and honesty, which above all other things I esteem.

Elizabeth Tudor to Edward Seymour, Lord Protector, 28 January 1549 (Elizabeth I, *Collected Works*, p. 24)

The king, the queen, and probably everyone at court was awaiting the birth. The women helping the queen during her labour knew the importance of this child, as did the pages and servants in the corridors. Thomas Cromwell knew, and Thomas Cranmer knew. The Boleyns probably knew as well as anyone. This child must be a healthy boy.

That was what all expected. Physicians and astrologers and friends and family had assured the king that this time, it would be a healthy boy. This time, the child would be the heir he had hoped and prayed for since taking the throne nearly twenty-five years earlier. King Henry VIII had confidence in the promises. After all, he had done his part. He had turned to scripture to find the problem with his marriage to Katherine of Aragon, the woman who had been at his side all those years and failed, in his mind at least, to provide him the needed son. She had borne him a daughter, one he loved but who could not succeed him on the throne. A strong country needed a strong king. So, God must have been displeased if He was denying Henry this most important gift.

The king, driven by his conscience and devotion, at least as he saw it, worked hard to secure an annulment. And, when that effort finally failed, he had taken the drastic step of breaking with Rome and becoming Supreme Head of the Church of England. For the rest of his reign, he would glory in his facing down the pope and going his own way.

At this moment, early in the morning of 7 September 1533, there was no need for justification. Anne Boleyn, his new wife, had promised him a son. He had based everything on that, put the two of them through a lengthy and tortured courtship that lasted nearly seven years. He had crowned her publicly at Westminster Abbey with St Edward's crown – something typically reserved for monarchs, not their wives. That crown reinforced the message that the son Anne was carrying was his true heir, his great accomplishment, the future of the Tudor dynasty.[1]

The letters were already written, ready to proclaim the birth of a prince. The celebrations were planned, great jousts and a grand christening. The birth of this son would make it publicly evident that Henry had been right to do the things that were so unpopular with his people: to put aside Katherine of Aragon, to break with Rome, to upend religion and politics, to create tensions with Catholic Europe and the Holy Roman Emperor, and to marry Anne Boleyn. God would reward him. After all, he was a faithful son of the church as far as he was concerned, named 'Defender of the Faith' in 1521. True, he had broken with the pope, but not with his faith and not with God. He was defending faith and his nation. God would reward him with a son who would rule England and extend the glories of the Tudor dynasty.

God did send Henry a child who would rule England for more than forty years and extend the Tudor dynasty into the next century. That child would be successful in the face of Spanish and Catholic threats and preserve the new religion in England. That child would oversee a flowering of music and art and theatre, a growth of trade and exploration, and an economic and cultural shift that would make London one of the world's most important cities. And that child would accomplish something Henry VIII could not have imagined: remain unmarried and refuse to provide an heir. That child was Elizabeth.

The birth of a daughter was a huge blow to Henry and Anne. Their marriage did not immediately fall apart, and Anne became pregnant again at least twice. But the focus on this child, the rush to make sure the marriage was proclaimed valid by Archbishop Cranmer, the visible presence of this child in Anne's coronation where her pregnancy was so obvious – all that was, as far as Henry was concerned, for nothing. A girl.

Elizabeth's birth did not provide Henry with the male heir he so desperately wanted, but it did provide him with a powerful tool for making alliances abroad. After all, that's what daughters of kings were for. They were useful to dangle in front of ambassadors as potential prizes when treaties brought nations together. Elizabeth became a potential pawn in an alliance with France a few months after she was born. But after three years of marriage to the king, Anne Boleyn had failed to provide her husband a son and heir. In 1536, everything changed for Elizabeth.

She was declared illegitimate and removed from the succession. Her status changed from favoured princess, a beloved daughter even if not a son, to child of a whore who had not been legally married to the king. Elizabeth was banished from court and the succession. Her governess, Lady Bryan, described the chaos in the young girl's household, with servants no longer certain of the child's status or how she should be treated. Lady Bryan also had to plead with Thomas Cromwell, one of the architects of Anne Boleyn's fall, for clothing for now Lady Elizabeth as she grew.

The failure of her mother to provide the king with a son and the dissolution of their marriage completely reshaped Elizabeth's life. Anne Boleyn's enemies had not only ended her marriage to the king, but they had also branded her as sexually depraved. She was charged with having seduced five men, even her own brother. Once her marriage was dissolved, this should have made the adultery charge void. But this wasn't about facts – in her day, even some of Anne Boleyn's enemies were surprised by the charges and the weakness of the prosecution against her. She was praised for the way she defended herself at her trial. But none of that mattered. Her executioner had been summoned from France even before her trial began. Her fate was sealed. She would die, and she would die an evil woman.

The spectre of her mother's reputation haunted Elizabeth for the rest of her life. Catholics did not accept the validity of her parents' marriage.

Even though Henry VIII himself never doubted her paternity, her half-sister Mary Tudor claimed Elizabeth looked like Mark Smeaton or Sir Henry Norris, two of the men Anne was accused of sleeping with. Slanders about Elizabeth often referred to her mother's failings. The destruction of Anne's reputation had been carefully planned to eliminate her, and it was used by Elizabeth's enemies for the rest of her life.

After the succession act of 1537 declared her legally illegitimate and officially removed her from the succession, Elizabeth's chance of becoming queen seemed over. It made it difficult for an advantageous marriage to be made for her. Elizabeth played some roles as the king's daughter for the rest of Henry VIII's reign. She was primarily away from court, but she did return for the christening of her half-brother Prince Edward. Since she was only 4 years old, she probably didn't understand much of what was going on. But she would have seen as she got older the obvious preference everyone had for her younger brother. No matter how well she or Mary did in their studies or tried to please the king, their brother would always be first.

Elizabeth attended and saw the fallout of her father's weddings. She was present at Henry's wedding to Anne of Cleves, and at age 6 she watched her father end that marriage and quickly move on to marry one of her very young ladies-in-waiting. She was 8 when the marriage to Catherine Howard fell apart and the teenage queen was sent to her death. She was 10 when her father married again, and she attended the quiet wedding to Katherine Parr at Hampton Court Palace.

Katherine Parr was a caring stepmother to her royal children. She created a family atmosphere, and although Elizabeth was still primarily away from court, she did spend more time there with Katherine as queen. When Henry left England in 1544 for his final attempt to conquer France, he named Katherine as Regent. Elizabeth had the opportunity to see Katherine in this role, working effectively with her male advisors. In conjunction with the dangers of warfare, Henry revised the succession once more. The third succession act returned Mary and Elizabeth to the line of succession after Edward and his heirs. Perhaps the influence of his intelligent and lively sixth wife encouraged Henry to think more highly of his daughters. In any case, the parameters of the act made it clear that if either Mary or Elizabeth married without the permission of the council, they would be removed from the succession (again). Elizabeth must have understood well that for her, marriage would not be primarily a personal decision. Controlling her marriage was a powerful way of controlling her.

During Henry's final illness, he sent his family away. Edward was brought to Elizabeth's household, where they were told that their father had died, and Edward was now King Edward VI. Elizabeth moved to Katherine Parr's household shortly after Henry VIII's death. It was here that another marriage possibility would emerge, one that would threaten her reputation and even her life.

As widow and queen dowager, Katherine Parr was expected to go into deep mourning for her royal husband. Those at court probably thought she would never marry again. After all, Henry had provided well for her. People assumed that a woman who had been widowed three times must be older and ready to just live quietly. Not so with Katherine. She wrote that she had been in love and had been planning to marry someone else before she caught the king's eye. This someone else was Thomas Seymour.

The Seymour family came into power at the Tudor court when Henry married Jane. Her two brothers, Edward and Thomas, had stayed at court and enjoyed comfortable status as Prince Edward's uncles. Jane had died at the height of Henry's love for her, just after she gave him a son, so her family remained in high favour as well. Henry VIII's will that dictated that upon his death, a council would help young Edward rule the country. Henry did not wish to have a Lord Protector named. But as the old king lay dying, Edward Seymour began negotiating for greater power. He arranged to have Henry VIII's death kept secret for a few days so he could finish his plans. He was the one who took Edward to be with Elizabeth, he was the one who informed them of Henry VIII's death, and then he was the one who told them that he was the new Lord Protector.

As Edward Seymour, now Duke of Somerset (hereafter called 'Somerset' to distinguish him from his brother), consolidated power, his brother Thomas hoped for a good position for himself. Somerset made his brother Lord Admiral of the Navy and Baron Sudeley, but Seymour wanted more. Some historians believe that immediately after Henry VIII's death and Somerset's consolidation of power, Seymour considered marrying one of the late king's daughters as a way to move himself into the inner circle and circumvent his brother's access to power. In particular, Seymour seems to have wished to marry Elizabeth.

According to the later testimony from Katherine Ashley, Elizabeth's governess, and Thomas Parry, her cofferer or accountant, shortly after Henry VIII's death and Somerset's recognition as Protector, Thomas Seymour wrote to Elizabeth asking her to marry him. Seymour was jealous of his older brother's power and resentful of having been shut out of the inner circle at court. For Seymour, a marriage to Elizabeth would catapult him ahead of his brother in the king's council as a brother-in-law. Elizabeth relied on her extensive education and wrote an eloquent refusal, stating she would continue to mourn her father for the next two years and would not consider any offers during that time.[2] Some historians doubt this happened despite the testimony of Elizabeth's servants. If true, this exchange demonstrates a technique Elizabeth would use for years with potential marriage partners. She kept her own heart close and closed to anyone else, waiting to see what others would offer. In the meanwhile, she moved into the household of Katherine Parr.

Whatever the truth of the rumour that Seymour reached out to Elizabeth, he quickly settled on Katherine Parr as his wife. Surprisingly, at the age of nearly 40, Seymour was marrying for the first time. It was a secret arrangement because marrying so soon after the death of her royal husband would cause trouble for Katherine. She would be assumed to be marrying for lustful reasons. As Elizabeth's guardian, Katherine's reputedly scandalous marriage raised concerns for Elizabeth as well. Mary Tudor, who had shared a good relationship with Katherine Parr prior to this, was offended by her stepmother's hasty marriage and encouraged Elizabeth to leave Katherine's household. Elizabeth, however, expressed appreciation for Mary's advice but remained where she was.

Elizabeth spent her time in Katherine's household pursuing her studies. Henry VIII was committed to the education of his daughters and had selected Katherine Champernowne as his younger daughter's governess. Katherine, or Kat (Kate) as Elizabeth referred to her, was a steadying presence in the life of the young girl. Given the dramatic and tense loss of her mother and the resulting reduction in status, as well as the frequent change in stepmothers, living with Katherine Parr and Kat at Chelsea provided consistency in Elizabeth's life.

While Seymour was away at court trying to gain more power and influence with Edward VI, Elizabeth enjoyed quiet times at Katherine's home. When he came home, things were more complicated and more exciting. Seymour was charming and handsome, and Kat Ashley was convinced he would eventually make an ideal husband for Elizabeth. Now that her position as governess had come to an end, Kat was possessive of the young woman and determined to retain her close relationship and position of favour. She had married John Ashley (or Astley), a member of Elizabeth's household and nephew of Anne Boleyn. If Elizabeth married out of England, she would likely leave Kat behind. A marriage to a nobleman such as Thomas Seymour would mean Elizabeth would remain in England and Kat would remain in her household. In addition, Kat was charmed by Seymour – at least in the beginning.

There is ongoing debate about exactly what happened in the months Elizabeth spent at Chelsea. When he married Katherine Parr, Seymour became the head of her household. He was in charge of the servants. He was in charge of the guests. He was in charge of his wife and all her possessions. Elizabeth saw the status of Katherine Parr change when she married Seymour. Marrying someone beneath her status (as dowager queen, anyone was beneath Parr's status) reduced her status as well. Her jewels were taken by the Lord Protector, the Duke of Somerset, who was determined to punish his brother and his wife. Her reputation was sullied by a hasty marriage that was considered disrespectful to the king and made for lustful purposes. Her independence in her own household was diminished because legally all power and possessions were now her husband's.

Elizabeth also saw the pleasure her stepmother had in marriage to a man she had reportedly loved for years. She sensed the change in the household. Elizabeth is frequently described as blushing when Seymour approached her. On the verge of her fourteenth birthday, Elizabeth was becoming a woman and talks of marriage were becoming more real to her. Seymour relied on his charm to court favour with the young princess. Things were about to become complicated.

Elizabeth slept alone, which was unusual for a young woman of her age and status. Kat Ashley wanted to sleep with her husband, and she didn't want anyone else to have the honour of sleeping with Elizabeth. The princess was alone when Seymour would unlock the door to her chamber and visit her early in the morning. According to later testimony of Ashley and Thomas Parry, Elizabeth's cofferer, Seymour would frequently visit the princess before she was out of bed and dressed, pulling back the bedclothes and tickling her. Reportedly, as the visits went on, Katherine Parr joined her husband in the early-morning romps. Elizabeth is said to have started getting up earlier so that she was already dressed when Seymour arrived.[3] There's also a description of a strange event in the grounds of the house. Elizabeth had always loved exercise and being outside. On one occasion, Ashley and Parry described Seymour catching a fleeing Elizabeth and, as Katherine Parr held the princess, Seymour cutting her black velvet dress into many pieces.[4]

After spending a few months away, Elizabeth returned in the spring of 1548, and Seymour's visits to her chamber resumed. At this point, Katherine Ashley scolded Seymour for the scandal of appearing in Elizabeth's room dressed in only his nightshirt. Affronted, Seymour denied any impropriety. The visits to the young woman's room continued.

How did Elizabeth feel about what was happening? As is so often the case, we have conflicting evidence. In June 1548, Katherine wrote a letter to her husband and asked Elizabeth to arrange for a messenger. Before she handed over the letter, Elizabeth wrote 'Noli me tangere' (Latin for 'touch me not') on it. Perhaps thinking she was being too bold in addressing Seymour directly, she amended this to 'let him not to touch me'.[5] In a haunting echo, Thomas Wyatt had used the same phrase, 'Noli me tangere', to describe Henry VIII's possession of Anne Boleyn, warning off other admirers. Did Elizabeth associate this phrase with her mother, and was she trying to avoid her mother's fate, having a reputation destroyed by powerful men? Even as we see Elizabeth attempting to resist, she is also described as being attracted to Seymour. Ashley certainly promoted Seymour's ongoing attentions to the princess in hopes of a future marriage.

To many of us today, this seems astoundingly inappropriate behaviour. However much Elizabeth might have been attracted to her handsome stepfather or have blushed when he came near, he was an adult, and she was a young teenager. Yes, the princess was approaching the age when marriage and cohabitation were common, but she was also Seymour's wife's stepdaughter. And what about Katherine Parr's participation? Was she condoning what was happening? Was she so enamoured or even afraid of her husband that she felt she had no choice but to go along? Or was she trying to use the only influence she had available, her presence, to stop things from going too far? Was she holding Elizabeth to stop her from escaping or to protect her?

According to historian Dr Tracy Borman, Elizabeth represented sexual attraction and power to Seymour. In the sixteenth century, the adult man's pursuit of a young teenager was not seen in the predatory way we might see it today. Instead, it was an example of an ambitious political nobleman preying on a royal young lady who because of her position in the royal family offered access to power. Elizabeth may have enjoyed Seymour's attention. Ashley also claimed Elizabeth was attracted to him.[6]

We only know about these events because of what happened after. At some point, something happened that shocked Katherine Parr into decisive action. On 11 June 1548, Parr came upon her stepdaughter and husband in some kind of embrace. Several months pregnant, Parr decided to send Elizabeth away from the household. To punish her stepdaughter and husband? To save everyone's reputation? We don't know. Ashley, describing the scene to Parry, said this discovery was the reason Elizabeth was 'sent from the queen, or else that her grace parted from the queen'.[7] The next day, Elizabeth left Chelsea to live with Sir Anthony and Joanne Denny, the sister of Kat Ashley.

However tense the parting was, Elizabeth wrote affectionate letters to her stepmother after she left. The first written after she left Katherine's household gives us a sense of Elizabeth's distress about what happened. The princess's letter expressed regret and appreciation. The original letter displays very careful writing and evenly spaced words,[8] which makes me think Elizabeth carefully planned what she wanted to communicate to her stepmother. She began by explaining that she 'could not be more plentiful in giving thanks for the manifold kindness receive[d] at your highness' hand at my departure', making it seem the princess did not leave on the friendliest of terms. She went on to assure Katherine that 'truly I was replete with sorrow to depart from your highness', especially during the pregnancy.[9]

Elizabeth then addressed directly but not explicitly the issue that seems to be behind the leave-taking: some threat to the princess's reputation. She wrote that, 'albeit I answered little' at the time, she later realised the importance of what Katherine said and why it mattered. 'I weighed it more deeper when you said you would warn me of all evils that you should hear of me; for if your grace had not a good opinion of me, you would not have offered friendship to me that way that all men judge the contrary.' Elizabeth must have known something she had done or was rumoured to have done could cause significant concerns in the way others thought of her. She ended by expressing her gratitude 'to God for providing such friends to me', a prayer for Katherine's health, and concern that she was not well.[10] The letter provides a sense of a young woman who was in some shock about what happened and what it represented for her future.

Katherine's pregnancy ended in sadness, as she died giving birth to a daughter, Mary, on 5 September 1548. After Katherine's death, Seymour was bereft of his wife and what he had hoped would be a male heir. He went to court to try again to increase his influence and power. He had not given up on his plan to marry Elizabeth, and once again Kat Ashley was supportive. She encouraged Elizabeth to write to Seymour to comfort him in his loss, but Elizabeth refused because it would appear she was pursuing him.[11] Seymour sent his nephew John to help Elizabeth move her household into Hatfield. According to Parry's later testimony, Seymour instructed John to ask if Elizabeth's great buttocks had grown any less.[12] Rumours began to spread at court that Seymour was interested in marrying the princess, and these rumours travelled to Hatfield. Elizabeth may have been aware of Seymour's interest, but she did not encourage him.

It is true that marrying Seymour would have offered Elizabeth some benefits. She knew him – something that would not be true of a foreign prince selected for the benefit of an alliance rather than any personal connection. She seems to have found him attractive. Marriage to Seymour would keep her in England among her friends and family and would allow her to continue in her faith rather than being forced into a Catholic marriage.

Historian Dr Elizabeth Norton believes that late 1548, after Katherine Parr's death and before his decision to take action against the king, Thomas Seymour represented Elizabeth's best chance of marriage. She was not expected to ever become queen. She was a royal daughter but an illegitimate one who might not be well received by a foreign prince. A marriage to a wealthy and powerful noble courtier was a reasonable choice. The king was fond of both of them and likely to give his approval. Had Seymour been able to persuade his brother, it might have happened.

But things did not work out that way. Somerset was opposed to his brother advancing, and he dominated the council. There was no chance the council would have approved a marriage between Elizabeth and Seymour. His drive to increase his power and curtail that of Somerset drove Seymour not only to pursue Elizabeth but also to attempt to gain more access to Edward VI. He was raising money and recruiting supporters, and the council got wind of his actions by January 1549. On the 17th, Seymour was arrested for treason and sent to the Tower. Elizabeth and her household were caught up in the events, with the Ashleys and Thomas Parry, her comptroller, arrested and sent to London. Elizabeth was left to face a fierce interrogation by Sir Robert Tyrwhitt.[13]

Katherine Ashley and Thomas Parry were imprisoned in the Tower of London. While there, they were questioned about Elizabeth's possible involvement in Seymour's plot and forced to testify about what had happened between the princess and Seymour. They knew their lives were in danger. Did they perhaps shape their stories in a way that would preserve their innocence and Elizabeth's? In particular, did Ashley emphasise or even embellish her protests to Seymour about his behaviour? After Ashley and Parry testified about what happened happened in Katherine Parr's house, Elizabeth was in great danger.

Elizabeth had once written to her brother, 'it is (as your majesty is not unaware) rather characteristic of my nature … not to say in words as much as I think in my mind'.[14] The princess would put this approach into action in 1549. She did not panic. Tyrwhitt assumed he would easily be able to gain the advantage on a young woman, and he reported happily that she had broken down and wept when he told her Ashley and Parry were in the Tower. However, Elizabeth's resolve was firm. She was devoted to her servants and despite anything Tyrwhitt tried, she refused to say that any of them had done anything wrong. In frustration, Tyrwhitt said he could see in her face that she was guilty, but she said nothing that he could use against her.[15]

The politics and public interest in the scandal taught Elizabeth a very important lesson about the dangers associated with sexuality and reputation. Women's worth depended on the preservation of their virtue. The loss of virtue or even the perceived loss meant a woman was undesirable and even unworthy of a good marriage and future. Elizabeth's virtue was already suspect. Her mother had been called 'the scandal of all Christendom'. Her stepmother Catherine Howard, who was Anne Boleyn's cousin, had also been executed because of a sex scandal. Even Katherine Parr had lost influence with Edward VI and been stripped of her royal status (and jewels) when her marriage to Thomas Seymour was seen as associated with lust.

Elizabeth's letter to Katherine Parr shortly after leaving Chelsea demonstrates Elizabeth knew the power of a good reputation and the danger of a tarnished one. If she were believed to have behaved in an immoral or lustful way, her future would be lost. Elizabeth continued to defend her virtue. She had tried to protect her body from Thomas Seymour, by shrinking back into the bed when he came at her and then by getting up early and being dressed by the time he arrived in the morning. She wrote 'let him not touch me'.[16] She was telling him hands off her body. She was doing what she could to protect herself.

While Seymour was facing trial, Elizabeth worked to protect her servants and her reputation. She wrote to Somerset, referencing the interrogation of Sir Robert Tyrwhitt and reinforcing her answers. She stated clearly that she would never consider marriage with Thomas Seymour without the Council's consent. She went on to advocate strongly for Kat Ashley. She assured him that she and Kat never spoke about marriage 'without the consent of the king's majesty, your grace's and the Council's'.[17] She ended the letter with a strong statement defending herself and her conscience: 'These be the things which I both declared to Master Tyrwhit and also whereof my conscience beareth me witness which I would not for all earthly things offend in anything, for I know I have a soul to save as well as other folks have.' She then directly addressed rumours: 'Master Tyrwhit and others have told me that there goeth rumors abroad which be greatly both against mine honor and honesty which above all other things I esteem, which be there: that I am in the Tower and with child by my lord admiral.' Elizabeth did not avoid the confrontation with the Lord Protector; instead, she clearly requested his assistance: 'My lord, these are shameful slanders, for the which, besides the great desire I have to see the king's majesty, I shall most heartily desire your lordship that I may come to the court after your first determination that I may show myself there as I am.' After all the interrogations have produced no clear evidence, she offered up herself as evidence. Although she ends the letter signing off as 'Your assured friend to my little power',[18] Elizabeth showed she could exercise great power in her determination to protect herself, her reputation, and her household.

In March, while Seymour was awaiting execution, Elizabeth wrote to the Lord Protector again and pleaded for Kat Ashley and her release from the Tower. She insisted that Ashley took such good care of her and 'Saint Gregory sayeth that we are more bound to them that bringeth us up well than to our parents… our bringers-up are a cause to make us live well', that Ashley didn't suggest a marriage between Elizabeth and the Lord Admiral unless 'he had the Council's consent thereunto', and finally that Ashley's continued imprisonment 'doth make men think that I am not clear of the deed myself'.[19] Elizabeth was firm and forthright in advocating for herself and requiring that she be cleared of the remaining suspicion.

Elizabeth's life changed when Henry VIII died, likely more than she expected it to. Her life with Katherine Parr offered time of study and enjoyment, but once Thomas Seymour entered the household, everything shifted. As she grew into womanhood, Seymour took steps that threatened her reputation and resulted in her being separated from her beloved stepmother. Elizabeth watched as Katherine's life ended with the birth of a child. Elizabeth also learned that her position was part of her attraction. Seymour's desire was for power as much as for her. As Professor Suzannah Lipscomb explains, 'As a result of Seymour's actions, Elizabeth knew that when a man came a-courting, he would have one eye on her and one eye on the throne, and she was determined not to let any of them get their hands on it, or on her.'[20] Perhaps the relationship with Seymour was both the closest Elizabeth came to being able to marry and the experience that taught her the dangers of marriage outweighed the advantages.

After the Seymour experience, Elizabeth spent the rest of her brother's reign living quietly, mostly away from court. Writing about Elizabeth in 1550, her tutor Roger Ascham described her as a religious and studious young woman: '...my illustrious mistress the Lady Elizabeth shines like a star, excelling them more by the splendour of her virtues and her learning, than by the glory of her royal birth.' He discussed her Greek and Latin studies, crediting the late William Grindal for her foundation in the classics. He praised her understanding of language and her love for the true religion. He also pointed out that 'with respect to personal decoration she greatly prefers a simple elegance to show and splendour, so despising "the outward adorning of plaiting of the hair and of wearing of gold," that in the whole manner of her life she rather resembles Hippolyta than Phaedra'.[21] In describing Elizabeth in this way, Ascham provided a deliberately crafted serious and sombre portrait of the young Elizabeth's actions and appearance. It's no coincidence that she adopted this posture to reclaim her reputation after the Seymour scandal.

When Mary Tudor successfully took the throne from Lady Jane Grey in 1553, she was eager to remove Elizabeth from the succession because of her 'heretical opinions, illegitimacy, and characteristics in which she resembled her mother'.[22] This made Mary hesitant to marry Elizabeth to anyone who might decide to fight for his wife's right to the throne if Mary died without heirs.[23] However, many of Mary's council felt differently. Despite Mary's marriage to Philip of Spain, there was concern about her ability to bear a child and heir. William and others felt that the best plan was to marry Elizabeth to an Englishman rather than take the chance that Mary's husband Philip would take the throne for himself if Mary died without children. Their selection was Edward Courtenay, a descendant of Edward IV who had been once considered a possibility as Mary's own husband.[24]

The next year, opinion changed and Paget proposed a foreign match. Mary's relation Charles V agreed, preferring Elizabeth marry a Catholic prince in case Mary died without children (that possibility seemed to be widespread among European leaders). Options included Archduke Ferdinand of Austria and Emmanuel Philibert, Duke of Savoy, a dedicated Catholic, royal, and not perceived as a threat to the English.

The problem was that both Mary and Elizabeth opposed the match. Elizabeth did not want to be associated with the Habsburg empire or the Catholic cause. Mary did not want to acknowledge Elizabeth as her heiress presumptive, one of Savoy's demands.[25] Despite Philip's attempts to move forward on the marriage, Mary provided surprising support for Elizabeth's refusal. In addition, most Englishmen opposed the match.

At the same time, the king of Sweden promoted the suit of his son Eric for Elizabeth. But the king's envoy made the mistake of going to Elizabeth directly instead of first approaching Queen Mary. Elizabeth was wise enough to turn the envoy away, not wishing to anger the queen. She told Mary she did not wish to marry the Swedish prince or anyone else. Several times during Mary's reign, Elizabeth declared she preferred to remain single. It may have been a political posture, ruling out marriage in general terms rather than turning down specific men. Paget, however, told Feria that there was no one in England or abroad that Elizabeth could marry.[26] It turned out to be more accurate than anyone realised at the time.

Philip's support of Elizabeth's position as Mary's heir increased as it became clear that Mary would not have children. After all, if Elizabeth did not become Queen of England, the Catholic alternative was Mary, Queen of Scots, who was married to the Dauphin and next king of France. The only thing more dangerous for Philip than a Protestant Elizabeth on the English throne was a queen of France on the English throne. Philip believed he could manage Elizabeth.

Therefore, with Philip's encouragement, Mary reluctantly agreed to recognise Elizabeth as her heir. When Mary died 17 November 1558, Elizabeth became queen.

Chapter 2

The Queen's Two Bodies, the Queen's Two Beds

There is a strong idea in the world that a woman cannot live unless she is married.

Elizabeth I (*Calendar of State Papers Spain*, 24 March 1559)

When Anne Boleyn went into labour in September 1533, all of England realised that Henry VIII was counting on his new wife providing him with a son and heir. He had taken the extraordinary step of declaring his first marriage, which had been sanctioned by the pope, his people, and all of Christendom, void. He had loved Katherine of Aragon and had been at her side for more than twenty years. But he set all that aside, and even broke his holy vow to the Catholic Church. He married Anne. He had her crowned queen in a spectacular ceremony. He defied the world and his own people. Now was the time for it all to be rewarded.

But the child was a girl. Her body was female. She was healthy, but that was not enough. As far as Henry was concerned, he was still without an heir. His new child had the wrong body: a female body.

Twenty-five years later, this female came to the throne as regnant queen. In many ways, she still had the wrong body. When Elizabeth succeeded Mary I, for the first and last time in English or British history, the crown passed from one regnant queen to another.

The succession from one monarch to the next was potentially a time of chaos and violence. At times, the crown passed through war and bloodshed. That was how Henry VII had come to the throne, by defeating Richard III on the battlefield. But more often, the king – or, in Mary's case, the queen – died and the throne passed to the successor. This event is sometimes described through the notion of the king's two bodies. According to historian Ernst Kantorowicz, the medieval theory of two bodies, one natural and one politic, allows the monarchy to survive when the monarch dies. Thus, 'the king is dead, long live the king'. According to Kantorowicz, 'The king has in him two Bodies, viz., a Body natural, and a body politic. His Body natural (if it be considered in itself) is a Body mortal, subject to all infirmities that come by Nature or Accident.'[1] This includes being a child or being ill or dying. 'But his Body politic is a Body that cannot be seen or handled, consisting of Policy and Government, and constituted for the Direction of the People and the Management of the public weal, and this Body is utterly void of Infancy, and old Age, and other natural Defects' that a natural body might be subject to. Therefore, 'what the king does in his Body politic cannot be invalidated or frustrated by any Disability in his natural Body'.[2]

When Elizabeth came to the throne, she invoked the idea of these two bodies in her accession speech:

> My lords, the law of nature moveth me to sorrow for my sister; the burden that is fallen upon me maketh me amazed; and yet, considering I am God's creature ordained to obey His appointment, I will thereto yield, desiring from the bottom of my heart that I may have assistance of His grace to be the minister of His heavenly will in this office now committed to me. And as I am but one body naturally considered, though by His permission a body politic to govern, so I shall desire you all, my lords (chiefly you of the nobility, everyone in his degree and power), to be assistant to me, that I with my ruling and you with your service may make a good account to almighty God and leave some comfort to our posterity in earth.[3]

Here, in the first public speech after becoming queen, Elizabeth draws attention to the notion of the monarch's two bodies: the body natural and the body politic. Embedded in that was the unique and more problematic element: her body natural was not simply young or aged or ill. It was female.

One way this unique tension between body politic and body natural was reflected in Tudor times was in the question of who was best suited to make decisions regarding the queen's body, personal and political. The question of the queen's body, and who was in charge of her body, was central to Elizabeth's life, her reign, and her success. In many ways, even Elizabeth's 'natural' body was never really her own. From the time she was born, her body was on display, literally as well as figuratively. It started as soon as she was born, when she was displayed to the French ambassadors, uncovered and completely vulnerable to the male gaze, while men evaluated her body to see if she would be a fit wife for a French prince. From then on, Elizabeth's fitness and vulnerability was essentially tied to her body.

When she was a young teenager, her body natural became an object of desire for Thomas Seymour, who violated her boundaries – a locked door, bed curtains, and clothing – to get at her body. During Edward's and Mary's reigns, rumours about Elizabeth's immorality and sexual depravity were used as a tool to threaten and weaken her. As was often the case in medieval and early modern times, 'sexual commentary was a strong way to diminish potentially powerful women'.[4] Elizabeth had but one body before she became queen, and it was seen as not her own even then.

After Edward VI died, Mary overcame the effort to put Jane Grey on the throne and secured it for herself. Once she was proclaimed queen, the questions about her ability to rule began. How did the existing ideas of monarchy, based on the assumption the monarch meant king, accommodate the notion of a woman on the throne? How was royal power and authority transferred? It was one thing to believe a 'body politic' moved immediately from the body natural of Henry VIII to the body natural of Edward VI when the old king died. But could a female body be a sovereign?

The essence of monarchy had been based on the assumption that the king's body was to rule, and the queen's was to provide for the succession. That set-up didn't work with a regnant queen. A regnant queen's body had to rule and to bear the child who would succeed her. Pregnancy and childbirth were dangerous in sixteenth-century England: two of Elizabeth's stepmothers had died following the birth of a child. A woman's body was removed from the public forum for weeks surrounding the birth of a child. After marrying Philip of Spain, Mary I believed she was with child. The pregnancy was announced in the fall of 1554, and she withdrew to Hampton Court Palace to await the birth of her child. The doctors believed the child would be born in May 1555. In April, word somehow got out that Mary had delivered a son. There was rejoicing in England and on the continent. But sadly, the rumours were untrue. There was no baby. At least not yet. So, Mary and Philip and the nation continued to wait.

May and June came and went. Mary remained in her chamber, certain she was still pregnant and that the time had been miscalculated. But by July, it became clear there would be no baby. Mary clung to her hope for a few more weeks, and in August left Hampton Court and went to a private residence. Gossip spread through the court. Had Mary miscarried and kept that a secret? Had she never been pregnant and instead been ill? Or had the queen invented the story to gain support from her people? The incident caused embarrassment for Mary and Philip in England and abroad. Philip left England and was reluctant to return. Mary is said to have believed she was being punished for being too lenient with heretics and was determined to strengthen her efforts. After the joy and hope the country had felt, the end of summer brought sadness and political turmoil.[5] Mary died on 17 November 1558. Despite her best efforts, she had not produced an heir to carry on her vision of a Catholic England. In other words, her body natural had failed in one of its primary responsibilities.

Elizabeth and Her Two Bodies

Elizabeth came to the throne because Mary I died without having a child. When Mary died, the notion of the 'two bodies' created this new reality: The queen is dead. Long live the queen. The queen's body natural had died, and the essence of monarchy had transferred to the new queen. At that time, Elizabeth officially embodied the queen's two bodies, her natural body now joined with her royal status. From this point on, Elizabeth's life was defined by a battle over her body: was it hers or did it belong to the state? When a queen ruled in her own right, as Mary and Elizabeth did, female flesh was tightly bound with the notion of monarchy.[6]

Henry VIII's decision to involve parliament and thus lawyers and the Inns of Court in determining the succession created tension in Elizabeth's reign. The matter of the succession was claimed as the responsibility of the government rather than the monarch, and not surprisingly Elizabeth objected to this. According to the French ambassador, when the privy council asked the queen to allow parliament to discuss the question of her marriage and the succession, the queen replied that 'not one of them should do it: she would reserve that for herself'.[7] Reluctant to give up the power, lawyers and ministers attempted to develop a concept to define the relationship between government and monarch.[8]

By 1561, it was deemed legally necessary to 'endow the queen with two bodies: a body natural and a body politic'. Her 'body natural' was known to be subject to infancy, infirmity, error, and old age. Contained within the natural body was a 'body politic', which was created out of 'faith, ingenuity, and practical expediency and which was immortal'.[9] The mingling of religious and political language that began when Henry VIII became Supreme Head of the Church of England meant Elizabeth's jurists were regularly discussing the queen's 'two bodies' in legal and religious terms. Ernst Kantorowicz, reviewing Edmund Plowden's *Reports* about the concept of the king's two bodies, sees new language emerging in 1560 stating that 'King is a Name of Continuance, which shall always endure as the Head and Governor of the People (as the Law presumes) as long as the People continue … and in this Name the King never dies'.[10] Note the male language, even in the reign of a sovereign queen.

Plowden was perceived by his contemporaries as a prominent common lawyer, and his writings influenced students at the Inns of Court throughout Elizabeth's reign. Some Catholic jurists who resented the religious decisions of Elizabeth used Plowden's theory of the king's two bodies to oppose Elizabeth's power. 'The judges affirmed their allegiance by exalting the Queen's body politic while at the same time they frustrated the wishes of her body natural.'[11] When Elizabeth sought to invalidate a grant made by Edward VI because the king was a minor and not allowed by law to grant land, judges opposed the queen and upheld Edward's grant because the law regarding age applied to his 'body natural' not his 'body politic'. According to Plowden, the king's 'body politic' was not subject to the perils of 'infancy' and 'what the King does in his Body politic, cannot be invalidated or frustrated by any Disability in his natural Body'.[12] The language enhances the power and continuity of the monarchy. The queen herself as an individual was less powerful than the monarchy.[13] That created an opportunity for Elizabeth to demonstrate that, as 'king' or monarch, she was not limited by any 'Disability' in her natural body, including her femaleness.

As queen, Elizabeth made effective use of the idea of two bodies to promote her majesty and her reign. She knew it was essential that her 'two bodies' be seen frequently by her people. Being on view was an important part of Elizabeth's approach to her rule. In 1586, she described her public life, 'We princes, I tell you, are set on stages, in sight and view of all the world.'[14] The notion of Elizabeth being on stages is clear throughout her reign. The queen was determined to control the stages and the way she was seen. Her coronation procession was an example of a public viewing of the queen as she travelled through London. She performed to the crowds, stopping to receive gifts and good wishes along the way. Her willingness to see her people and to let them see her, the shared view, was an important component of her approach to being sovereign. Throughout her reign, she went on progresses into the country so more of her subjects could see her. She most often journeyed in open carriages so she could be seen travelling through the country on her way to various destinations. She was ever concerned about displaying her political and her natural self, her political and natural body.

Elizabeth was healthier and more active than her sister had been. She walked vigorously every morning and loved hunting and riding. She danced frequently and enjoyed the more athletic or 'male' dance moves. Sometimes this level of physical activity was described as manly, in contrast to the more socially acceptable image of women sitting and sewing (or, even better, pregnant and bearing children). Elizabeth enjoyed physical exercise and used her health to show she was powerful and able to manage the heavy burden of rule. But she could not fully control her body natural. When she did fall sick with smallpox in 1562, it plunged the council into panic about who would succeed her on the throne. After Elizabeth recovered, she was furious that her council had attempted to choose her successor. The queen was determined not to be forced to name a successor. She took special care to project an image of near immortality, publicly participating in physically taxing activities, gaining a reputation for dancing and riding frequently, and showing herself in carefully curated ways that concealed any hint of ill health. The hours she spent dressing and creating her royal images every day was not simply an exercise of vanity; it was a way of demonstrating that she was healthy and would rule for years to come. The health of her body meant she could keep her throne; her body natural was strong so the body politic could survive.

Elizabeth used the notion of being having both male and female attributes and 'bodies' creatively and played on concerns about her gender to turn them in her favour. Elizabeth used language of power, gender, and sexuality to describe herself and her role(s) to her council, her suitors, and her people. It is perhaps the fluidity of the queen's use of both male and female attributes and titles that made it possible for playwrights such as Shakespeare to fill his stage with boy characters who played young women who dressed as men. Viola in *Twelfth Night* and Rosalind in *As You Like It* take on male clothing and characteristics to hide their vulnerability and move more freely in court settings.

Elizabeth often took on male language, describing herself as 'prince' and 'king', and compared herself to Henry VIII to position herself as more powerful and therefore less vulnerable in her position as ruler and head – or governor – of the church.

Cross-dressing allowed theatre to explore and disrupt expectations of what women were capable of. Think of Portia, clad in professional legal garb she could not legally wear, represented as the only character who could see the specific details of the legal case clearly enough to save Antonio. Behind the dress and manners that disguise Portia's identity, she speaks with confidence and power. The audience knows it is a woman doing so. Elizabeth did not dress herself as a man, but she did dress herself as a king, displaying her body in all the finery of clothing and jewels equal to that preeminent station.

In this and other ways, Elizabeth was able to rule because her 'body politic' compensated for the weak characteristics associated with being female. Thus, Elizabeth could be thought of as 'King Elizabeth', or having, as she herself claimed, 'the heart and stomach of a king'.[15] Elizabeth was not a solely masculine figure but was king and queen at once. She sometimes used her sex as an 'ideological and diplomatic tool'.[16] She used her feminine and her kingly style to suit a particular audience and purpose. For example, when she was dealing with issues of courtship, marriage, and providing an heir, she used specific language to describe herself. She often pushed back at pressure to make a decision about a husband by claiming she was only a woman and couldn't make such a decision. Of course, she was not about to let men make the decision for her!

Gender, power, and sexuality were also reflected in the drama of the time. Elizabeth managed to 'redefine the limits of traditional gender expectations'. An interesting although possibly fabricated story in the memoirs of Sir James Melville described a conversation between Melville and Elizabeth about the desire of the queen to meet the Queen of Scots. As an official meeting seemed impossible, Melville suggested Elizabeth dress as a male page and travel to Scotland to see the queen that way. The idea of the powerful queen dressed as a powerless male symbolises the ways Elizabeth disrupted expectations of king and queen.

Elizabeth used language intentionally. She regularly referred to herself as 'prince' and 'king'. She was dedicated to crafting people's perception of her as king and queen. She compared herself to famous men. For example, during her coronation procession, when she came to the Tower of London, she compared herself to Daniel the prophet. There were women in the Bible she could have used, but she specifically chose Daniel.[17]

There was power for the queen in embracing and using the ambiguity of male and female rule. In 1560, George Lord Seton described Elizabeth as having 'manly courage, and Sex ambitions of Command' that could embroil Spain in a long war. This is 'a description of a woman who causes others to fear her because of her unwomanly attributes'.[18] Later in the reign, when all were alarmed by the sight of Spanish ships, a Spanish informant described the queen as having 'a stouter heart than any of them'.[19]

The most famous example of Elizabeth describing herself as king and queen is in her speech at Tilbury when she addressed her troops as they prepared to face the Spanish Armada. The very real possibility of an invasion from Spain and Catholic Europe was one of the most dangerous moments in Tudor history. Elizabeth, knowing the value of her presence, travelled to meet the troops at Tilbury. James Aske described her in male terms as a sacred 'general' and mentioned her 'marching like a king'.[20] Camden described her as male and female: 'the Queen with a masculine Spirit … sometimes with a martial Pace, another while gently like a Woman'. He went on to emphasise how she encouraged the hearts of her captains and soldiers 'by her Presence and Speech to them'.[21] Even when she was processing gently like a woman, as Camden had it, the action of visiting troops preparing for battle was a typically male endeavour. Elizabeth could not lead her troops in battle, as her father had done in France, but she was there in their midst. And her words expressed her male and female support of them.

The Tilbury speech includes Elizabeth's own description of herself as both male and female, man and woman, king and queen. She described herself as having 'the body but of a weak and feeble woman' and at the same time 'the heart and stomach of a king, and of a king of England too'. Elizabeth then put herself firmly in the camp of kings when she promised that if any dared to invade her realm, 'I myself will take up arms, I myself will be your general, judge, and rewarder of every one of your virtues in the field.' She acknowledged that as she would not actually be leading them, whatever language she used, 'my lieutenant general shall be in my stead'. Still, she referred to herself as male, describing Dudley as 'whom never prince commanded a more noble or worthy subject'.[22] The speech was read aloud in subsequent days, creating another layer of complexity as male officers read the queen's speech in which she described herself and queen and king.[23]

There are some doubts about whether this speech was given according to the version in the British Library, or whether other versions are more accurate, or if the speech was given at all. Historian Janet Green believes there is plenty of evidence that the speech is genuine and that the copy in the British Library was written by Dr Leonel Sharpe (or Lionel Sharp), a contemporary of Elizabeth.[24] She goes on to say that the form and phraseology of the speech indicate that it was composed by the queen herself, the culmination of her years of excellent education.[25] Elizabeth's reference to 'king of England' would almost certainly remind her army of her father, Henry VIII. She frequently associated herself with her father as a way of reinforcing her place on the throne, and this allowed her to associate herself with his warlike attributes. She may have referred to herself as a 'weak and feeble woman', but in fact her body was not weak or feeble. She had been ruling successfully for thirty years and had overcome every challenge – all as a queen on her own. This was not the only example of her use of two bodies, queen and king, to claim her power, but it is an exceptionally successful one. In this moment, she made her body her own.

But she was unable to maintain full control of her body, as it belonged to the nation as well. Even after her death, battle for control of Elizabeth's body continued.

The Death of the Body Natural

By late 1602, Elizabeth was nearing the end of her life. John Harrington, the queen's godson, wrote to his wife in December 1602 that he met with the queen and found her troubled by illness and grief about the Earl of Tyrone in Ireland and the death of the Earl of Essex. The next month, she moved to Richmond Palace. The queen continued her official duties from Richmond through February, but by March her symptoms worsened.[26] De Beaumont, the French ambassador, blamed her sorrows for her final illness.[27]

Elizabeth's health continued to deteriorate. For days, the queen refused to go to bed, as if she knew she would never get up again. Eventually, the Lord Admiral was summoned, and he persuaded her to go to bed. According to lawyer Sir John Hayward, in her final hours the queen was unable or unwilling to speak but made gestures to indicate her wish that James succeed her. These narratives present the queen's death in a way that promoted the smooth transition to James VI of Scotland as king.[28] Elizabeth I died at 3.00 in the morning of 24 March 1603. John Manningham, an English lawyer who kept a diary while he was a student at Middle Temple, described the event this way: 'This morning about three at clocke hir Majestie departed this lyfe, mildly like a lambe, easily like a ripe apple from the tree.'[29]

There was speculation about how the queen's body was handled. Elizabeth had left clear instructions that her body was 'not to be opened'. According to an account written years later by Elizabeth Southwell, one of her maids of honour, Robert Cecil gave a contrary secret order that the barber surgeons open and examine the late queen's body. The rest of the council went along with the order.[30] The question of how the queen's body natural was treated after her death had potential implications for the way the body politic and in particular the transfer of monarchy to King James proceeded and was accepted by the people.

The process of disembowelling was typical in the case of royalty. Several of Elizabeth's contemporaries and even family members were disembowelled, including Henry VIII, Mary Tudor, Katherine Parr, and Mary, Queen of Scots. It would have likely been seen as standard process, unless the queen specifically asked it not to be done. According to Southwell, Elizabeth had done just that.[31] Why would the queen have wanted her body to be left alone? Perhaps after having her body be the property of the country for so long, Elizabeth simply wanted to be left alone.

But there were political implications as well. There were many rumours that, despite her carefully crafted image as the Virgin Queen, an examination of her body would reveal she had been sexually active. Perhaps it would reveal she had given birth. Or perhaps it would confirm the rumour that she was unable to have sex, as some rumours had stated. A disruption in the worthiness of Elizabeth was a statement about her right to rule. And, as the nation was preparing for the coronation of the man the privy council said Elizabeth had chosen to succeed her, it was essential that the narrative remain clear and uncomplicated. Southwell's account said Cecil and others had the body 'seared up', but the council claimed the body was not opened. Why? Was Elizabeth's desire not to be opened well known and the council wanted to be seen as obedient to her final wishes? Were they worried that the possibility of an examination of her internal organs might call the succession into question? Were they striving to preserve her reputation as a virgin?[32] Without their statements, it's impossible to know. It is also possible that Southwell was influenced by someone to create or change the story in an attempt to cause trouble for King James and his government.

The account doesn't end there. According to Southwell, while waiting for burial, the corpse exploded and 'brake the coffin with such a cracke, that it spleated the wood, lead, and cer-cloath, to the terror and astonishment of all that were present'.[33] Given the fact that Elizabeth wasn't buried for five weeks, 'the Council would have been ill-advised to leave Elizabeth's corpse unopened'. If unopened, the possibility of a body encased in lead and kept with candles burning around it for more than a month might well have exploded or burst. Years later, Reverend A. P. Stanley looked into Elizabeth's tomb and reported seeing a simple lid on the queen's coffin bearing only the date, the outline of a Tudor rose, and the letters ER. Given the elaborate nature of the queen's monument, this seemed understated. Perhaps it is the result of a new coffin having been quickly assembled to replace the one that had cracked.[34]

The description of the opening of the queen's body and of its bursting is not found anywhere else. According to Southwell, Cecil silenced everyone around him. The notion of an exploding corpse was horrifying and linked to moral corruption.[35] It could also be an image of a divided kingdom. The queen's corpse coming apart could symbolise the destruction of the near-divine Virgin Queen image, the breaking apart of the idea of monarch as head of church and state, and the violation of England by an army of Catholics, either from abroad or from within the country. Elizabeth's mother had been destroyed by her head being removed from her body, as had the Catholic martyr Mary, Queen of Scots. Traitors were hung, drawn, and quartered, literally taken apart to demonstrate what happened to those who betray their loyalty to king (or queen!) and country.

It's no wonder Robert Cecil and the council would have made any attempt necessary to suppress the story. They were determined to preserve the image of the Virgin Queen and her choice of James VI of Scotland as king. Cecil and members of Elizabeth's council had been building a relationship with the Scots king for years. On the other hand, Catholic Robert Persons promoted the rumour of the queen's body being a reflection of her evil and the decay of the nation, assuring readers of his *Judgement of a Catholicke English-man Living in Banishment for his Religion* in 1608 that he could, if he wished, share a story of a 'miserable end' of the queen. Bishop Barlow responded vehemently to Persons, comparing the Catholic to a dog and blaming him for Elizabeth not being able to rest in peace. He connected her silences to 'princely resolution' and her salvation. He gave his own eyewitness account of the queen's final hours to counter Persons's claim.[36]

The battles over Elizabeth's body continued after her death. In addition to the sensational descriptions of secret disembowelling and exploding corpses, the question of Elizabeth's sexuality and stories of possible secret children have continued to reverberate through the years. While there are many questions that are posed even now about kings, the focus on sexual immorality, moral depravity, and hidden children tends to be especially true of how queens are remembered and reimagined. We still see and hear debates about questions related directly to the queen's body: 'Was she really a virgin queen?' or 'Was Dudley more than just a friend?' and even 'Was Elizabeth I really a man?' For Elizabeth, her body had defined her since she was born the 'wrong' gender as a child. Throughout her life and her reign, she used the notion of 'two bodies' – natural and politic, male and female – to craft a reign and an image.

'Because questions of marriage and the succession connected her natural and physical bodies in ways that Elizabeth constantly sought to control, the queen herself became the most politically significant sign of her reign.'[37] Elizabeth's body – politic and natural – was the most important symbol of her reign. It turned out that Elizabeth's body natural was a lasting and capable vehicle for the body politic. Throughout her life, she enjoyed good health. She outlived eight popes and four kings of France, and her forty-four-year reign was among the longest of English monarchs. Until right before her death, her physical well-being impressed Venetian Ambassador Giovanni Scaramelli, who reported that she was healthy, and people believed her death was far off. John Manningham wrote in his diary that the queen's physicians thought she would live many years. Christophe de Harlay, Comte de Beaumont and French ambassador to England, reported he was impressed with her good health. She displayed healthy habits, continuing to dance, ride, and walk daily until shortly before she died. Her body, like her reign, defied expectation.

Chapter 3

'An Inconsiderate Folly' – Parliament and Marriage

God send our mistress a husband, and by him a son, that we may hope our posterity shall have a masculine succession.

William Cecil to Nicholas Throckmorton (14 July 1561)

The Tudor monarchs had a fascinating relationship with parliament. Common Law in England, as taught by the Inns of Court, was a force that not even a monarch could fully control. Parliament was the means of interpreting, adapting, and applying the law. Parliament also held the ability to impose taxes to pay for whatever the monarchy could not cover through its own funds. So, legislation and taxation were the means through which parliament exercised its own power alongside the Tudor monarch.[1]

As the Tudor dynasty progressed, parliament exercised control in shaping the future of the monarchy itself. Henry VIII established parliament's essential role in the royal succession. As he repeatedly changed his mind about wives and marriage, he used parliamentary acts to declare his daughter Mary was illegitimate and remove her from the succession and establish his daughter Elizabeth as his heir (Act of 1534), then to declare Elizabeth was illegitimate as well and remove her from the succession (Act of 1536), and finally to return both Mary and Elizabeth to the succession, although both daughters were still illegitimate (Act of 1543).[2] Henry also used parliament to give himself a great deal of power in determining the line of succession and naming his heirs and in deciding to eliminate the descendants of his elder sister Margaret.

Prior to Henry VIII, the succession had been considered as ordained by God. When Henry began to adjust the succession to meet his own needs, he needed to show parliament approved to create the appearance that the nation was behind him (which was not necessarily the case). He also used parliament to demand adherence to his actions. It became treasonous to oppose the king's control of the succession and his position as Supreme Head of the Church of England. Even Sir Thomas More and Bishop John Fisher, two loyal Catholics and widely respected leaders in church and state, expressed support for parliament's ability to determine the succession.[3] Less than ten years after Henry's final succession act, the force of the act was challenged by Edward VI and the Earl of Northumberland, who attempted to name Lady Jane Grey as heir instead of Mary Tudor. Faced with the attempt to replace her on the throne, Mary responded by referring to her appointment as Edward VI's heir 'by act of parlement'.[4]

Mary I made the decision to hold her coronation before parliament met, as had her predecessors, so that her claim to the crown did not appear to depend on parliament. After the coronation, her first parliament clarified her role as monarch, passing 'An Act declaring that the Regal Power of this Realm is in the Queen's Majesty as fully and absolutely as ever it was in any of her most noble Progenitors Kings of this Realm'.[5] In other words, parliament stated explicitly that her rights and powers were equal to those of kings. Parliament then helped the queen create a marriage contract that attempted to dispel concerns that a foreign king would hold ultimate control over England and her resources. The marriage contract with Philip of Spain was groundbreaking in terms of providing the queen regnant the ability to retain her land and possessions, something not available to other women who married.

As she realised she might not produce the child she so desperately wished for, Mary turned her attention to the succession. As her brother Edward had been, she was loath to leave her throne to the heir her father had named, in this case her half-sister Elizabeth. Mary was vocal about wishing to bypass Elizabeth and instead leave her crown to Lady Margaret Lennox, descendant of Margaret Tudor.[6] Mary expressed concern to her supporter Simon Renard that Elizabeth's 'heretical opinions, illegitimacy, and characteristics in which she resembled her mother' made Mary wish to name another heir. However, as parliament considered Elizabeth the proper heir, Mary knew it would be very difficult to disinherit her.[7] So Mary made no changes, and Elizabeth inherited the throne.

Elizabeth came to the throne despite the debates over legitimacy and plans for religion. That made it even more important for Elizabeth to move boldly and decisively to gain and hold the crown. As her sister had, Elizabeth chose to hold her coronation before her first parliament met. After the coronation, she called her first parliament, which passed the 'Acte of Recognition of the Quene's Highness Title to the Imperyall Crowne of this Realme'. This act stated that it had 'pleased God of his merciful providence and goodness towards us and this our Realme, not onely to provide but also to preserve and kepe for us and our wealthes … our most rightfull and Lawfull Sovereigne liege Ladye and Quene most happily to Reigne over us'.[8] It also referred to Henry VIII's act of 1543 to reinforce Elizabeth's right to the throne.[9]

Given the role parliament had played in the reigns of Henry VIII's children thus far, it's not surprising the institution would consider it proper to counsel Elizabeth about her marriage and heirs. But they found the final Tudor queen even more reluctant than her sister to take the advice of her council and parliament on these issues. Parliament tried to persuade Elizabeth to quickly marry and to influence her choice of husband. However, her accession speech clarified her desire to rule on her own. After expressing sorrow for the death of her sister, Elizabeth states she is amazed at the burden that has fallen upon her and went on to say she was:

> God's creature, ordeyned to obey his appointment … desiring form the bottom of my harte that I will have assistance of his Grace to be the minister of his Heavenly Will in this office now committed to me, and as I am but one Bodye naturallye Considered though by his permission a Bodye Politique to Governe.[10]

Parliament opened in late January 1559. The queen's opening speech was read by Sir Nicholas Bacon. The Commons elected Sir Thomas Gargrave as their speaker. The body then moved to address the important issues of the reign: recognising Elizabeth's right to the throne, refuting the divorce of Henry VIII and Anne Boleyn, and restoring Elizabeth's legitimacy – all focusing on the present situation rather than bringing up the past. Then there was the careful ecclesiastical return to the church of Henry VIII and Edward VI and Elizabeth's supremacy.[11] The initial focus was on the Act of Supremacy, the Act of Uniformity, the Treason Act, and the First Fruits and Tenths Act, establishing uniform religion and to ensuring continuation for the navy and its coastal defences. Uncomfortable with a woman holding the title 'Supreme Head', Elizabeth and the House of Lords agreed she would take the title 'Supreme Governor' of the Church of England. This did not mean the queen agreed to hold less power, although some bishops were more loyal and helpful than others. Religious services returned to English, and England was established as a Protestant nation. However, there were efforts to allow for compromise in some areas of religious reform.

On 6 February, the focus turned to something the struck the queen closer to her personal life. Parliament officially requested that she marry. According to a letter from Paulo Tiepolo, the Venetian ambassador, the parliamentary petition was focusing primarily on English candidates for the queen to marry, with William Pickering identified as an early favourite.[12] The practice of asking Elizabeth to marry and settle the succession became a familiar component for future sessions of parliament. Also familiar was the queen's reply that she understood the desire of parliament to advise her and cautioning that it was not their place to plan her marriage or force a choice on the succession. It was a 'dance she did with Parliament again and again'.[13]

There are different versions of parliament's request and of Elizabeth's responses. According to William Camden, Thomas Gargrave, speaker of the lower house, went to the queen and stated, 'There is nothing which with more ardent affection we beg of God in our daily prayers, than that our happiness hitherto received by your most gracious government may be perpetuated to the English nation unto all eternity.' He went on to say that the options for this were that the queen reign forever or that she marry and have children. This desire, the queen's marriage and children, was 'the single, the only, the all-comprehending prayer of all Englishmen'. This might sound like an exaggeration, but given the assumptions of the day, it is probably not far off the mark. Camden's account goes on to quote Gargrave emphasising the necessity of the children of the queen to the safety and peace of the country, as well as how they would be an ornament and strength to the realm.[14]

Camden gives Elizabeth's response as an attempt to give an answer that will please them but not commit her. She said this:

> Concerning marriage, which he so earnestly move me to, I have been long since persuaded, that I was sent into this world by God to think and do those things chiefly which may tend to his glory. Hereupon I have chosen that kind of life which is most free from the troublesome cares of this world, that I might attend the service of God alone.

She said that with the cares of the kingdom laid upon her, to take upon herself the cares of marriage as well would be an 'point of inconsiderate folly'. She cautioned parliament not to 'upbraid me with miserable lack of children' because they were, all the country, her children.[15]

The speech includes a commendation from the queen regarding the nature of the nature of the petition that she marry: 'I do well like of and take in good part, because that it is simple and containeth no limitation of place or person.' Elizabeth had no interest in being told whom or when to marry. She also assured parliament that 'I will never in that matter conclude anything that shall be prejudicial to the realm.' She qualified somewhat, 'albeit it might please almighty God to continue me still in this mind to live out of the state of marriage', she said not to worry because God 'will so work in my heart and in your wisdoms as good provision by His help may be made in convenient time, whereby the realm shall not remain destitute of an heir'. The final statement is a something she is famous for. There are two primary versions: 'And to me it shall be a full satisfaction, both for the memorial of my name, and for my glory also, if when I shall let my last breath, it be engraven upon my marble tomb Here lieth Elizabeth, which reigned a virgin, and died a virgin',[16] and 'And in the end this shall be for me sufficient: that a marble stone shall declare that a queen, having reigned such a time, lived and died a virgin.'[17]

Elizabeth may well have written the speeches herself. There are some parts in her own hand, and the style is reflective of her other speeches and written works, displaying her phrases and clarity.[18] Her thoughts spread through the Houses of Lords and Commons, stating her ability to rule and make her own decisions.[19] It was the first step of a dance that would go on until nearly the end of her reign, with Elizabeth on one side, parliament and privy council members on the other, and the question of the queen's marriage at stake.

By the time Elizabeth's second parliament was called, there was greater urgency for the queen to marry. Mary, Queen of Scots was now in Scotland, eager to marry a politically powerful Catholic husband, and a definite danger to Elizabeth. The two queens initially made overtures of peace and even considered meeting, but religious violence in France and French pleas for Elizabeth to help support the Protestants there raised tensions in England with the Catholics and Mary. After several delays, Elizabeth abandoned the idea of a meeting. Despite Mary's continued requests for the two queens to meet in person, and despite the meeting being portrayed on stage and screen, Elizabeth and Mary, Queen of Scots never met in person.

In September 1562, Elizabeth announced she would send troops to France to offer protection from the Guise family. A few weeks later, the queen began to feel ill, and it soon became clear she had contracted smallpox. By mid-October, she was so sick she was unable to speak. Her privy council were convinced she could die, and they held meetings to try to conclude who would succeed the queen. Generally, the council was split into three groups: one supporting Henry VIII's preference that Katherine Grey, the granddaughter of his sister Mary; was next in line; another supporting the more distant but male claim of the earl of Huntingdon; and the third believing that the matter should be sent to the judiciary. After lively debates, the council was unable to reach any consensus. This created the possibility that the death of Elizabeth would plunge the country into chaos and civil war.

The queen's recovery was unexpected and an enormous relief. By the end of October, she was well enough to attend to government business. Elizabeth was dismayed and angry that the council had taken it upon themselves to try to settle the succession, but the members of the government could not avoid the reality that the nation was utterly unprepared for the death of the queen, something that could not be prevented should God or an accident or foul play intervene. This created a renewed determination that Elizabeth marry and settle the succession. Parliament met on 12 January 1563, and the question of the succession was evident even at the opening church session.[20] The privy council sought the support of parliament in pressuring Elizabeth to commit to marriage or at least to name a successor.[21]

The Commons sent a petition to Elizabeth at Whitehall in late January 1563. It combined the need for clarity about the succession with expressions of fear about the queen's health and gratitude for her recovery:

> Forasmuch as your said subjects see nothing in this whole estate of so great importance to your majesty and the whole realm, nor so necessary at this time to be reduced into a certainty, as the sure continuance of the governance and th'imperial crown thereof in your majesty's person and the most honourable issue of your body, which almighty God send us to our highest comfort, and for want thereof, in some certain limitation to guide the obedience of our posterity; and where almighty God to our great terror and dreadful warning lately touched your highness with some danger of your most noble person by sickness, from which so soon as your grace was by God's favour and mercy to us recovered…[22]

The urgency of the request was not overstated. Years of civil war in the late fifteenth century had stemmed from a debate over competing claims to the throne.

The petition continued by praising Elizabeth's grandparents, Henry VII and Elizabeth of York, who established the Tudor dynasty and, importantly, provided for the future by producing an heir – Elizabeth's father, Henry VIII. This ensured the security of the realm. Now,

> As your majesty hath upon your own danger most graciously considered for our comfort and safety so we your humble subjects, knowing the preservation of ourselves and all our posterity to depend upon the safety of your majesty's most royal person, have most carefully and diligently considered how the want of heirs of your body, and of certain limitation of succession after you, is most perilous to your highness, whom God long preserve us.[23]

The 'Lords both temporal and spiritual assembled in Parliament in your Upper House' also petitioned the queen. William Paulet, the marquis of Winchester, was speaker of the House of Lords and delivered the suit. It stated that 'with all humbleness and obeisance they are come hither to present to your majesty' a petition for 'matters most dearly touching your most royal person, th'imperial crown of this your realm, the th'universal weal [well-being] of the same'. The suit contains two points:

> The former is that it would please your majesty to dispose yourself to marry where it shall please you, with whom it shall please you, and as soon as it shall please you. The second, that some certain limitation might be made how th'imperial crown of this realm should remain if God call your highness without any heir of your body (which our lord defend).[24]

The marriage question was, by this point, not only tied to but also in some cases separated from the question of succession. If the queen continued to postpone her marriage, parliament now asked her definitively to name an heir.

The separation of marriage and the succession was reinforced by the next portion of the petition. Referring again to the marriage, the lords 'do in their hearts most earnestly wish and pray for as a thing that must needs breed and bring great and singular comfort to yourself, and unspeakable joy and gladness to all true English hearts'. But there was much more emphasis on the request for a named heir, for 'it carrieth with it such necessity that without it they cannot see how the safety of your royal person the preservation of our imperial crown and realm, shall or can be sufficiently provided for'. The petition referred again to Elizabeth's illness, which was what brought them to make this request. The petition went on at some length, detailing the dangers inherent in the current state without a named heir, giving examples of other nations and times and in scriptural accounts. It finished by reminding the queen that without an heir, the kingdom shall 'be in more dangerous state and condition than ever it was that any man can remember'.[25]

Elizabeth's reply, delivered on 10 April 1563, exists in two formats, one in Elizabeth's own hand and one in the hand of Lord Keeper Nicholas Bacon, who delivered the speech on the queen's behalf. Both copies are held at the British Library. The copy in Elizabeth's hand shows her corrections and word changes and demonstrates her concern about presenting the most appropriate information to achieve her ends. There are several strikeouts and notes in the margins. A corrected copy in Bacon's handwriting, with some changes from Elizabeth's marked-up copy, is the most likely to be the one read in parliament. Elizabeth chose to have Bacon read the speech even though she attended the session.

Elizabeth agreed to address their concerns: 'the two petitions that you presented me, expressed in many words, contained in sum as of your cares the greatest: my marriage and my successor'. She agreed to address the second, believing that about her marriage 'a silent thought may serve', although she went on to say, 'if I can bend my will to your need I will not resist such a mind'. About the succession, she reasoned:

> the greatness of the cause thereof and need of your returns doth make me say that which I think the wise may easily guess: that as short time for so long continuance ought not pass by rote (as many tell their tales) even so as cause by conference with the learned shall show me matter worthy utterance for your behoofs, so shall I more gladly pursue your good after my days than with prayers whilst I live to linger my living thread.

She hoped for good outcomes other than those they called for, hoping to die in peace, 'which cannot be without I see some glimpse of your following surely' after her death. In the draft held at the British Library, written in the queen's hand, the multiple changes she makes, with strikeouts and marginal notes, demonstrate the care with which she chose her words. She ended by urging parliament to put the notion of her marriage out of mind, seeking to pacify them but refusing to make a firm commitment other than that if she could persuade herself to want what they want, she would do so.[26]

After this was read, Elizabeth gave assent to bills and Bacon announced the queen had asked him to prorogue the parliament. There was still hope the queen would marry and have at least one child. After all, she was only 29 years old. Elizabeth also proposed a marriage between Robert Dudley and Mary, Queen of Scots (more about that in Chapter 7) to settle the succession. The issue was left unresolved, and the second session of this parliament would not meet for another three years, by which time several things had changed.

In 1565, Elizabeth was beset with concerns about marriage and the succession. Activities in the previous three years had seen her plans for the marriage between Mary, Queen of Scots and Dudley come to nothing. Instead, in July 1656 the Scots queen had married Henry, Lord Darnley, another grandchild of Margaret Tudor and possible heir to the English throne. Elizabeth saw this as a clear act of defiance on Mary's part, as it strengthened the Catholic claim to the throne. Tensions were further raised when Mary gave birth to a son the following year. The marriage between Mary and Darnley might be publicly falling apart, but her son was the only male heir on the island at a time when even a baby boy might be preferable to a female ruler. That shifted power to Mary, who had fulfilled the expected womanly duties of marrying and producing an heir.

Elizabeth did understand parliament's concern and was stepping up her desire for courtships, even if she was still seemingly reluctant to go through with a marriage. The French ambassador was pleading the case of Charles IX, son of Catherine de Medici (a marriage partner initially requested by Mary, Queen of Scots). Princess Cecilia, the sister of Eric XIV of Sweden, was on her way to England, possibly to renew the courtship of her brother. There were renewed efforts to arrange the marriage to the Archduke Charles as well. Robert Dudley was ever-present, attempting to promote his own suit for the queen's hand. Watching the various negotiations, Spanish ambassador de Silva was keen in his support of the archduke, who was Spain's choice, but reported that he believed Dudley was the only one who had a real chance with the queen.[27]

The second session of that parliament was held in the midst of all this, from September 1566 to January 1567.[28] Both houses of parliament petitioned the queen to marry and settle the succession. The succession debate was finding its way into public discourse as pamphlets were published extolling the virtues of various claimants. John Hales of the Chancery wrote a tract promoting the case of Katherine Grey. Elizabeth took this seriously and was worried that Grey's marriage to Edward Seymour might be recognised as legal despite the queen's attempts to discredit it. Hales was charged with sedition and imprisoned in the Tower. Anthony Browne, a Catholic judge, published a tract advocating the claim of Mary, Queen of Scots. After Mary's son was born, a Scottish minister in Paris published a poem celebrating the baby boy as prince of Scotland, England, France, and Ireland. The evidence of public opinion about the succession was a worrying development for Elizabeth. A paper found among those of Thomas Sampson, a Marian exile, stated that if the queen would not hear the words of her people crying for progress in the marriage and succession question, the people would turn to parliament instead.[29] Parliament was ready to force the issue.

In an attempt to soften the queen and her resistance, when Elizabeth attended the council meeting on 12 October, her relative the Duke of Norfolk addressed the queen. He stated that, as a councillor, he had taken an oath to have regard for her well-being and for the safety and well-being of her subjects. He reminded the queen of the petitions presented to her at the previous meeting of the parliament and 'most humbly begged her to let parliament discuss both the succession and her marriage'. The queen angrily replied that she believed she had governed the nation well enough and that she had given her subjects no reason to complain. She did not wish parliament to discuss the succession; she would do that herself for she had 'no wish to be buried alive, like her sister'.[30]

Elizabeth realised that parliament was preparing to present another formal petition asking her to marry and name a successor. She summoned a parliamentary delegation of Lords and Commons, stating that the speaker need not attend because she 'intended to be speaker herself'.[31] Again, there are different versions of the queen's speech, including one in her own hand. It appears both versions were created after the fact. The notes in Elizabeth's hand may have been the queen's initial thoughts or her memory of what she said, with strikeouts perhaps indicating changes in delivery or her memory. The other version is longer and more complete.[32] The primary message is the same in both versions. Elizabeth was clearly angry about the continued pressure parliament was putting on her, especially the Commons, whom she said would not have dared to behave this way in the reign of her father.[33]

The queen railed against the idea that any of her actions had caused her subjects distress or concern, and denied that any would have greater care for her people than herself: 'Is there any cause I should alienate myself from being careful over this country? Is not my kingdom here?' She went on to tell them she knew what was coming, a 'petition, as I am informed consisteth in two points: in my marriage and in the limitation of the succession to the crown'. She reminded the group she had sent her answer that she would marry even though she was not naturally inclined to do so, but that her answer 'was not accepted nor credited'. She went on to say, 'and therefore I say again that I will marry as soon as I can conveniently, if God take not him away with whom I mind to marry, or myself, or else some other great [hindrance] let happen'.[34] Negotiations were underway at this time for a marriage to Archduke Charles, and some members of parliament were opposing it. So, Elizabeth might have been reminding the members that she was not the only one who was standing in the way of a possible marriage.

She also addressed the succession. 'The second point was the limitation of the succession of the crown, wherein was nothing said for my safety, but only for themselves.'[35] The general feeling of the time was that a named successor to the queen would provide the country safety and eliminate or at least greatly reduce the likelihood of civil war in case of her death. A named heir would also provide security for Elizabeth, because assassinating her would not leave the country without a leader, as her appointed heir would immediately step up. This would make rivals less likely to move against the queen. But Elizabeth didn't see it this way. She had spent time as the assumed heir in the reign of Mary I, and she had been sent to the Tower during the Wyatt rebellion. She saw her heir as more of a threat than an assurance. As Mary, Queen of Scots would learn less than a year after Elizabeth delivered this speech, even an infant son could be seen as a better alternative than a ruling queen.

After explaining her own value and assuring her audience that her courage was equal to her father's, she stated unequivocally, 'I am your anointed queen.' Although she might have been tentative when she came to the throne, this statement is expressed with confidence. It is significant that, even though she often referred to and channelled her father, and often referred to herself in male monarchical terms as a 'prince', here she called herself an anointed queen. She was positioning herself to participate in an arena formerly reserved for men – being able to stand in front of a group and claim her rights, using language to set her limits. Those limits included refusing to turn over to parliament the future of her nation.

Parliament challenged the queen's demand that they not discuss her marriage and heirs, stating it was their prerogative to do so. Elizabeth claimed her greater power, her right as a monarch and a woman to exercise her authority.[36] She assured her listeners that she thanked God for having endowed her with such qualities that 'if I were turned out of the realm in my petticoat, I were able to live in any place of Christendom'. Again, she was positioning herself as a woman, stripped of royal robes, but still able to live in control of her life. She was denying parliament the power to challenge that.

She ended by claiming that, instead of protecting the realm, having parliament 'deal in the limitation of the succession' would not be convenient and would cause danger to her and to her realm. Those perils were such that they could not be disclosed at the time. But, she assured them, 'as soon as there may be a convenient time and that it may be done with least peril unto you, although never without great danger unto me, I will deal therein for your safety and offer it unto you as your prince and head, without request. For it is monstrous that the feet should direct the head'.[37] She was head of the kingdom and would not be moved out of her place.

Prior to this speech of the queen's, Cecil had written that 'To require both marriage and stablishing of succession is the uttermost than can be desired. To deny both is the uttermost that can be denied.' This was not the first or final time he expressed a desperate desire for the queen to marry and have children. In 1561, he had written to Throckmorton candidly in what sounds like a prayer, 'God send our mistress a husband, and by time a son, that we may hope our posterity shall have a masculine succession.'[38] He believed marriage was the natural state for a woman, essential for a peaceful succession, and expected by the people. He recognised, however, the difficulty of addressing these issues with the queen, and concluded that if they could not get traction on the marriage question, 'then proceed to discussion of the right of the successor'.[39]

One thing these exchanges with parliament reveal is how the focus within the institution shifted over the years from marriage itself, with whatever comfort and counsel and stabilising influence a husband might have had on the queen, to a focus on the succession. Previous Tudor monarchs had also been focused on the succession. Henry VII had married Elizabeth of York shortly after his coronation. Their first child, Arthur, was born that September, just over a year since Henry had defeated Richard III at Bosworth. The first Tudor quickly provided the necessary heir and provided the spare male on 28 June 1491. In less than six years, Henry VII and Elizabeth of York had done the most successful job any Tudor monarch would do in providing for the succession. Other Tudors were not as successful, but not for lack of trying. Henry VIII made history in marrying six women in his desperation to have at least one son. When he realised he would leave just one male heir behind, he went to extraordinary lengths by devoting most of his will to describing his wishes for the future over several generations. Although Edward VI didn't marry and have children of his own, he was so serious about the succession he attempted to override a parliamentary act and his father's will to put the Protestant Lady Jane Grey on the throne. Mary I was keen on marriage and motherhood, marrying Philip of Spain and then apparently convincing herself she was pregnant. As she worried about being able to bear a child, she explored options other than Elizabeth to succeed her.

Elizabeth, on the other hand, seemed more ambivalent about the notion of an heir. She certainly showed less inclination to marry. And when she spoke of children, she was no champion of motherhood. When the Scottish ambassador spoke to her about how her children could strengthen and support her, she retorted, 'Think you I could love my winding sheet?'[40] She saw an heir as a potential rival, much as she herself had been during the reign of Mary I. She dangled the possibility of naming Mary Stuart as her heir in an attempt to coerce the Scots queen into abandoning her claim to Elizabeth's throne while Elizabeth was living. But it's not clear Elizabeth would have come through even if Mary had agreed. Elizabeth seemed to be convinced her greatest security was in leaving the question of her successor unanswered, with vague and unconvincing assurances that she would not leave the country comfortless and that God would take care of things in his own way.

Her subjects, and particularly her parliament, did not agree. Cecil reported to the full parliament the message of the queen and her refusal to entertain their petition. 'And as to her marriage, she said she thought she had so satisfied by her answer thereto that she looked rather for thanks than for request.' With a vague assurance three years prior and no firm action since then, it's easy to see why the members were not fully satisfied. He raised the succession issue directly: 'The other matter for limitation of the succession: she said as it was necessary, which she would not deny so did she know therein such perils to enter into the decision thereof at the present time.' But facing the threat of Mary, Queen of Scots and her son, as well as the memory of Elizabeth nearly dying of small pox only four years previously, parliament was not satisfied. Ultimately connecting the passage of bills the queen desired with permission to petition her, parliament was successful to some degree. On 24 November, Elizabeth sent a message lifting her demand that parliament not discuss marriage and the succession.[41] Parliament did pass the subsidy bill the queen wanted and presented a final document that thanked the queen for remitting part of the subsidy, for determining to marry, and for promising to settle the succession. But the language was softened to read that the queen would 'have due regard' to the issue 'when time shall thereunto serve conveniently'.[42]

As the end of the year approached, Cecil drew up his 'Memorial to the queen at the end of parliament', a document it's not clear the queen ever saw. His document demonstrates his discontent:

> The succession not answered.
> The marriage not followed.
> A subsidy to be levied.
> …
> General discontentations…[43]

With the world 'full of offences' according to Archbishop of Canterbury Parker, and with the privy council, Lord Keeper Bacon, and both houses of parliament expressing discontent, the queen went to the closing ceremony of this parliament. At the end of his remarks, the speaker again thanked the queen for her promise to marry and name someone to succeed her. Bacon, after addressing governmental business, also thanked the queen and expressed hope for seeing her married. Then Elizabeth rose to deliver her address. In addition to other areas, the queen was pointed in her response to their ongoing desire to require from her action on the succession.

> The Prince's opinion and good will ought, in good order, have been felt in other sort than in so public a place [to] be uttered. It had been convenient that so weighty a cause had had his original from a zealous prince's consideration, not from so lip-laboured orations out of such subjects' mouths.

Elizabeth's original draft calls those subjects 'wrangling', a word that can be read even though she crossed it out. It's also possible to read her revision to add 'lip-laboured'.[44]

Elizabeth ends with this counsel:

> Let this my discipline stand you in stead of sorer strokes, never to tempt too far a prince's patience [Elizabeth first wrote 'power'], and let my comfort pluck up your dismayed spirit and cause you think that, in hope that your following behaviours shall make amends for past actions, you return with your prince's grace; whose care for you, doubt you not to be such as she shall not need a remembrancer for your weal.[45]

She then instructed Bacon to dissolve parliament. De Silva reported that she chose to dismiss rather than prorogue parliament because she was dissatisfied with the members and hoped to have different men in the next group.[46] She might not have achieved everything she wanted, but she had made clear she would not allow parliament to dictate her choice of marriage or determine the succession. She had told parliament to do as they wished, and 'as for me, I shall do no otherwise than pleases me'.[47]

By the time this parliament was dismissed, Elizabeth had ruled nearly a decade. She had resisted attempts to be coerced into marrying someone she did not wish or turning over the power of marriage and or the succession to parliament or her privy council. She saw parliament becoming more focused on the succession, something that would continue through the rest of her reign. She was aware of the threats at home and abroad, and she took steps to publicly project her ability to address and overcome them. She was emerging as a monarch in her own way, and she was managing the demands of the men around her, from her council to her parliament to her suitors, in her own way.

Within the context of parliament and the queen dancing around the subject of her marriage, let's look at Elizabeth's potential partners, foreign and domestic.

Chapter 4

'Everything Depends Upon the Husband This Woman May Take'

If she does not marry and behave herself better than hitherto, she will everyday find herself in new and greater troubles.

Alvaro de la Quadra, Bishop of Aquila, to Philip II of Spain (4 August 1560)

The evolutions associated with the 1559 Treaty of Cateau-Cambresis provide an example of the complexities associated with the theory of the queen's two bodies when Elizabeth becoming Queen of England.

When negotiations began in October 1558, England was squarely aligned with Spain through Philip II of Spain's marriage to Mary I of England. But the ground shifted when the monarchy passed from Mary I to her half-sister Elizabeth on 17 November. England was no longer Spain's long-term ally, and the hope for Mary's child to carry England's return to Catholic Europe into the future was gone. Instead, England was now under the control of the young Protestant-leaning queen. Although everyone involved believed the treaty would involve marriage arrangements, no one had anticipated the monarchs of Spain and England would end up among the eligible partners.

It was now in Elizabeth that the body politic resided, and her natural body would bear the burden of trying to survive long enough to carry out her own religious, marital, and political plans.

Within a few days of Mary I's death, Count de Feria, Ambassador to Spain, wrote to Philip II about the late queen's death and Elizabeth's accession. He wrote 'it is very early yet to talk about marriage', but goes on to say, 'the confusion and ineptitude of these people in all their affairs make it necessary for us to be the more circumspect, so as not to miss the opportunities which are presented to us, and particularly in the matter of marriage'. Feria was already concerned about possible marriages for Elizabeth and what that would mean for Spain. He raised caution about the Duke of Savoy's potential suit, 'they fear he will want to recover his estates with English forces and will keep them constantly at war'. After describing his unhappiness about Elizabeth's appointments to her council and suggestions that Philip's servants in England believe they are already dismissed, Feria went on to summarise where things stood overall with Elizabeth now on the throne: 'The more I think about this business, the more certain I am that everything depends upon the husband this woman may take.'[1]

Feria was both well placed to give an accurate assessment of how things stood and biased by his support for Spain, the Habsburg empire, and Catholicism. Despite his bias, however, I think he summed up exactly how everyone felt in the first weeks of Elizabeth's reign: her choice of a husband would dictate everything.

Everyone assumed Elizabeth would marry. Her half-sister Mary had quickly begun negotiations for a husband after taking the throne. The country, the council, and foreign courts expected Elizabeth to do the same.

After all, people felt a queen regnant was bad enough. An unmarried queen heightened fears. Women were believed to be inferior to men in all ways. The refusal of any woman to follow nature and God's will and submit herself to a man would surely lead to disorder. Women's bodies were thought to be in constant flux and in need of a man and marriage to settle them. Marriage protected against the unstable qualities inherent in a woman's constitution. From the fall of Eve, women had been morally and intellectually inferior to men.[2] Therefore, for the good of herself and the country, the question was not if the queen would marry, but whom.

That was the question with which Feria was concerned. Just as the Cateau-Cambresis treaty had been thrown into confusion by Mary's death, so were the carefully constructed roles of England in regard to Spain, France, Catholic Europe, and emerging Protestant countries.

Elizabeth's own claim to the throne and her legitimacy would be affected by her choice of (and the reputation of) her husband. The presence of Philip of Spain at Mary's side counteracted any question of her legitimacy and right to sit on the throne of England. Elizabeth, too, would be strengthened by a strong foreign support system upholding her right to the English crown.

Religion was another area that Elizabeth's marriage would shape. If Elizabeth married a Catholic, the efforts of Mary and Philip in religious counter-reform would continue. If Elizabeth married a Protestant, England would return to the church of Edward VI. This would disrupt the new alliance with the pope and Catholic Europe, and align England firmly with reform-minded nations, resetting the balance in Europe. Finances would also be affected by the queen's marriage. The English economy was weak when Elizabeth came to the throne, and trade partnerships would be strengthened or perhaps destroyed based on the husband she chose.

As Feria surveyed the likely candidates, he was encouraged that the privy council seemed to be leaning toward a foreign choice for Elizabeth. After all, a foreign marriage would offer the strength of another country, financial and military support, and a bolstered reputation – something important for a relatively weak England. Feria was encouraged about the benefit for Spain, writing to Philip, 'I am very pleased to see that the nobles are all beginning to open their eyes to the fact that it will not do to marry this woman in the country itself.'[3]

So, who were the most likely of the foreign suitors seeking (to different degrees, certainly) a marriage with the new Tudor queen?

The Scottish Options: James Stewart and Lord James Hamilton, Earl of Arran

When Mary I of England died, Henri II of France saw his chance to gain power in England because his son was married to Mary, Queen of Scots, who was the Catholic claimant to the English throne. Henri instructed his son and daughter-in-law to claim the English throne. Mary, Queen of Scots started presenting herself as queen of England as well as the next queen consort of France. She appeared to be less interested in Scotland, creating an opportunity for the lords governing Scotland to begin to control of their own futures and that of their nation. They saw a chance to align with Elizabeth and England and protect Protestant gains in Scotland. Even John Knox supported this notion. According to John Aylmer, Knox said the greatest problem with female rule was that the realm would be transferred to strangers because the power of the queen would be transferred to her husband.[4] In their minds, the union of the weak English queen could be saved by a marriage to an appropriate Scottish Protestant.

The men who dominated Scottish and English state affairs in the first months of Elizabeth's believed marriage would 'counteract, if not obviate, some of the "inconveniences" attached to female rule' and godly Protestant husbands could prevent the return of Mary's Catholicism to Scotland. Elizabeth's male heirs would eliminate the chance that Mary would inherit the English throne. Furthermore, the birth of a male heir would also make Elizabeth's husband king in his own right, as custom dictated the husband the possession of the queen's dignity upon the birth of a child. As far as these men were concerned, marriage between Elizabeth and a Scottish lord promised the solution to the problem of Elizabeth's gender and the problems of Mary, Queen of Scots' Catholicism.[5]

The two Scottish contenders to become Elizabeth's husband were Lord James Hamilton, Earl of Arran, and Lord James Stewart, who became Earl of Moray in 1562.

James Stewart was the illegitimate son of King James V of Scotland and Margaret Erskine, who was married to Sir Robert Douglas of Lochleven. Stewart had been an early supporter of his half-sister Mary and attended her wedding to the Dauphin of France in early 1558. On his return from France, he visited England and met William Cecil. He was a strong supporter of the Scottish Reformation and was committed to preventing Catholicism taking hold in in Scotland.

Lord James Hamilton was the oldest son of James Hamilton, Duke of Chatellerault, and Margaret Douglas. He was Regent for the baby Queen of Scots when James V died. He attempted to arrange a marriage between his son and Mary. That fell through and he went to France as part of young Mary's entourage in 1548 when she was betrothed to the Dauphin. When Mary I died, Hamilton was considered as a possible husband for a member of the French court, but he did not marry. When Mary I died in England, Chatellerault and Hamilton openly declared their allegiance to Protestantism. Hamilton met with English diplomats Thomas Randolph and Ralph Sadler. This set the stage for a possible alliance with England and marriage between Hamilton and Elizabeth.

Hamilton was proposed as Elizabeth's husband in 1559 and Stewart in 1560. The Lords of the Congregation, who came to power in Scotland in 1560 following the death of Marie of Guise, proposed marriage between Queen Elizabeth and the Earl of Arran, believing he would stand in for a king and would bring 'the friendship and force of a kingdom'.[6] Cecil agreed, believing if the English queen were to marry a Protestant husband, the government of Scotland would be transferred to Elizabeth's son after her death.[7]

The English privy council considered Arran a better candidate to become king of Scotland than Stewart. In June of 1560, Cecil reported to the queen that Lethington believed Arran had all his father's honour valid upon him. He ended with a fervent plea that the queen marry: 'So most humbly of Almighty God I doo require that it may please him to direct your Majesties hart to make choice of a husband that may be a father to your posterite; for without it for my part I wish to my self no posterite.'[8] However, if Elizabeth was not interested in Arran, the Scottish Lords and English council agreed that Stewart would be an acceptable alternative.[9] The important thing was to unite Elizabeth with a Protestant husband and unite the two kingdoms.

However, before Elizabeth had a chance to really consider the possibility, let alone make a choice, the opportunity for a Scottish marriage disappeared. Henri II died in 1559, and Francis II and Mary, Queen of Scots became king and queen of France. Their reign was short. When Francis died in December 1560, and Mary, Queen of Scots was no longer queen of France. In 1561, she returned to Scotland to take control of her native country. She and Elizabeth ruled neighbouring nations for a few years, then battled for control of Elizabeth's crown after Mary came to England. Despite the efforts of the Lords of the Congregation, England and Scotland would not be united for another forty years, and it would ultimately be Mary's son who brought the nations under one king.

The Spanish Option: Family Ties

An immediate option for Elizabeth's husband and England's king was a familiar name: Elizabeth's brother-in-law and England's previous king, Philip II of Spain. There were several reasons this marriage would have positive political outcomes for England. Philip offered the strength and support of the Habsburg empire, something that had been highly favoured by Mary and was attractive to many English politicians. With the Queen of Scots claiming the English throne for herself, England was vulnerable to a French invasion. Many believed that with Philip at her side, Elizabeth could strengthen her own position and that of her kingdom.

Elizabeth faced serious challenges from the beginning of her reign for a host of political and religious reasons. There was tension over England's recently passed religious settlements, the Act of Uniformity of 1559, the third such act passed in England during the Tudor dynasty. The first Act of Uniformity, passed in 1547 during Edward VI's reign, enforced the use of the *Book of Common Prayer* in worship services. This was overturned during Mary's reign with a second act that restored Catholicism. Elizabeth I's act authorised a prayer book similar to that used in Edward's reign but with some Catholic elements retained.[10]

Even though Elizabeth's act did not go as far as Edward's had, the settlement was unacceptable to Philip as a Catholic king. Furthermore, the marriage of Mary, Queen of Scots and the French Dauphin created a possible political firestorm if France pushed Mary's claim to the English throne. There were also questions about international trade and specifically England's position with the Netherlands. Elizabeth's insistence on the return of Calais to England was another sticking point in international circles beyond her battles with the French.[11]

Philip recognised that marriage with Elizabeth would disrupt a union between France and England. The most direct way for Philip to continue his own unity with England and prevent a new alliance between England and France was to marry Elizabeth himself. Whatever his personal thoughts about Elizabeth or her religion, from a political perspective, marriage to Elizabeth was a clear path to a positive outcome.

Although Philip knew he would not be able to immediately continue his 'return England to Catholicism' plan by marrying Elizabeth, marrying her could represent a way to eventually bring her and then her country back to the 'right' path. In any case, even were she to cling to her heretical views, that was still better for Spain because as king of England he would have influence over a Protestant queen. Philip may have been devoted to the Catholic cause, but his religious zeal was always tempered by politics. He protested the pope's plan to excommunicate Elizabeth shortly after her coronation in 1559 to keep Elizabeth on friendly terms with Catholic nations and her own Catholic subjects. Maintaining good relations with Elizabeth helped Philip, and marriage with England would neutralise the power of Spain's traditional enemies.[12]

The union offered benefits for Elizabeth as well. For one thing, she knew him. Philip had spent time in England, and he had supported Elizabeth's position as heir to the English throne. Some even suggest that Elizabeth survived Mary's reign because of Philip's looking to his own future and intervening on her behalf when Mary's other councillors were calling for Elizabeth's execution.[13] Rumours about Philip being attracted to Elizabeth had begun to spread during his marriage to Mary and increased during discussions about a marriage between Philip and Elizabeth. Although only rumours, in the mid-seventeenth century, the bishop of Gloucester stated directly that Philip had been attracted to his sister-in-law during his marriage to Mary I.[14] Whether the rumours were true or not, Elizabeth appreciated talk about Philip's interest in her.[15]

Marriage to such a prominent European ruler and member of a powerful royal house would increase Elizabeth's recognition in Europe. This was something Feria played upon when he began serious negotiations on Philip's behalf. Feria was convinced that Elizabeth would be eager to marry Philip, assuring the Spanish king that, 'If she decides to marry out of the country she will at once fix her eyes on your Majesty.'[16] The reputation of the Spanish king would enhance Elizabeth's disputed claim to the throne and dampen the enthusiasm of Mary, Queen of Scots in her pursuit of the throne. Feria described Elizabeth as 'vain' and reasoned that she was competitive and would not wish to 'hold herself less than her sister', who would never have married a subject.[17] It was true that marrying a common subject or a lesser royal would present Elizabeth as potentially less desirable or powerful than her sister, who had married the king of Spain.

Despite having personal and political reservations, Philip came to the conclusion that given the 'enormous importance of such a match to Christianity and the preservation of religion which has been restored in England by the help of God', he would set them aside. He told Feria he was 'resolved to render this service to God, and offer to marry the queen of England, and will use every possible effort to carry this through'.[18] He saw the marriage as political and religious in nature, securing Spain's interests and promoting Catholicism in England to avoid problems with Habsburg dominions and allies. Hardly the words of an eager suitor. And, not surprisingly, he had some conditions.

First and foremost, Philip insisted that Elizabeth convert to Catholicism and commit to ongoing efforts to restore her country to the Catholic faith. Her efforts must include 'all that may appear necessary to me', he stated. He also expected the queen to request absolution from the pope for her heresy and gain a dispensation so that she would be a Catholic in good standing when they were married. Philip wanted it evident to the world that 'I am serving the Lord in marrying her and that she has been converted by my act.' Politics were also important, and Philip insisted that although when he married Mary I he agreed that their children would inherit his rule of the Netherlands, he would not agree to the same with Elizabeth. He wanted Elizabeth's agreement to all the conditions before the pope was approached for his support.[19]

Philip instructed Feria to make the offer to the English queen, which he did in early February 1559. The two men seemed confident Elizabeth would eagerly, or at least willingly, accept. England was a small and, in their view, weak country in need of the power and support of the man who was ruler of Spain and the Netherlands and was establishing an empire in the Americas. A significant portion of English overseas commerce was transacted through the Low Countries, which were in Philip's control.[20] Surely, it was unthinkable Elizabeth would not wish to marry and to marry as well as her sister had and enjoy the significant benefits of marriage to the king of Spain. The English council seemed willing to move forward. What Philip and Feria had not taken into consideration was the person the king had never understood and always seemed to underestimate: Elizabeth herself.

Elizabeth was eager for a good relationship with Spain and an amicable one with Philip. She was aware of the economic and political benefits of the alignment between them. But she did not jump at the chance to marry the Spanish king. Ironically, the proposed marriage between Philip and Elizabeth echoed the marriage between Henry VIII and Katherine of Aragon: marriage to a dead sibling's spouse. It was the objection to Henry and Katherine's union that was the basis of Elizabeth's claim to the throne. Henry VIII had insisted the pope had no authority to override the biblical injunction not to marry his brother's wife. Therefore, he was not married to Katherine and was free to marry Anne Boleyn. If Elizabeth were to marry Philip, the action would revive the disputes over the marriage of her parents and could effectively undercut her legitimacy. A marriage between Philip and Elizabeth would be within the prohibited degrees. Even though Feria assured her that the pope would be willing to issue a dispensation, Elizabeth, like her father, believed the pope did not have the authority to override scriptural injunction.

Feria was surprised Elizabeth was reluctant to give him a speedy and positive response. For several weeks she continued to avoid the question and resist pressure to give an answer. In February, she told Feria she did not wish to marry at all, but he did not believe she was being serious. He believed the queen wanted to 'shelve the business with fair words'. Feria pressed and they agreed he would 'have no answer that was not a very good one' and they left the matter open. Feria still sounded positive that a favourable response was possible, stating 'it seems to me that if the marriage is carried out the rest will soon be arranged, and all will proceed in accordance with the glory of God and wishes of your Majesty'.[21] After more discussion with the queen, Feria reported that she mentioned again she did not wish to marry and reiterated she did not believe the pope could grant the dispensation. Still, he believed this was not a final answer.

In mid-March, Feria wrote to Philip that Elizabeth told him she could not marry the Spanish king because she was a heretic. Feria described himself as 'much surprised to hear her use such words and begged her to tell me the cause of so great change since I last discussed the subject with her', but Elizabeth chose not to discuss it with him.[22] She had waited as long as she could, but the queen could no longer pretend she would remain in the Catholic Church. She was also encouraged about the progress in talks about making peace with the French. For his part, Philip was probably relieved. He moved quickly to marry Elisabeth of Valois, daughter of Henri II. Elizabeth responded by expressing disappointment that he would replace her so quickly, but she was probably as relieved as he that it was over.[23] At least for the short term, it appeared the matter had been resolved amicably and that the two rulers and the two nations would maintain a positive relationship moving forward.

Philip's marriage to the French princess had unintended consequences that disrupted Elizabeth's reign and marriage plans. While celebrating his daughter's marriage on 30 June 1559, Henri II participated in several jousts. At the end of a long day, he decided to take the field one more time and was mortally wounded. He died on 10 July and his son, Francois, and daughter-in-law, Mary, Queen of Scots, became king and queen of France.

While those matters were playing out in Spain and France, Elizabeth moved on to other foreign suitors seeking her hand.

A Protestant Among Catholics: Eric of Sweden

About twenty years before Elizabeth took the throne, after the death of Jane Seymour in 1537, Henry VIII and his council had to find a wife for the king. Thomas Cromwell was eager to find an ally who would support England's religious reform. With limited options, he selected Anne of Cleves. Elizabeth and her council faced a similar challenge in 1559, with most European princes being Catholic. Eric XIV of Sweden was a rare Protestant monarch at the beginning of Elizabeth's reign.

Eric had pursued Elizabeth before either of them ascended to the throne. In 1558, when the ambassador from Sweden had bypassed Mary I in London and gone to Hatfield to approach Elizabeth directly,[24] Elizabeth had displayed an early understanding of the politics of royal proposals. When Thomas Pope informed her of the offer, Elizabeth replied, 'I so well like of this estate, as I persuade unto myself there is not any kind comparable unto it.' Pope did not take Elizabeth's expressed preference for the single life seriously and speculated that 'her Grace would be right well content to marry so there were some honourable marriage offered her'.[25]

The next year, the Swedish offer returned. In October 1559, Eric's younger brother Duke John of Finland came to England to promote his brother's suit.[26] The duke believed his brother's commitment to Protestantism would convince Elizabeth to marry him. There was some initial popular support for the Swedish suit.[27] Duke John came to England, initially assuming his fine welcome meant Elizabeth had already agreed to marry Eric. He put on airs, expecting those receiving him to kiss his hand. It was not a good beginning. The duke tried to make amends and gain favour with the English.[28] He distributed silver coins widely and promised that after a marriage between Elizabeth and Eric there would be more to come, but it turned out that much of the money was counterfeit and of no value.[29] Still, the duke spent lavishly in other areas, and popular support grew for the possible marriage.[30] Eric became king of Sweden at the death of his father and continued his pursuit of the English queen. Cecil believed that the French also favoured the Swedish marriage as it would prevent an alliance between England and the Habsburgs or the Scots.[31] Engravings of Eric and Elizabeth together began to appear,[32] in what feels like a very early version of royal wedding tea towels and mugs.

With all the momentum for the Swedish marriage, there was one person (at least) who was decidedly against the match: Elizabeth herself. When she had told Thomas Pope she was very happy in her single state, she meant it. Elizabeth attempted to put Eric off with fair words but no firm answer. She said she would not agree to marry a man she had never seen, harking back to her father's experience with Anne of Cleves. Eric surprised her by stating his wish to come to England and court her in person. When Elizabeth learned in February 1560 he was actually planning to travel to England, she wrote to clarify her position and tell him to stay home. Stating that she understood the sentiment offered in the letter presented by the duke of Finland, and acknowledging with appreciation his love and zeal for her, she went on to say 'we are grieved that we cannot gratify your Serene Highness with the same affection'. She assured him this was not because she doubted his love or honour, but because 'as we have testified both in words and in writing, that we have never yet conceived a feeling of that kind of affection towards any one' (or as we would say today, 'it's not you, it's me'). She then begged the king to 'be pleased to set a limit on your love, that it advance not beyond the laws of friendship for the present not disregard them in future'. She reiterated this came from her desire to remain single, ending 'we do not conceive in our heart to take a husband but highly commend the single life', telling the king to spend no more time waiting for her to change her mind.[33]

As was often the case, Elizabeth was righ to trust her instinct. Eric XIV suffered from severe and violent mental instability later in his life and lost his throne in 1569.[34]

Archdukes Ferdinand and Charles of Austria

In April 1559, Spanish ambassador de Quadra wrote to Philip II of Spain that a marriage was being discussed between Elizabeth and the Archduke Ferdinand.[35] Marriage with Ferdinand or his brother Charles became an appealing possibility after Elizabeth decided not to marry Philip.[36] Emperor Ferdinand I and Philip agreed that a marriage between the English queen and one of the emperor's sons would be beneficial to the Habsburgs and Spain. Baron Casper Breuner, the emperor's ambassador, arrived in England in May 1559 and began negotiations for a marriage. He had some concern about the other possible suitors for the queen's hand.[37] Breuner was particularly annoyed at the presence of Duke John promoting the suit of the king of Sweden. The duke's public display frustrated him, and he accused the Swedish king of having stolen their crown. The dispute between the duke and Breuner became so pronounced that Elizabeth had to take steps to keep them apart.[38]

De Quadra, who had replaced de Feria as Spanish ambassador, was more positive than his predecessor about the potential for Elizabeth being convinced to marry. He cautioned Philip that there was opposition to Ferdinand because of his devoted Catholicism. De Quadra had learned from Cecil about the objections to Ferdinand, so he went back to talk to Elizabeth and told her it was the younger brother, Charles, that they were suggesting. Having said she would not consider a marriage to someone she had not seen, Elizabeth asked de Quadra if Charles would come visit. The ambassador explained he doubted the emperor would send his son without a marriage agreement in place. After leaving the queen, de Quadra and Breuner also met with Cecil, Bacon, and other members of the council to emphasise how pleased the Spanish king would be were Elizabeth to marry Archduke Charles. De Quadra ended his letter to Philip by admitting he remembered how sceptical Feria had been about Elizabeth ever marrying. Still, he believed that, 'so clearly is the need for her to marry being daily more understood by herself and her advisers, nothing withstanding her disinclination to say yes, I need not despair of her listening to the proposal' of Archduke Charles.[39] However, despite all de Quadra's attempts, Elizabeth was not yet ready to commit, and the negotiations stalled. A few years later, they would be picked up again, and this time at the instigation of Elizabeth and the English.

By 1563, things had changed for Elizabeth. Katherine Grey, younger sister of Lady Jane Grey and potential heir to the throne, married without permission of the queen. Elizabeth was already suspicious of those close to her crown, and Katherine's secret marriage to the Earl of Hertford made the queen fear a potential dispute over the succession. Elizabeth reacted dramatically, especially after Katherine gave birth to a son, and sent the couple to the Tower. Even more concerning for the English queen was Mary, Queen of Scots returning to Scotland in August 1561 after her husband's death. Mary's presence as the Catholic claimant to the English throne living just across the Scottish border sent shock waves through Elizabeth's court. With Mary searching for a second husband and making overtures toward Spain, the notion of an alliance with the emperor became very appealing for England. In 1563, Elizabeth promised parliament she would try to overcome her reluctance to marry. It was time to try again with Archduke Charles.

In 1565, the emperor sent an Imperial envoy, Baron von Mittenburg, to negotiate a marriage between Elizabeth and Archduke Charles. There were two important obstacles to Elizabeth agreeing to the marriage: the archduke's religion and Elizabeth's insistence that she meet any suitor in person before making a final decision.[40] Elizabeth was unwilling to rely on portraits so she could avoid disappointment after the betrothal was arranged. It's also possible that, knowing how inappropriate it would be for a foreign prince to visit her to be evaluated, Elizabeth used this as a way to delay or avoid having to make a decision about the marriage. The request for a visit might have been simply posturing. The question of religion was a more serious one.

Elizabeth was determined that Charles convert to Protestantism, stating that two people with different faiths could not peaceably live together. The English believed that Charles's commitment to Catholicism was less zealous than that of his brother Ferdinand's and expected agreement. Another controversial English demand was financial support to cover the archduke's household expenses. Cecil felt these requests would be met and optimistically sent Mittenburg off to take the English terms to the emperor. He told Sir Thomas Smith he believed the terms would be accepted, Charles would come to England, and the marriage would proceed.[41]

Despite earlier concerns about the dangers of a foreign marriage, support for Elizabeth's marriage to Archduke Charles increased. It was championed and promoted by Cecil, who was actively supported by several of the council including the Duke of Norfolk and the Earl of Sussex. English Catholics and Protestants supported this marriage, which points to the real concern in the country about a disputed succession. The possibility of the queen's death had become all too real in 1562 when she had nearly died of smallpox. Years of civil war over the succession had devastated the country in the latter half of the fifteenth century and remained an ominous memory. The confusion and fears over Elizabeth's successor, with Katherine Grey in disgrace and Mary, Queen of Scots attempting to marry herself to a European powerhouse, were a powerful motivator for the marriage to move forward.

Despite agreement among some leading English Protestants and Catholics that the importance of the marriage overshadowed religious differences, for the archduke religion was a deal breaker. De Silva, one of Philip's primary advisors, felt that agreement on the practice of religion would prove the greatest obstacle to the marriage. Elizabeth was dedicated to her religion and to her role as Supreme Governor of the church. Archduke Charles was more devoted to Catholicism than the English had anticipated. Elizabeth had already stated she felt marriage could only be successful if the partners shared a faith, and it became clear that neither of them wanted to change. There were other difficulties as well. The emperor wanted the English to pay for the archduke's court expenses, to name him king, and to have him reign jointly with Elizabeth. Furthermore, he desired that should Elizabeth die without an heir, the archduke should remain in England and continue to hold influence in government. The last request was dismissed immediately, while the others were considered as worthy of negotiation.[42]

De Silva told Elizabeth the emperor was willing to allow the archduke to visit England, but he wanted some areas of the agreement settled before he did so. In addition, de Silva reported having told Robert Dudley, the queen's closest courtier and ongoing suitor for her hand, that the queen had assured him she wished to marry someone out of the country and that he would do his best to bring the marriage between the queen and archduke to a successful conclusion.[43] Adam Zwetkovich, the ambassador to Emperor Maximillian II, returned to Vienna to present Elizabeth's wishes. The question of religion continued to be the sticking point, as Elizabeth did not want Charles to attend mass in England. The emperor said unless Elizabeth modified that requirement, the matter would be abandoned. Reluctant to end negotiations, Elizabeth sent Thomas Dannet to continue discussions in May 1566. Dannet discovered that Charles was determined to hear mass. Furthermore, the emperor refused to consider Elizabeth's religious conditions.[44]

With parliament pressuring her, Elizabeth sent the Earl of Sussex to meet with Maximilian. The two came to an agreement that Charles could attend Catholic worship in private if he would attend Anglican services with the queen in public. Sussex sent his colleague Henry Cobham to present the terms to Elizabeth and the council. Cecil, Lord Admiral Clinton, and Lord Howard of Effingham stated their strong support for the marriage, reasoning that the fear of a disputed succession and chance of civil war overcame any other consideration, even religion. Pembroke, Northampton, and Knollys spearheaded the opposition, stating that allowing the queen's husband to attend Catholic service even in private would lead to religious disputations throughout the country. Eventually, Elizabeth decided she could not allow Charles to attend mass, even in private. Sussex continued to try to negotiate, but finally in 1568 he returned home empty handed.[45] Despite positive signs and years of effort, marriage negotiations with Archduke Charles were truly at an end.

With the opportunity to gain Imperial support through a marriage to the archduke at an end, Elizabeth would face the late 1560s and a series of significant events without the benefits of foreign support.

Might she, instead, face the future with an Englishman at her side?

Chapter 5

The Favourite and Court Favourites

Sir Christopher Hatton was wont to say the Queen did fish for men's souls, and had so sweet a bait that no one could escape her network.

Sir John Harrington to Mr Roberte Markham

Despite all the international drama, the first decade of Elizabeth's reign was not all about foreign suitors. She was presented many opportunities to avoid some of the pitfalls of her half-sister's reign by marrying one of her own subjects. Ambassador de Feria wrote to Philip of Spain little more than a month after Elizabeth came to the throne, 'Everybody thinks she will not marry a foreigner and they cannot make out whom she favours, so that nearly every day some new cry is raised about a husband. They have dropped the earls of Arundel and Westmoreland, and say now she will marry William Howard's son or Pickering.' A letter of Tiepolo to the Doge and Senate in February 1559 included a note describing parliament's request that the queen marry within the realm. After proclaiming her preference for a single life, Elizabeth said she would marry and would prefer to avoid the 'inconveniences' Mary was subjected to by marrying a foreign prince.[1] Domestic suitors were ready to take her up on her offer.

Early Suitors

Henry Fitzalan, the 12th Earl of Arundel, served in the courts of Henry VIII, Edward VI, and Mary I before Elizabeth took the throne. Although he signed Edward's letters patent making Jane Grey queen, he shortly denounced Northumberland and proclaimed Mary queen.

He served in many capacities in Mary's reign and helped suppress the Wyatt rebellion. His name had been put forward as a possible husband for Elizabeth while Mary was queen. When Elizabeth came to the throne, he retained his offices and believed he could now be seriously considered as the new queen's husband. He showered gifts on the queen's ladies-in-waiting in hopes of a commendation. According to Feria, he gave jewels worth 2,000 crowns. He also entertained the queen lavishly the summer after her accession at his home, Nonsuch. Seeing the queen's enjoyment of his attention, he believed he would be her choice.

However, no one else seemed to have shared that view, least of all Elizabeth. Feria reasoned the marriage was unlikely because the earl was 'a flighty man, of small ability'. In response to rumours about Elizabeth's interest in Arundel, Venetian ambassadors Surian and Tiepolo believed Elizabeth was humouring her people's desire for her marriage by implying she would marry the earl.[2] Despite his generous gifts and Elizabeth's enjoyment of the festivities, she was not interested in the 50-year-old earl as a potential husband. Baron Breuner monitored Arundel's efforts and concluded the earl was the only one who thought he had any chance of winning the queen.[3] Eventually, Arundel realised his efforts were in vain.

Sir William Pickering seems to have been a rival for Arundel and a more serious contender for the queen's hand. Pickering publicly criticised Arundel as impudent and discourteous, and called him a knave. Arundel, in turn, told friends he would leave England if Elizabeth married Pickering.[4] Tiepolo described the opinion of the time that the queen would marry someone of 'not much lineage' who was in Flanders, whom he thought was Pickering.[5] Later that month, Tiepolo described Pickering as 'about 36 years old, of tall stature, and handsome, and very successful with women'. Pickering spent the beginning of Mary's reign in exile because of religion, then went to Flanders to recover from an illness. Italian ambassador 'Il Schifanoia' wrote that the people of England were convinced the queen would marry Pickering.[6]

Feria described Pickering's standing with Elizabeth in mid-1559: 'She saw him secretly two days after his arrival, and yesterday he came to the palace publicly and remained with her four or five hours. In London they are giving 25 to 100 that he will be king.' De Feria went on to describe how another of the queen's favourites, Robert Dudley, was put out by the amount of time and favour Elizabeth was giving to Pickering. All this was playing out during the period de Feria was negotiating for a Habsburg match for the queen, so it's not surprising he was unimpressed with the rivalries among the English suitors: 'If these things were not of such great importance and so lamentable some of them would be ridiculous.'[7]

Feria's replacement, de Quadra, picked up on the reports of Pickering. Deeply involved in and committed to the proposed marriage between Elizabeth and Archduke Charles, de Quadra was eager to believe Pickering's case was not seriously being considered. He reported that Pickering believed that the queen meant to die a maid.[8] Although de Quadra frequently stated he did not believe Elizabeth when she told him she preferred not to marry, he was happy to associate Pickering with the belief the queen would not marry. During the summer, Pickering's health declined and by autumn his hope of marrying the queen seemed to have evaporated.[9] He remained loyal to Elizabeth, never marrying, and serving as one of her lieutenants during the Northern Rebellion.[10] In some ways, by treating Elizabeth with lavish attention, recognising and respecting her desire to remain single, and continuing to support and serve her, Pickering was a more ideal suitor for the queen than those who expected their courtship to end in a marriage.

Thomas Heneage was a member of parliament for Stamford (1553), Arundel (1559), Boston/Lincolnshire (1563), Lincolnshire (1571–72), and Essex (1584, 1586, 1589, and 1593).[11] He became a member of Elizabeth's privy chamber in the mid-1560s. As far as the queen's courtships went, Heneage was primarily known for Elizabeth's public flirtation with him in order to make Robert Dudley jealous.[12] The flirtation was significant enough to merit a mention from de Silva, who wrote to Philip II that Elizabeth 'has begun to smile on a gentleman of her chamber named Heneage, which has attracted a good deal of attention'. Having observed Elizabeth for some time, de Silva realised that 'people think however, that it is all make-believe' and only intended to punish Dudley.[13] Four months later, de Silva mentioned the matter again, telling Philip he had asked Cecil about it. Cecil stated that the 'talk about Heneage was baseless nonsense' and the 'queen made a show of it for purposes of her own'.[14] Dudley took it more seriously than the rest, storming off to lavish attention on Lettice Knollys.[15] Heneage remained on good terms with the queen, and it's thought she gave him the spectacular jewel known as the Heneage Jewel that is held by the Victoria and Albert Museum. Like Pickering, he turned out to be a supporter more than a suitor, something Elizabeth enjoyed and appreciated.

Sir Christopher Hatton

Sir Christopher Hatton was not considered a typical suitor of the queen and was not taken seriously by his contemporaries. Naunton commented primarily on his being tall and a good dancer and stated that despite his having 'a large proportion of gifts and endowments', he was a lightweight at court that 'sprung up at night, and sunk again at noon'.[16] Nicolas countered that Naunton's assessment had likely originated in envy or misinformation. Camden gave a similar report and mentioned the 'modest sweetness of his manners'.[17] But none ever believed the queen considered marrying him.

Hatton came from a modest gentry family and lacked the connection and wealth of others at Elizabeth's court. Although he probably was good-looking and a good dancer, common attributes of Elizabeth's courtiers, he was also intelligent. He patterned himself on the model provided in *The Book of the Courtier* by Baldassare Castiglione, which was the 'ultimate how-to guide for aspiring courtiers'.[18] The *Courtier* provided the court and Elizabeth a working model for the royal court.[19]

During the reign of Mary I, Hatton attended St Mary's Hall, Oxford, leaving without a degree and enrolling at Inner Temple in 1560 at age 20. He studied Latin and classical rhetoric and remained to study common law and 'become proficient in gentlemanly pursuits'. This was not unusual at the Inns of Court, which functioned not only as training for lawyers but also as a 'finishing school' for young men hoping to join the royal court. Instruction was offered in fencing and courtly pursuits such as singing and dancing. Hatton likely attended lectures and perhaps qualified as a barrister but did not become a senior member.[20] He participated in the Inn's social life, writing and performing in several entertainments there.[21]

The glimpse of Hatton while entertaining and possibly while dancing marked the beginning of a relationship that would be important to the queen for years. In addition to his skills in the arts of the courtier, Hatton would come to play pivotal political roles in Elizabeth's reign. Hatton's rise seems to reflect a more general shift at court, where defending and promoting the queen's reputation through court gallantry was as favoured as battlefield success.[22] This courtliness became associated with the Order of the Garter. Hatton's becoming a Knight of the Garter and political player in Elizabeth's court after coming to her attention as an entertainer demonstrated the growing value of courtly gallantry.[23]

That did not mean Hatton lacked physical strength or diplomatic skill. In 1564, Hatton joined the group of fifty men who formed Elizabeth's personal and ceremonial bodyguards. In this position, Hatton was expected to accompany the queen to chapel and on royal progresses, to participate in tilts and other exercises, and to attend regularly at her request. Hatton was a skilled rider and enjoyed athletic pursuits. Hatton also became a member of the privy chamber. He did not figure in contemporary accounts during the 1560s, as his relationship with the queen was more private than her relationship with Dudley or her foreign suitors. The first grant from Elizabeth to Hatton was recorded in April 1568, which was a lease on Holdenby property in Northamptonshire. He later built a house on the property. He was appointed Keeper of the Royal Parks in 1568. Still, he was not considered to be as important to the queen as Heneage and Dudley until into the 1570s.

Once he became a member of the privy council in October 1572, Hatton was firmly established as one of Elizabeth's courtiers. Perhaps because he was less ambitious than Robert Dudley, Hatton's intimacy with the queen remained mostly out of the public eye.[24] Still, the time they spent together fuelled some speculation. Recognising the queen paying attention to Hatton and aware of the pitfalls of the ever-shifting sands at court, Hatton's friend Edward Dyer told him that there were rumours about his relationship with the queen. He also warned Hatton that however much the queen valued him and however close he felt to her, he must not forget that Elizabeth was queen and he a humble servant: 'though she do descend very much in her sex as a woman, yet we may not forget her place and the nature of it as our sovereign'.[25] Perhaps Dyer thought Hatton was being reckless or that his actions could leave him vulnerable to attacks from other courtiers.

It would be easy to imagine how Hatton might forget the vast difference in status between him and Elizabeth. When Hatton fell with some kind of kidney trouble in May 1573, the queen visited him nearly every day to see how he was feeling.[26] The queen's attention was particularly important to Hatton, as prior to his illness, he had worried that the queen would be so flattered by the attentions of the earl of Oxford that she would abandon him. The queen valued Hatton, and he was a true admirer who remained unmarried and devoted just to her. Hatton is recognised now as one known for expressing more than 'average capacity for Elizabetholatry', showering praise and attention on Elizabeth and expecting little in return.[27]

Robert Dudley – Elizabeth's True Love?

Of course, the primary English suitor and possibly the love of Elizabeth's life was Robert Dudley. Although he was a descendant of traitors and had participated in the effort to remove Mary and Elizabeth from the succession, Robert Dudley was the queen's longest lasting and closest companion. The Dudley family had been at the heart of the Tudor government since the reign of the first Tudor monarch, Henry VII, and a Dudley would hold the heart of the final Tudor monarch, Elizabeth I.

As Henry VII worked to strengthen his hold on the throne, he faced a double disaster when his son and heir Arthur died in 1502 and his wife, Elizabeth of York, died the next year. The Tudor dynasty now depended on the young Prince Henry, and the king feared his reign was under threat. He set in motion a plan to weaken the nobility and raise money to fund a vast security force, and he relied on Edmund Dudley to make this a success. Edmund was one of Henry VII's central ministers, and he raised thousands of pounds (more than £150 million in today's money) to support the king's efforts.[28] Edmund married Elizabeth Grey, and in 1504, the Dudley star of the next generation, John, was born.

Edmund might have been central to the success of Henry VII's final years, but when the old king died, he discovered his efforts were not appreciated. Henry VIII came to the throne eager to throw off the reputation of his father as miserly, greedy, and feared. Eager to disassociate himself from the unpopular decisions of his father while at the same time maintaining the power of the Tudor name, Henry VIII made Edmund Dudley and his colleague Richard Empson scapegoats and sacrifices. Both men, whose real crime was serving their king so well they had become the face of his most unpopular policies, were executed on 17 August 1510. It seemed the family reputation would be destroyed, but the Dudleys came to prominence again.

John Dudley was at court and in favour during the reign of Henry VIII. We don't know exactly when Robert Dudley and Elizabeth Tudor met. As an adult, Dudley claimed he had known Elizabeth since she was 8 years old, when she had informed him she would never marry. This would have been around the time of the execution of Catherine Howard, Elizabeth's third stepmother. We don't know how much Elizabeth would have been told about the sudden disappearance of her stepmother, but she might have begun to be wary of marriage after seeing stepmothers come and go quickly. It's also possible that Dudley thought it a handy reference point to claim a lengthy relationship with Elizabeth. In any case, Dudley was one of Prince Edward's companions and Elizabeth and Edward sometimes shared lessons and tutors. Both Elizabeth and Dudley studied under the tutelage of Roger Ascham.[29] It's certainly possible the two became close during childhood.

They certainly spent time together during Edward VI's reign, with John Dudley playing a prominent role in Edward's government and bringing his sons regularly to court. After Edward's death, the Dudley family played a leading part in the effort to remove both Mary and Elizabeth from the succession and put Jane Grey on the throne. Robert himself was given the role of arresting Mary Tudor to prevent her from raising supporters and making a play for the throne. It's fascinating to wonder how Elizabeth felt about his involvement in the effort to disinherit her.

The Dudley family was imprisoned when Mary I came to the throne, but the new queen was merciful to Jane Grey, her husband Guildford Dudley, and Guildford's brothers. They were imprisoned in the Tower, but initially only John Dudley, Duke of Northumberland, was executed for treason. Only after the Wyatt rebellion in early 1554 did Mary order the execution of Jane Grey Dudley and her husband Guildford on 12 February of that year. John Dudley, earl of Warwick (son of Northumberland), Ambrose, Henry, and Robert all remained in the Tower as prisoners. In March 1554, Elizabeth was arrested on suspicion of her involvement in Wyatt's plot and sent to the Tower as well.

Although she and Robert Dudley were in the Tower at the same time, as they were both suspected of treason it's unlikely they ever spent time together. The idea of a budding romance between the two of them as prisoners is impossible under the circumstances. With a father and brother already executed and his known involvement in the plan to help Jane Grey become queen instead of Mary, Robert would not have been allowed to roam freely and meet other prisoners. Nor would Elizabeth, who was imprisoned in the same apartments that her mother had spent her final days in before her execution. Still, it was a shared experience, living in constant fear that their lives would come to a violent end. That experience affected Elizabeth for the rest of her life, and she referred to it when she became queen. It was something she shared with Robert Dudley and no other suitor. Elizabeth was released from the Tower on 19 May 1554 – the anniversary of her mother's execution. She then went into house arrest. The Dudley brothers were pardoned and released in 1555. Warwick died shortly after his release.

The surviving Dudley brothers served Philip and Mary and fought in the war against France. Henry Dudley was killed fighting the French in 1557. Both Ambrose and Robert continued to serve Queen Mary until her death in 1558. By this time, Robert had established a relationship with Elizabeth, sharing interests such as hunting and dancing. As Mary's illness progressed in 1558, Dudley was one of those who began spending time with Elizabeth at Hatfield House as it became more evident she would soon become queen. One of Elizabeth's first appointments upon inheriting the throne on 17 November 1558 was to name Robert Dudley as Master of the Horse. It was a prestigious position, ranking after only the lord steward and lord chamberlain in the household.[30] He would be the person who would accompany Elizabeth whenever she rode or hunted, pastimes she participated in frequently. He was also the only man in the kingdom with permission to touch the queen, helping her mount and dismount. In the early weeks of the reign, Elizabeth and Dudley spent more and more time together.

It seemed to be something of a fairy-tale romance: two friends who grow up in danger, overcome time in the Tower of London, and eventually rise to success. Surely a romantic wedding was the next step in the relationship. There was one clear problem, though: Dudley already had a wife. He had married Amy Robsart in May 1550 during the reign of Edward VI. Amy was the heiress of Sir John Robsart of Syderstone, strengthening the Dudley support in Norfolk. While Robert was imprisoned in the Tower, Amy was allowed to visit him. Once Elizabeth took the throne, Dudley was at court and in regular attendance on the queen. Elizabeth preferred her married courtiers leave their wives at home, something Robert Dudley seemed happy to do. As the weeks went on, the queen granted Dudley property in

Kew. Members of the family benefitted from Elizabeth coming to the throne: Dudley's sister Lady Mary Sidney became a gentlewoman of the privy chamber and his brother Ambrose became Master of the Ordnance and was granted lands.[31]

During the first year of Elizabeth's reign, the relationship between the queen and her devoted Master of the Horse progressed enough to spark gossip in court, throughout the country, and abroad. It was a classic way to attack a woman – accuse her of sexual depravity. The general consensus of the time was that women were more sexually depraved than men, and that only marriage could contain their sexual impulses in an honourable way. Elizabeth's stated preference for the single life worked against her – morally sound women desired marriage, and a woman who proclaimed a desire not to marry was considered immoral and unnatural. Given Dudley's background as the descendant of traitors and Elizabeth's reputation as the daughter of 'the scandal of Christendom', rumours about their inappropriate behaviour spread quickly and widely.

When Kat Ashley begged the queen to marry and end her relationship with Dudley and thereby save her reputation, Elizabeth was angry. In fact, it's unlikely that anyone other than this long-time servant and friend would have been able to say such a thing to the queen. Elizabeth responded that she had experienced so much sorrow and hardship in her life that no one should deny her those few pleasures available, particularly as Dudley had shown himself to be honourable in all his dealing with her.[32] Elizabeth was described as having been shaken by Ashley's comments, feeling melancholy and determined not to give the members of her kingdom any reason to think ill of her. But the queen kept spending time with her favourite, and rumours continued spreading.[33] Mary, Queen of Scots, for example, seemed eager to convince others that the queen and Dudley were lovers.[34]

According to de Quadra, Spanish ambassador, the Duke of Norfolk spoke openly in England about the rumours of Elizabeth and Dudley having an affair, and people in the country were embarrassed by the queen's behaviour.[35] Less than a month later, de Quadra reported to

Philip II that he had 'heard from a certain person who is accustomed to give me veracious news that Lord Robert has sent to poison his wife'. De Quadra said he was initially sceptical about the level of intimacy his source reported between Dudley and the queen, but went on to say the frequent accusations by Dudley's enemies made him believe it was possible.[36]

In the fall of 1560, something happened that changed the queen's relationship with Dudley forever, although not in the way most people expected. According to de Quadra, William Cecil, who was out of favour because of his criticism of Elizabeth's obvious favouritism towards Dudley, believed the queen's plan to marry Dudley would cause 'the ruin of the realm'. De Quadra claimed that Cecil said Dudley was thinking of killing his wife, who was known to be ill, and that Elizabeth said Dudley's wife was dead or nearly so, calling the entire business 'most shameful and scandalous'. A note added at the bottom of the letter read: 'Since writing the above I hear the queen has published the death of Robert's [wife], and, said, in Italian, "She broke her neck." She must have fallen down a staircase.'[37] It's difficult to imagine that Cecil would speak so openly to the Spanish ambassador, however concerned he might have been. But on this final point, de Quadra was correct.

On 8 September, Amy Robsart Dudley sent all her servants to the Abingdon Fair for the day, despite their reluctance to leave her alone.[38] When they returned, they found her dead at the bottom of a short flight of stone stairs. Exactly what happened remains a mystery to this day. It is certainly strange that anyone of Amy's status would send all her servants away and wish to remain alone. According to her servants, she had been depressed and had been praying for God to deliver her. There is reason to believe Dudley could have wanted her dead – he had not visited his wife in more than a year.[39] Others might have also wanted Amy dead. Perhaps if not Dudley himself, his supporters or servants might have thought her death would help him. After all, two friends of Dudley's were living at Cumnor Place, where Amy died.[40] William Cecil might have reasoned that the surest way to eliminate Dudley from the group of potential marriage partners was to involve him in a scandal so serious that Elizabeth would not be able to marry him. Perhaps Amy was so depressed that she decided to end her life and, after sending her servants away, threw herself down the stairs. Or perhaps the death was the result of the illness that Amy had been said to be suffering. She was reported to have had a 'malady in her breast', which might have been advanced breast cancer. This could have made her bones so weak that even a stumble down a short staircase might have broken her neck.

Whatever the exact cause of Amy Robsart Dudley's death, the aftermath shook the English court. The timing, with Dudley travelling with the queen, intensified the rumours of foul play. Many believed Dudley himself was responsible. He immediately ordered a thorough investigation.[41]

Elizabeth responded by sending Dudley to Kew until the death was investigated. The inquisition was held at Cumnor in Oxfordshire on 9 September to investigate the death. John Pudsey was the coroner took evidence and called jurors and held assizes. The result was that it was determined that Lady Amy Dudley

> intending to descend the aforesaid chamber by way of certain steps of the aforesaid chamber there and then accidentally fell precipitously down the aforesaid steps to the very bottom of the same steps, through which the same Lady Amy there and then sustained not only two injuries to her head – one of which was a quarter of an inch deep and the other two inches deep – but truly also, by reason fo the accidental injury or of that fall and of Lady Amy's own body weight falling down the aforesaid stairs, the same Lady Amy there and then broke her own neck, on account of which certain fracture of the neck the same Lady Amy there and then died instantly.

Ultimately, the verdict was 'misfortune'.[42] The coroner and jurors affixed their seals to the verdict, officially closing the case.

Scottish surgeon Ian Aird revisited the possible causes of Amy Robsart Dudley's death in 1956 and concluded that the best explanation was that she died from a disease that caused her spine to fracture.[43] Was her spine weak from a disease such as breast cancer, perhaps hinted at by rumours she had a 'malady' in one of her breasts? Perhaps weakened by poison? After all, poison was a common danger at the Tudor court. William Cecil was so worried about Elizabeth herself being poisoned that not only her food but anything that might touch her body had to be examined and tested before it reached the queen.[44] It may never be clear exactly what caused Amy Robsart Dudley's death. What is clear is the complicated fallout.

Despite the coroner finding that Dudley's wife's death had been the result of 'misfortune', key figures believed Dudley to be involved. De Quadra reported to Philip II that Henry Sidney, Dudley's brother-in-law, told him no one believed the death was accidental and that 'even preachers in the pulpits discoursed on the matter in a way that was prejudicial to the honour and interests of the queen'.[45]

Immediately after the incident, Elizabeth put physical distance between herself and her favourite. But once the inquest was over, he returned to court and to the queen's side. Dudley seemed to renew his determination to woo and wed the queen, something he continued for more than a decade. He saw himself as a single man and believed there was no reason he should not court the queen.

For Elizabeth, though, the incident of Amy's death made her marriage to Lord Robert less, rather than more, likely. Elizabeth's conflicting statements on marriage make it impossible to know what the queen might have done had Amy died in a natural, uncomplicated way. But given the suspicious nature of her death, and the scandal that would surely follow were Elizabeth to marry the man most suspected in the death, she could not marry him. The evidence presented at the inquest was simply not enough to convince people of Dudley's innocence. Dudley's general unpopularity, compounded by the scandal that now marred his reputation, meant that many in the country would absolutely refuse to recognise him as their king. The danger that 'the kingdom would split into hostile factions' was demonstrated when Arundel's servant said any such marriage would cause trouble among the nobility.[46]

In addition, a marriage to Dudley would do damage to Elizabeth's reputation as queen. Her half-sister had bolstered her claim to the English throne by a marriage to Philip of Spain. With the public support of Spain and the Habsburg empire, few were likely to question Mary's legitimacy or right to the throne. Elizabeth's marriage to a commoner, particularly one mired in a murder scandal, could only make things worse for a woman who had been declared illegitimate by her father, her half-brother, and her half-sister. The power of rumour to weaken Elizabeth's standing in the European community was expressed by her ambassador to the French court.

Sir Nicholas Throckmorton complained to Cecil about the mockery of the French court, which would only worsen were the queen to marry Lord Robert. He described the sentiment he was hearing: 'some let not to say, what religion is this, that a subject shall kill his wife, and the Prince not only bear withal but marry with him?'[47] It's possible no one was more pleased with the scandals surrounding the death of Amy Dudley than Mary, Queen of Scots and France, who cried that the queen of England was about to marry her horsekeeper, who had killed his wife to make way for her. Throckmorton made certain Elizabeth would hear this, believing such an insult might shock her into breaking off her relationship with Dudley. Throckmorton even sent his secretary, Mr Jones, to England to meet with the queen and convince her of the danger of choosing Lord Robert as her consort. Elizabeth was impatient, laughing at Jones's warnings and defending Dudley. The audience did not allay Throckmorton's worries.[48]

Cecil, on the other hand, recognised that attacking Dudley caused the queen to defend him. Therefore, he took the calm approach, allowing Dudley's own unpopularity to weaken his case with the queen. Cecil believed that Elizabeth, given time to consider the matter, would come to realise the imprudence of such a match. He even counselled Throckmorton not to 'be too busy' about the queen's relationship with Dudley.[49] Elizabeth's independence was something Cecil fought against in many situations; he was very keen that she should marry, and he regularly encouraged her to do so. However, in this instance, her resistance to take a husband worked in his benefit as it meant she was unlikely to abandon her independence and lessen her control, even to her long-time favourite.[50]

Dudley eventually made an attempt to involve the Spanish ambassador in his quest to marry the queen. He sent Henry Sidney to ask de Quadra to 'recommend the queen to marry him'.[51] Dudley assured de Quadra that once he married Elizabeth and became king, Catholicism would be restored to England.[52] Philip seemed to believe there was some possibility, counselling the ambassador to continue to have conversations with Sidney and Dudley and 'give them to understand that I have the same good will towards the latter that I ever had, and take every opportunity you may see to express affection and attachment to him, so as to forward the affair by this means'.[53] Elizabeth may have been in on the plan; although she had no intention of allowing the return of Catholicism, making Philip believe she was willing to do so would mean she was less likely to face excommunication or be directly challenged for her throne by those supporting Mary, Queen of Scots. As always, she declined to give an absolute answer, but she agreed that she had affection for Lord Robert and appreciated his good qualities and said she believed she would be best served by marrying an Englishman.[54]

The matter proceeded far enough to create the possibility that the Papal Nuncio might visit England, something Cecil opposed vehemently. He was able to intercept a letter from a bishop about the potential visit and used that to create concern regarding English Catholics and imply de Quadra was to blame. This resulted, not surprisingly, in anti-Catholic sentiments at court, which Cecil encouraged. In May, the council recommended the queen not receive the Papal Nuncio, and she wrote to Throckmorton expressing her 'denial for the Nuncio to come into England'.[55] Cecil was pleased, telling Throckmorton, 'God and the queen (the one by directing and the other by yielding) have ended the matter well.'[56] Dudley was discouraged by the withdrawal of Spanish support, but the queen then arranged for him to have apartments near her own, creating new hope of success.[57]

Through the turmoil of 1560 and 1561, there were many who believed that the queen would marry Dudley. He himself seemed to be convinced his chances were good, and his commitment to this quest is evidenced by his even aligning himself with Spain and Catholicism, at least to some degree, for a period of time. Elizabeth continued to encourage his affection and to return it in her own way. She certainly gave him ongoing and questionable physical access to her through these years and beyond, and she also allowed him to play a role in dampening the chances of other marriage possibilities. She would continue to have Dudley at her side, in pursuit of her hand, for many years to come.

At the same time, she did not give up her position as monarch or surrender herself or her power, even to him. It was, according to Naunton (whose record was, admittedly, written much later), to Dudley himself that Elizabeth declared her famous line: 'I will have here but one mistress and no master.' For the next decade, the queen would satisfy herself with an ongoing courtship with her favourite that would not end in marriage.

Elizabeth continued her dance of deception. She kept her council, her parliament, and foreign courts wondering how she really felt about marriage and what she would do next. She accomplished this by speaking in a way that appeared to respond to a question but didn't really provide a commitment. Elizabeth excelled in the skill of using 'answers answerless'.

Chapter 6

Questions and Answers Answerless

> Courtships were part of statecraft; they were also flattering and amusing yet from an early age Elizabeth never intended them to be anything more.
>
> Lisa Hilton, *Elizabeth: Renaissance Prince*

In 1586, Elizabeth faced one of the greatest personal and political challenges of her reign: what to do with Mary, Queen of Scots. She had been arrested for participating in a plot to assassinate the English queen. She had been found guilty. The sentence for treason was death. Elizabeth's council, her parliament, and her friends were clamouring for her to sign Mary's death warrant and eliminate one of the dangers that had threatened Elizabeth and England for years. In her hesitation to do so, Elizabeth called attention to the verbal strategy that she used throughout her life and reign: delivering answers answerless.

Elizabeth's hesitation was based on several things – her own insecurities, the fear of retaliation from abroad, and the dangers posed by English Catholics who objected to Mary's death. There were also possible repercussions from the person Elizabeth was seeking to cultivate as her ally and potential heir, James VI of Scotland. There seemed to be no 'right' answer. So, in her own words, she told her councillors they 'must take an answer without answer at my hands' and be content with 'this answer answerless'.[1] This phrase, 'answers answerless', was a hallmark of Elizabeth's rhetorical strategy through her reign, and even before she became queen. From the time she was a young woman, she employed the use of language that seemed to answer a question but actually left the listener with nothing more than contradictory words. She might have first used the phrase at this

'Elizabeth I when a Princess', c. 1546. (*Wikimedia Commons, public domain*)

'Thomas Seymour, 1st Baron Sudeley', Nicolas Denizot, c. 1509–1549. (*Wikimedia Commons, public domain*)

'Elizabeth I, the Hampden Portrait', attributed to George Gower, formerly attributed to Steven van der Meulen, c. 1567. (*Wikimedia Commons, public domain*)

'Philip II of Spain', Alonso Sanchez Coello, c. 1570. (*Wikimedia Commons, public domain*)

'Robert Dudley', Steven van der Meulen, active 1543–died 1563, Netherlandish, active in Britain (from 1560), naturalised 1562, Robert Dudley, first Earl of Leicester (1532/3–1588), ca. 1565, Oil on panel, Yale Center for British Art, Paul Mellon Collection, B1981.25.445. (*Public domain*)

'Sir Christopher Hatton KG', Nicholas Hilliard. (*Wikimedia Commons, public domain*)

'Elizabeth I, Pelican portrait', Nicholas Hilliard, c. 1573–1574. (*Wikimedia Commons, public domain*)

'Robert Dudley, first Earl of Leicester', Unknown artist, sixteenth century, Robert Dudley, first Earl of Leicester (1532/3–1588), ca. 1595, Oil on panel, Yale Center for British Art, Paul Mellon Collection, B1975.1.7. (*Public domain*)

'Francois, Duc of Alencon/Anjou', unknown artist, 16th century. (*National Gallery of Art, public domain*)

'Sieve Portrait of Queen Elizabeth I', Quentin Metsys the Younger, 1583. (*Wikimedia Commons, public domain*)

'Robert Devereux, Earl of Essex', Print by Jacobus Houbraken, after Issac Oliver, 1738. (*Wikimedia Commons, public domain*)

'Elizabeth, Queen of England', Crispijn de Passe I, 1592. (*The Metropolitan Museum of Art, public domain*)

point, late in her reign, but this was a strategy she relied on from her childhood and youth, and then throughout her reign.

Elizabeth's childhood was unpredictable, to say the least. She was born as heir to her larger-than-life father, Henry VIII. Before she turned 3, her father not only had his marriage to Anne Boleyn annulled, making Elizabeth illegitimate, he had Anne Boleyn accused of sexual depravity and treason. She was beheaded on 19 May 1533, and from that point on, Elizabeth's enemies used her mother's manipulated bad reputation against her.

During her brother Edward VI's reign, Elizabeth was subjected to sexual advances by her stepfather, Thomas Seymour, while living with Katherine Parr. After Parr's death, Seymour tried to marry her. As a result, Elizabeth was subjected to accusations of being involved in Seymour's treason and was subjected to lengthy interrogation. She learned then to give careful answers that provided just enough information to protect her from the plots of others. During Mary I's reign, Elizabeth was again suspected of treason after the Wyatt rebellion. Despite Wyatt's testimony that Elizabeth was not involved, Mary suspected her half-sister and sent her to the Tower to be interrogated. Again, Elizabeth gave careful answers that revealed only what was necessary and remained ambiguous and noncommittal. Through her first twenty-five years, Elizabeth developed 'a verbal style that would stand her in good stead throughout her reign'.[2]

Once Elizabeth became queen, she took her use of language as a political strategy to new heights. To effectively rule as a woman, Elizabeth used her education and experience with rhetoric as an instrument of power. She relied on her speaking skills to manage the men in parliament. Her strategy was often to promise an answer and then speak carefully, considering the moment, the topic, and the style that would be most effective. Often, 'her responses could be construed as answers only because she described them as such'.[3]

Sir John Neale described the queen as a great actress who viewed her addresses to parliament as an opportunity to show off her personality and project her leadership capabilities on the public stage.[4] The queen also used and deliberately confused language about gender expectations. When she wanted to appear decisive and like her royal forebearers, she frequently described herself as a 'prince'. When she wanted to resist making a decision, she was not above hiding behind the image of a woman unable to decide or take action. In a reply to the House of Commons, she said:

> The weight and greatness of this matter might cawse in me being a woman wanting both witt and memory some feare to speake, and bashfulness besides, a thing appropriate to my sex: But yet the princely seate and kingly throne, wherein God, (though unworthy) hath constituted me, maketh these two causes to seme little in myne eyes, though grievous perhaps to yor eares, and boldeneth me to saye somewhat in this matter, which I meane only to towche, but not presently to answer.[5]

Whatever the queen may have thought about women in general, she did not consider herself wanting in wit or memory or afraid to speak. Describing herself in this way was a tool she could use to resist being forced into revealing her true thoughts or intentions. She used this tool well and frequently. Elizabeth was savvy enough to use her gender to her benefit, playing into and against contemporary assumptions about women's personality, attributes, and capabilities (or lack thereof). She was typically effective in shutting down petitions and requests for answers, at least temporarily. As queen, the weight of her presence and language were considerable; often even brief comments were enough to end the discussion. Nowhere did Elizabeth employ the power of 'answers answerless' and rhetorical devices more than in her courtships. She had stated since she was a youth that she did not wish to marry, but no one seemed to take that seriously at the time.[6] She also stated she would marry, if God willed it, allowing the confusion from her contradictory statements to work in her favour.

Political marriages were the norm for royals at the time, but the Tudors had regularly expected personal satisfaction from marriage.

Henry VII married Elizabeth of York so he could reinforce his claim to the throne and gain support from Yorkist loyalists. Elizabeth of York proved a successful consort, providing the king with a son just eight months after their marriage. She went on to have several children, with two sons and two daughters surviving early childhood. When their son Arthur died in 1502, Henry and Elizabeth were described as comforting each other in ways that demonstrate genuine affection and concern. After Elizabeth's death, Henry VII withdrew from court for weeks in his grief. What had started as a political marriage had become a genuine and personal one.

Henry VIII is often thought to have been casual about marriage – a conclusion drawn from his having more wives than any monarch in history. But in fact, Henry was ardently seeking a lasting and personally fulfilling marriage. He had a lengthy marriage to Katherine of Aragon, and if she had managed to give the king even one living son, he would not have abandoned her. Had Anne Boleyn given the king a son, Henry would not have sent her to her death. After Jane Seymour's death, which Henry greatly regretted and mourned, he ended his marriage to Anne of Cleves of his own accord. But had there not been evidence Catherine Howard had betrayed him, he would have kept her at his side, and he hoped to have children with Katherine Parr (according to his will) before he died. Henry deeply believed in marriage.

Mary I recognised how important marriage was for her position as first crowned regnant queen, for England's safety, and for her goal of returning England to Catholicism. But it's clear from the time she saw Philip's portrait that she was also very attracted to him and wished for a strong personal connection and relationship. She was genuinely distraught when he left England and spent so much time out of the country. She, like her father and grandfather, sought a genuine and personally rewarding relationship in her marriage. None of the Tudor monarchs before Elizabeth were satisfied with a purely political union of countries and leaders – they all wanted more.

Likewise, Elizabeth expressed desire for more than a political marriage. She made it clear she would not be told whom to marry.

She resisted being pushed into marriage during Mary I's reign, and she was even more determined that marriage would be her own choice and not that of her male advisors during her own reign. She did not wish to share governance of her kingdom with a husband, despite the tradition and expectation that women were less able to lead than men were. Early on, she expressed no desire to marry quickly as her sister had. She repeatedly explained to William Cecil how much she enjoyed her single state and her reluctance to end it. At the same time, she hinted at a willingness to marry if God were to inspire her to do so. The queen's willingness to express a preference to remain single and a willingness to marry, while never quite committing fully to either, was a hallmark of her conversations with suitors, ambassadors, and her own councillors throughout her reign.

Elizabeth was aware of the political advantages associated with being courted by foreign princes, dukes, and the leading courtiers in England. She therefore said she was ready to consider individual suitors who were politically appropriate and personally desirable, someone she found 'physically, emotionally, and intellectually appealing – an astonishing notion for a monarch at that time'.[7] Perhaps in part it's the contradictory nature of her desires that leads to the contradictory nature of her language when discussing marriage. After all, she knew that the political appropriateness of a suitor was perceived political realities that were changing all the time, on religious questions that were fraught with the potential of violence if she or her potential husband went too far, and on the complicated notion of a woman who wished to rule her own kingdom while married to a man who would expect to be her superior and lord. There were always as many reasons not to make a match with a foreign or an English suitor as there were reasons to make a match, and parliament knew that.

From the start of her reign, Elizabeth was petitioned by parliament and her council to marry quickly and provide an heir. The notion of the queen's marriage as a topic of public debate would last through much of her reign. She was often faced with direct petitions that she needed to answer. In fact, five of the queen's speeches to parliament directly addressed the topic of marriage and the succession.[8]

According to some accounts of her first speech to parliament, Elizabeth spoke clearly about her reluctance to marry. William Camden includes this passage in his account of the queen's address to the House of Commons: 'I am already bound unto a husband, the kingdom of England, and that may suffice you.'[9] This version of her speech, and this phrase in particular, has been frequently quoted for centuries. However, some scholars doubt that the queen spoke those words. John King questions the validity of the account, particularly since Camden was writing many years after the speech was given and lacks citations for his account. King argues that Camden was describing Elizabeth's reign, start to finish, through the lens of a Jacobean representation of her as a virgin queen – something that was not yet evident in 1559.[10]

At the same time, Elizabeth certainly made statements that seemed to call her commitment to marriage into question. In the version of the speech held at the British Library,[11] Elizabeth stated she 'chose this kind of life in which I yet live, which I assure you for mine own part hath hitherto best contented myself and I trust hath been most acceptable to God'. Even so, she understood parliament's petition for her marriage. She liked it because 'it is simple and it containeth no limitation of place or person'. Had it been more prescriptive, she 'must needs have misliked it very much'. She understood the Commons wanted her to marry and she could accept that request, since they didn't presume to dictate the choice of husband or the timeframe. So, 'whensoever it may please God to incline my heart to another kind of life', she assured them they should not imagine she would do anything that would displease the kingdom.[12]

On the other hand, just moments later she expressed the possibility 'it might please God to continue me in this mind, so live out of the state of marriage'. That must have surprised listeners who had felt they had just been told she wouldn't do anything to displease them or the realm, and they wished to her to marry and provide an heir. She alluded to the need for an heir without committing herself to providing one, even though that was one of the primary responsibilities of the sovereign: 'He will so work in my heart and in your wisdoms as good provisions by His help may be made in convenient time, whereby the realm may not remain destitute of an heir that may be a fit governor, and peradventure more beneficial to the realm than any offspring as may come of me.'[13]

At the end of her address, she included one of the most famous statements attributed to her about marriage: 'And in the end, this shall be for me sufficient: that a marble stone shall declare that a queen, having lived such a time, lived and died a virgin.'[14] John Neale's account contained the same statement.[15] In the clarity that came when Elizabeth died as the only adult sovereign of England never to marry, it's tempting to see this statement as a prophecy, something she was certain of from the very beginning of her reign. She would live and reign alone and then die a virgin.

And yet even in that same speech she had acknowledged the possibility that God would inspire her to adopt a different way of life, that He would inspire her to marry. And other statements to parliament gave members reason to believe the queen would, eventually, marry. The people around her wanted her to marry. Her privy council and her parliament regularly requested, counselled, and begged her to marry. Most people believed all women should marry to achieve their highest place in life, to control their wild sexual impulses within the holy bonds of marriage, and to find happiness in producing children. The men around Elizabeth believed the queen needed the steadying hand of a husband to help her share the burdens of rule, which were too burdensome for a woman. They were consistent in their words and meaning: marry and give the kingdom an heir.

Elizabeth was consistent only in her inconsistency. With her government officials and even with her closest advisors, she delivered contradictory messages about her marriage. She presented a wide range of responses to the prospect of marriage, depending on her audience, the time and context, and the suitor under consideration. William Cecil was Elizabeth's first and closest advisor from the very beginning of her reign. And even he didn't seem to know whether or not the queen would ever marry. In 1561, he wrote to the Earl of Sussex that he found the queen's attitude toward marriage 'strange', and that he prayed that God would change her mind. That same year, he wrote to Sir Nicholas Throckmorton that he believed the queen was not disposed seriously toward marriage, and that he believed evil would come to the kingdom if she did not quickly marry. As time went on, he seemed to fall into greater despair as she appeared reluctant to marry. In letters to his friend Sir Thomas Smith, Cecil bewailed the queen's resistance to marriage, believing that it threatened the safety of the kingdom. Even when he had serious reservations about suitors, as he did with Dudley and the Duke of Anjou, he feared the results of the queen remaining single.[16] He participated actively in negotiations from the first options shortly after she came to the throne in 1558 until she eventually moved past negotiations in the 1580s, and he was never fully convinced of the outcome.

Elizabeth pushed back against expectations and created confusion with her council and parliament about her plans to marry. It appeared to many she was reluctant to make up her mind, and when she did, was as likely to change her mind as not. Councillors Francis Knollys and Thomas Smith complained about her unwillingness or perhaps inability to come to an 'irrevocable decision' in marriage and other matters. They credited this to the fact she was a woman and frequently made long speeches that included digressions that strayed from the original point.[17]

The queen's interactions with her foreign suitors and their representatives also demonstrated her ongoing use of 'answers answerless' to keep negotiations going. In many cases, Elizabeth's goal was to keep marriage opportunities open long enough to convince ambassadors and other foreign dignitaries that there was reason to ally themselves with England. She tried to keep them happy without making any firm commitments, dropping hints about desiring marriage and at the same time protesting that she favoured her single state. She learned as a young woman not to show her hand or reveal any more than she wished. As English suitors came into view and foreign ambassadors from the Spanish empire, the Holy Roman empire, the Baltics, and Scotland came into the royal court, she employed language with the suitors and ambassadors in the same way, remaining uncommitted to moving forward or ending the suit for as long as possible.[18] She did this through rhetorical practices that kept those around her guessing. 'Elizabeth used the rhetoric of courtship so deftly that it looks almost like a calculated political strategy.'[19]

This was clear from her interactions with one of her earliest suitors, Philip II of Spain. Philip had left England before Mary's death, but his representative the Count of Feria negotiated on his behalf. As ambassador, it was his duty to mediate marriage negotiations in ways that would benefit Spain and Philip.[20] Feria expressed a mix of confidence and frustration about his success in understanding and being able to work with the English queen. He wrote to Philip about a month after Elizabeth came to the throne, 'Everybody thinks that she will not marry a foreigner and they cannot make out whom she favours, so that nearly every day some new cry is raised about a husband.' He attributed the confusion to Elizabeth herself: 'I do not know which way the queen is inclined, for on the one hand she complained to me of her sister's having married a foreigner, and on the other I see she is very vain and unlikely to settle for a non-royal English suitor.' At the end of this letter, he concluded, 'She is a very strange sort of woman.'[21] Feria couldn't make out what Elizabeth would ultimately decide about Philip's proposal, although he was confident he had done his part in making a strong case about the benefits of the Spanish marriage.

The new year brought no new clarity as Feria continued his attempts to arrange the marriage or at least get a firm answer. In February 1559, he met with the queen. They returned to the question of marriage with Philip. Elizabeth began 'to answer me by keeping to her old arguments for not wishing to marry but seeing whither she was tending I cut short the reply' so he would not allow her to 'helve the business with fair words. It ended, however, in our agreeing that I would have no answer that was not a very good one, and so I left the matter open.'[22] Feria felt his best option was to leave the matter unresolved lest the queen repeat that she didn't wish to marry. He also did not want to give her the opportunity to rehearse all her objections again.

Later that month, Feria prepared a memorandum for Philip summarising the queen's responses to Philip's offer: 'That she had no desire to marry, as she had intimated from the first day; that she quite understood that this marriage would be advantageous to her honour and the preservation of both states … that these ends could be attained by the maintenance of the good friendship with your majesty.' He added that Elizabeth stated more clearly than ever that the pope did not have the authority to grant a dispensation and that the people did not wish her to marry a foreigner.[23] Less than three weeks later, Elizabeth had given another reason she could not marry Philip: 'she was a heretic'. Feria was surprised by this and 'begged her to tell me the cause of so great change since I last discussed the subject [religion] with her, but she did not enlighten me'.[24] More answers answerless.

Even after the courtship came to an end, and Philip married Elisabeth of Valois, Elizabeth continued to plague Feria with her language. Feria reported to Philip that when she met with him in April, she mentioned the king's marriage. Feria replied that he had hoped that she would marry Philip instead. She replied, 'that it was your Majesty's fault it had fallen through … as she had given me no reply'. Feria protested that she knew this was not true. She admitted this, 'and afterwards went on to say that your Majesty could not have been so much in love with her as I had said, as you had not patience to wait for her; and many things of the same sort, as if she was not at all pleased at the decision of your Majesty'.[25] Throughout, Elizabeth had spoken in ways that contradicted her previous statements, that confused Feria about her intentions, and that rewrote what had happened to suit her own narrative. It was a pattern she would continue throughout her courtships.

It's not surprising Feria was eager to leave England shortly after this experience. His job had been to listen, ascertain the unspoken possibilities, unpack rumours and conjectures, and convely all of this to his king. As was always the case, the failure or success of a specific negotiation was most often dependent on the ability of the ambassador and his relationship with the queen and her court.[26] Frustrated by Elizabeth, their conversations, and his inability to push her to clarify decisions, Feria was glad to be replaced by Alvaro de la Quadra, the bishop of Aquila, who became the Spanish ambassador to England.

Within a couple of months, de Quadra was already frustrated. He wrote to Philip, 'I have lost all hope in the affairs of this woman … her language (learnt from the Italian heretic friars who brought her up) is so shifty that it is the most difficult thing in the world to negotiate with her. With her all is falsehood and vanity.'[27] After the end of Philip's marriage negotiation, the Spanish king supported the suit of the Archduke Charles as Elizabeth's husband. About this, Feria wrote to Quadra about his distrust of Elizabeth and the 'crew she is surrounded by', and reasoning that 'it seems the Emperor up to the present refuses leave for his son to go [to England], and, to tell the truth, I cannot persuade myself that he is wrong, nor do I believe that she will either marry him, or refuse to marry him'.[28] Shortly thereafter, de Quadra wrote to the emperor, explaining 'we have inquired in all possible quarters as to the queen's intentions about the marriage'.[29] And so the suit continued.

De Quadra wrote to the Duchess of Parma in early 1560 expressing concern that Charles's suit might be over, saying that the queen was now expected to marry the Earl of Arran.[30] A month later, de Quadra wrote to Philip that he was able to promote the archduke's suit, although Elizabeth had responded 'she could not include herself to change her state'. Elizabeth also introduced her unique barrier to marrying Archduke Charles at this time, declaring that 'she would never desire to marry until she had seen the person who was to be her husband'. This would become an ongoing issue for the queen, a repeated request that foreign leaders were unwilling to meet. Perhaps Elizabeth's knowledge about diplomatic affairs and her recognition that it was almost impossible for a foreign royal to come to England to be evaluated in person by a queen who had not committed to marry him convinced Elizabeth to name this as a requirement. She presented her terms in all seriousness, knowing that they could not possibly be met.

De Quadra realised this as well: 'Since, however, we know that the emperor will not send his son until she is willing to treat of marriage, nothing more can be done than to urge her afresh to consider how desirable it is for her to come to a decision.' De Quadra also attempted to assuage the queen's concerns: 'I manifested dissatisfaction at her reply, and said that as the emperor was content not to bind her until she had seen and approved of the person of the archduke.' He thought this would be enough and not leave her any excuses, but 'she again answered me that nothing would suffice to make her think or marrying, or even treating of marriage; but the person she was to marry pleasing her so much as to cause her to desire what at present has no wish for, and if this was not the case it was no good thinking she would ever marry at all'. As the emperor would not send his son unless marriage negotiations were open, this seemed to end the discussion. But Elizabeth wasn't finished.

She told de Quadra 'she still thought she would consider the matter and ordered me to wait whilst she entered her chamber, where she remained an hour with Cecil. When she came out she repeated what she had already said, but in such a way as to try to persuade me that, in any case, the visit of the archduke might not be altogether fruitless.' After such a confusing conversation, de Quadra gave up and said he saw no alternative than to leave the question to the emperor.[31] The emperor appointed two ambassadors to England, Count Helfenstein and Baron Casper Breuner. Generally, these two were more positive about Elizabeth than their Spanish counterparts, and Helfenstein even thought the religious issue could be overcome.[32]

In mid-February, de Quadra wrote to Philip that the queen met with him and raised the question of marriage with the archduke. He told the queen that 'if she had anything fresh to say to send for Count Helfenstein'. Elizabeth continued to 'complain of the emperor, and make out that the difficulty arises from him', continuing the queen's tendency to shift blame for her procrastination. He described their next conversation, which included Helfenstein:

> Yesterday she sent for the count and for me, and gave us to understand in a roundabout way that the fault of the business not being concluded lay with the emperor for not sending his son. The count thought well to show her the last instructions he had from the emperor, in which his majesty agrees to send his son if she only wants to satisfy herself as to his person. In sight of this she said that although she thought the needs of her kingdom and the pressure of her subjects would render it necessary for her to marry soon, she will not say that she is determined to marry the archduke, even though his person should satisfy her, until she has seen him.

Helfenstein then tried to turn the tables on Elizabeth, according to de Quadra: 'He told her plainly that if she did not promptly make up her mind, and that in a better way than hitherto, he expected orders to return home, which seemed to trouble her exceedingly, as she perceives that her tricks are being seen through.'[33]

There were several reasons that the marriage with the Archduke Charles floundered in 1560, including the significance of the religious difference and the queen's relationship with Robert Dudley. But in addition, in this and the other cases of her negotiations, the queen enabled lengthy and protracted negotiations through her extraordinary use of language. Elizabeth enjoyed and benefitted from the rituals of courtship, being the centre of attention and the object of expressed desire. It reinforced her needs on a personal level, and it also strengthened her position as a desired ally and counterpart with European nations. Sir Henry Sidney suggested that Elizabeth was 'greedy for marriage proposals', and the idea was shared by foreign ambassadors.[34] For the majority of her reign, Elizabeth received, considered, negotiated, and declined various marriage offers by prevaricating, procrastinating, and obfuscating in her replies.

In some ways, the queen's way of speaking about her possible marriage signalled a shift in the way cultural sources portrayed that language. For example, in her 1566 response to the House of Commons insisting she agree to marry or name an heir, she replied, 'I shall do not otherwise than pleases me.'[35] About twenty years later, when Shakespeare wrote *Much Ado About Nothing* around 1598, his independent and highly vocal character Beatrice claimed she would marry only when it suited her and actively resisted male counsel to make herself more appealing in order to find a husband. She also counselled her cousin Hero to take her own wishes into account when her father arranged a marriage, and if she was not pleased to decline, saying, 'Father as it please me.'[36] These words are similar to the queen's earlier speech when she also declined instruction to marry.

Beatrice was tagged as 'curst' for her outspoken character, as was another of Shakespeare's characters, Katherina in *The Taming of the Shrew*. One of Shakespeare's earliest works, written in about 1593, the play is the story of a 'shrew' who was outspoken and therefore unmarriageable. Her father would not allow his younger, milder, much sought-after daughter Bianca to marry until the elder and troublesome daughter found a husband. The feisty Katherina was 'tamed' and changed through marriage to the bombastic Petruchio. One of the things he took control of was her language. At the end of the play, Katherina delivered a subservient speech counselling women to be subject to their lords and husbands – something that recent productions have made all kinds of attempts to modify to make the ending more palatable for a modern audience.

Both Beatrice and Katherina resisted marriage. Petruchio eventually controlled Katherina, which seemed to rob her of her independence and spirit. Beatrice, on the other hand, ended up with Benedick, someone who exchanged barb for barb with her and who, in a moment of crisis, chose Beatrice and her truth over the actions of his army buddies. Beatrice was not tamed by marriage, and even when she was planning to marry at the end of the play, she continued to speak up.

It's interesting to consider these plays as they would have been performed and received at the time of a queen who was nearing the end of her life and reign, a woman who had spoken frequently about a preference for the single life even when she admitted she would probably need to marry. As a woman, Elizabeth was subject to the constraints of the expectations of society, law, and religion about her independence and the necessity of her marrying to fulfil her destiny. As a queen, Elizabeth had the power to challenge these assumptions, speaking at times openly about her reluctance to marry and questioning why it was considered the only possible way for her to live and rule. In this way, 'Elizabeth's words played a central role in the political and cultural scene',[37] as well as in the political one.

Ultimately, the queen could not control the behaviour of her suitors or their ambassadors, she could not control the desires of her parliament or privy council, she could not control the wishes of her subjects regarding their expectation she would marry. She did, however, play an active role in the marriage negotiations throughout her reign.[38] And she always controlled her response.

From the time she was a young woman, Elizabeth relied on the careful crafting of language to provide information that protected and suited her, revealing only so much, keeping her counsel, and avoiding being manipulated into saying something that would limit her options. She developed this unique voice in the reigns of her half-brother and half-sister. When she became queen, Elizabeth gave full range to her use of language to create her own approach to queenship and monarchy. Through her unique use of language, 'Elizabeth gave the traditional discourses of politics and love a female body and a female voice.'[39] She used that female voice when it suited her, demurring about her wit and wisdom when pushed to make a decision and providing 'answers answerless' that left men wondering what exactly would happen next. And in the end, those words she possibly spoke in her first address to parliament turned out to be the most accurate and direct ones to describe her approach to marriage: that she 'lived and died a virgin'.

As she neared ten years on the throne and approached her mid-30s, Elizabeth was soon to face additional challenges at home and abroad. And she would continue to face them unmarried and on her own.

Part II

Politics, Courtly Love, and the Virgin Queen

Chapter 7

The Widowed Queen of Scots

> So, the Queen of England is to marry her horsekeeper, who has killed his wife to make room for her!
>
> Mary, Queen of Scots on hearing of the death of Amy Robsart

Mary Stuart was part of Elizabeth Tudor's life from the time she was born. As the granddaughter of Margaret Tudor and daughter of James V, Mary was at the heart of the Scottish royal family. When her father died in December 1542, the six-day-old princess became Queen of Scots. At that point, Elizabeth Tudor was 9 years old, legally illegitimate, and out of the English succession. Henry VIII considered infant Queen Mary the perfect future wife for his toddler son Edward and began pursuit of her as a daughter-in-law. Henry's plans naturally favoured himself and English interests. Mary's mother, Marie of Guise (who had turned down Henry himself as a husband after the death of Jane Seymour) was not convinced the English marriage was best for her daughter. The men who were governing Scotland in the early days of young Mary's reign, however, were pro-English and pro-Protestant. Henry VIII hoped the Earl of Arran would promote Mary's marriage to Edward. But Arran realised the marriage was unpopular and shifted his support to Marie of Guise. Alongside Marie's supporter Cardinal Beaton, Arran participated in the coronation of the nine-month-old Mary as queen of Scotland at Stirling Castle on 9 September 1543.[1]

In January 1543, a new possibility for Mary's future emerged with the birth of Francis, grandson of King Francis I of France and son of the French heir. Marie of Guise strongly preferred an alliance for her daughter with France, where her family lived. She resisted the efforts of Henry VIII's ambassadors to push her into an agreement or to send her daughter to England, as the English king wished. Things changed quickly in 1547. In January, Henry VIII died, and his young son Edward became king of England. Two months later, Francis I died, and his son Henri became king of France. Mary, Queen of Scots could be betrothed to the king of England or heir to the French throne. At the Battle of Pinkie Cleugh, English forces prevailed and sought to take possession of the young queen. With the support of her French relatives, Marie arranged for a marriage between Mary and the French heir and in August 1548 sent Mary to France.

This experience had been the first path for Mary, Queen of Scots toward becoming queen of England. In those years, Edward was expected to live and reign for years, marrying and producing a heir who would succeed him. It seemed unlikely or even impossible that Elizabeth would ever come to the throne. Until Mary left for France, she was much closer to becoming queen of England than Elizabeth was.

Whilst Mary grew up as the darling of the French court, Elizabeth navigated the dangerous court of England during the reigns of Edward VI and Mary I. She was under suspicion in both reigns because of her relationships, her religion, and her popularity. In the final months of Mary I's reign, Mary, Queen of Scots married the heir to the French throne. When Mary I died, under the direction of Henri II, the young couple in France claimed the English throne. Henri II was counting on the pope officially declaring Elizabeth illegitimate, which could catapult Francis to the English throne – a double victory as he was male and Catholic. For Mary, the hope of becoming queen of England and one day queen of France, in addition to being queen of Scotland, presented a glorious dream of uniting the three kingdoms under one crown.[2]

Francis and Mary became king and queen of France when Henri II died in July 1559. They claimed the throne of England as well. The presence of Mary in the French royal family was one of the key reasons that Philip of Spain encouraged Mary I to name Elizabeth as her heir. Philip feared that if Mary, queen of Scotland and France, were to become queen of England as well, that would create a power base that would cause serious trouble for Spain and reset the European power balance.

Mary's ambition for the English crown also helped propel Philip into offering to marry Elizabeth himself. Philip's candid comments to Feria make it clear he considered the possible marriage a duty, not a pleasure. His obligation to show his duty to God and his religion was at odds with drawbacks including financial and religious concerns and 'many other difficulties no less grave'. Even so, he reasoned that he could not 'lose sight of the enormous importance of such a match to Christianity and the preservation of religion which has been restored in England with the help of God', he concluded that he was 'resolved to render this service to God, and offer to marry the queen of England'.[3] Feria believed Philip was the best possibility for Elizabeth and was confident about his success.

Philip was a significant early suitor. Although he did not mention Mary as a contributing factor in his decision to undertake the apparently burdensome task of agreeing to marry Elizabeth, Philip admitted that relationship with France was one of the things he considered. However, despite realising Philip would provide support against Mary, Queen of Scots' claim to her throne, Elizabeth was not willing to bring Philip back for another round as king of England.

The possibility of Elizabeth's marriage to the Archduke Charles was also linked to Mary, Queen of Scots. When it became clear that Elizabeth would not marry Philip of Spain, he supported the suit of his relative the Archduke Charles. As early as May 1559, Philip instructed Feria to explore 'the marriage of the queen with one of the archdukes my cousins', referring to Ferdinand and Charles, the sons of Emperor Ferdinand I.[4] By the end of the month, the focus was on Charles.

One of the obstacles to this phase of the archduke negotiations was the presence of other suitors, particularly Robert Dudley. Dudley took full advantage of his frequent access to the queen and her willingness to publicly show her preference for him. Unrest in Scotland and rumours of possible war with France made marriage with the archduke popular with the people. Cecil believed that marriage with Charles was far preferable to marriage with Dudley despite the religious issue. Elizabeth continued to vacillate, refusing to proceed further unless he came to England. De Quadra reported to the emperor that when he pushed Elizabeth about whether she was seriously considering marriage with the archduke, 'her answer was that she did not want to marry him or anybody else'.[5] Quadra was not convinced Elizabeth was sincere and added, 'I therefore say that as the necessity is evident, and she is doing now what she never would do before in allowing the Archduke to come, she is receiving him for the purpose of marrying him, and your Majesty may well send him on this conjecture for, although it is not more than a conjecture, the circumstances are such as to make it a manifest demonstration.'[6] De Quadra wrote to the Duchess of Parma, 'the queen is very pleased and gay, as she thinks the archduke is coming ... I am sure if the archduke comes she will marry him'.[7]

Feria was more cautious, having spent more time with Elizabeth: 'I am still of the opinion that the archduke should not come.'[8] By mid-November, Quadra had come to agree with Feria that the marriage with Elizabeth was unlikely even if the archduke came to England. He devised another plan:

> I am of the opinion if the archduke comes and makes the acquaintance and obtains the goodwill of these people, even if this marriage – of which I have now no hope except by force – should fall through, and any disaster were to befall the queen, such as may be feared from her bad government, the archduke might be summoned to marry Lady Katherine [Grey] to whom the kingdom falls if this woman dies.[9]

De Quadra was right about one thing: at that point, there was no real hope of the marriage.

Because of the circumstances surrounding Mary, Queen of Scots, Elizabeth's view of marriage to the archduke changed. When Francis II died in December 1560, his younger brother Charles became king. As Charles was unmarried and a child, the most powerful person at court was the young king's mother, Catherine de Medici. Mary, Queen of Scots, asked to marry the new French king, but Catherine refused. Catherine was determined to move Mary's Guise relatives out of the French court and to send her former daughter-in-law packing. In August 1561, Mary sailed for Scotland, returning to take control of a country she had not set foot in for thirteen years. Mary was now in search of a husband. That changed things for Elizabeth. Mary had never relinquished her claim to the English throne. The possibility of Mary forming an alliance with a Catholic prince proved a real threat to Elizabeth and the survival of England as a Protestant nation.

Less than a month after Francis's death, Throckmorton wrote to the English council about the question of Mary's possible husband: 'one of the special things your lordships have to consider, and to have an eye to, is the marriage of that queen'. He continued with some concern,

> The ambassador of Spain has been with her above an hour together, which is thought to be for more than the ceremony of condoling required. He has also since that time dined and had great conference with the Cardinal of Lorraine, and though the writer thinks the Council of Spain too wise to think of marrying her to the prince of Spain without other commodity, yet it is not amiss to hearken to the matter.

Throckmorton was impressed with Mary for being 'content to be ruled by good counsel and wise men', something he didn't always feel about his own queen.[10] Mary's possible marriage to Don Carlos of Spain, Philip's heir, was being discussed within a few weeks of Mary becoming a widow. Such an alliance would represent a threat to Elizabeth and England.

Mary's entrance into the European marriage market and her return to Scotland was a danger for Elizabeth and for England. Mary was interested in remarrying and she 'was not to be swayed by anything but a great foreign power'.[11] She had refused to sign the Treaty of Edinburgh and recognise Elizabeth as rightful queen of England, something Elizabeth required before she would grant Mary a safe-conduct pass through England. Mary wanted to be named as Elizabeth's heir, something Elizabeth refused until the treaty was signed, which Mary wouldn't do until she was named heir. It was a standoff the two women would continue for years.

Elizabeth did favour the choice of Mary as her heir, but she wouldn't say so publicly until it served her purposes. Mary tried to win over Elizabeth on a personal level, seeking a meeting and writing friendly letters, some of which were full of flattering poetry. She believed she could work her charm on the English queen.[12] In the autumn of 1562, when Elizabeth nearly died, Mary hoped the fears of the council and country about civil war would help her chances in the English succession. But she was not popular with the council. In fact, Cecil had tried to exclude her from the succession earlier that year. Mary decided to keep her focus on gaining favour with Elizabeth herself.

Mary's choice of husband provided an opportunity to gain favour, as Elizabeth insisted that Mary select a husband who posed no threat to England. Mary wanted to pacify Elizabeth, but she needed a partner who would strengthen her own power. Her misplaced trust in her half-brother, James Stewart, whom she created earl of Moray, caused resentment of the previous holder of the title, the earl of Huntly. There was a rumour that James Hamilton and the earl of Bothwell planned to kidnap the queen, carry her off to Dumbarton Castle, assault her, and force her to turn over the government to them. This raised widespread concern about Mary's well-known trust in Bothwell. When she toured northeast Scotland, she was threatened by Huntly, still angry about losing his title. He ordered her barred from Inverness Castle, and she and her supporters had to fight to get in. The next February, one of her French courtiers was found hiding under her bed. She banished him from court, but he returned and tried to attack her.[13]

With her nobles fighting each other and threatening her, Mary was desperate to marry. She began to wonder whether she should try to please Elizabeth or counteract her. The Scots queen eagerly pursued a Spanish marriage, which would offer support against Elizabeth. Spain's Don Carlos's health came into question, so Mary had to look elsewhere. Her Guise relatives suggested marriage to Archduke Charles to gain the emperor's support. In 1563, rumours were spreading that Mary would marry Archduke Charles. Christopher Mundt, one of Elizabeth's agents, reported to Cecil that Cardinal Lorraine was meeting with the emperor about the marriage 'of the Queen of Scots with the Archduke Charles'.[14] A month later, Sir Thomas Challoner (who had been involved in the original negotiations for a Charles/Elizabeth marriage) reported the same thing to Cecil: Lorraine was promoting the marriage of Mary and the archduke.[15]

These reports worried Elizabeth's council and court. However, Mary lost interest in Charles because of his previous pursuit of Elizabeth. Even so, Mary was still considered a threat, and that led Elizabeth and her council to reopen her negotiations with him. Elizabeth discovered Mary was pursuing the option of marrying Archduke Ferdinand and told Mary she would consider any marriage with a foreign power the end of their good relationship.[16] Elizabeth's council believed it was imperative that the English queen marry immediately. Even though Charles was Catholic, which had brought negotiations to a standstill a few years earlier, William Cecil was committed to the marriage. Simply put, with the possibility Mary might form an alliance with Spain or France or another European power, Charles's religion was considered less dangerous than Elizabeth's not being married.

Furthermore, Charles had shown sympathy or at least had tolerated Lutherans within his territories. The Imperial ambassador, Caspar Breuner, allowed the confusion about Charles's religious commitment to continue as the talks progressed. For more than two years, from 1563 to 1565, the Archduke Charles was the leading candidate for Elizabeth's hand.[17] It's possible that Elizabeth's support of these negotiations was more about countering and confusing Mary, Queen of Scots than about a real interest in marrying Charles, and that Elizabeth was at least as interested in Mary's marriage prospects as in her own.[18] Elizabeth's marriage to the archduke would maintain Elizabeth's position as the more powerful queen, whomever Mary chose as a husband.

Cecil and his agents worked to convince the emperor and his envoys that they were serious about marriage negotiations. He and Mundt assured the duke of Wurttemberg, who was acting as ambassador after the death of de Quadra, that this time things would end in success. In January, Elizabeth expressed her personal interest in negotiating with the emperor. At this point, thanks in part to dangers associated with Mary, Queen of Scots, it was preferable that Elizabeth marry a foreigner who could offer militlary support rather than an English Protestant.[19]

Elizabeth's willingness to commit to marriage was still a concern. Her hesitations were well known by this point, and she continued to raise them them herself. De Silva wrote to Philip that he had considered the issue of Elizabeth's unwillingness to marry Philip as an example of her overall unwillingness to marry. She responded, 'If I could today appoint such a successor to the crown as would please me and the country I would not marry, as it is a thing for which I have never had any inclination.' She went on to explain that 'My subjects, however, press me so that I cannot help myself, but must marry.' She continued, 'There is a strong idea in the world that a woman cannot live unless she is married, or at all events that if she refrains from marriage she does so for some bad reason.'[20] This seems an accurate description of the attitudes she faced during her reign. Everyone expected her to marry, and when she hesitated to do so, they assumed there was something wrong with her. It's not entirely clear she never desired marriage, but she knew she was being pushed toward specific candidates for political reasons not her personal wishes. The danger posed by Mary, Queen of Scots focused the conversation on political advantages of marriage.

So as Elizabeth positioned herself as ready to negotiate for a marriage with the Archduke Charles, Wurttemberg became enthusiastic about the march. It served the Habsburgs as well as Elizabeth, as this would align the English queen and England with them instead of leaders of reform states. In addition, Wurttemberg was interested in extending principles of toleration, and the Austrian/English alliance would be a major step forward. Elizabeth and Cecil seemed to agree with the Lutheran Confession of Augsburg.[21] Elizabeth seemed to see it as a way to hold off Mary, Queen of Scots and the Catholic threat and to emphasise that religion in England and Catholicism differed only in 'things of small importance'.[22]

After the death of the Emperor Ferdinand and accession of Maximilian, Cecil suggested an envoy come to England. The emperor's councillor, Adam von Zwetkovich, came to London, by which time the news of a possible marriage between Elizabeth and the archduke was well known through much of the country. The marriage had several supporters in the council, including leading Catholic Thomas Howard, Duke of Norfolk, and Thomas Radcliffe, Earl of Sussex.[23] The two primary factors that had proven obstacles in the earlier negotiations, however, remained: Elizabeth's insistence on seeing a prospective husband before making up her mind and the still-complicated problem of religion.

Elizabeth's requirement to see her potential suitor before committing herself was a technique she employed regularly. It nearly backfired when Eric of Sweden offered to come to England, an offer that pushed her to end the negotiation and tell him not to come. In the case of Archduke Charles, she was able to use it to continue the negotiation. She supported her requirement with the contemporary medical belief that personal attraction for a partner made conception much more likely. After all, the goal was a husband and an heir.

The larger issue was religion. Ferdinand's death had removed part of the religious obstacle, as Ferdinand had not wanted his son to marry a Protestant. The new emperor, Charles's brother Maximilian, had seemed to adopt a more flexible approach to religion. The Lutheran Confession reinforced a hope that Charles might be willing to convert to Protestantism. Even after he learned that Charles had a stronger personal commitment to Catholicism than originally thought, Cecil still believed the issue could be overcome as long as the archduke conformed to the law and accompanied the queen to church services in public. Cecil thought he could manage the way Charles chose to worship in private, but others were concerned this would open the door to English Catholics wanting the same rights.

As things went on, it became clear that Charles wanted to practise his religion openly, and Elizabeth wanted assurance that the archduke would not attempt to bring about any religious change in England. Mary's position as the Catholic claimant to the English throne made Elizabeth especially anxious about anyone who might support and promote the growth of Catholicism in England. In response, Maximilian insisted that his brother not be limited in his practice of his faith in any way – and this requirement extended to his courtiers as well.[24] What had been considered a defence against the growth of Catholicism in England was becoming something that could promote that growth instead.

Maximilian wanted the financial and political elements of any agreement to favour his family at the expense of Elizabeth and her court. Recognising the growing concerns about the queen's safety as the possibility of widespread Catholic rebellions rose, he asked for the archduke to continue to have power in England even after Elizabeth's death. Guzman was well aware that the last requirement was 'a thing they cannot concede, and will never agree to'.[25] Elizabeth's reaction was definite on this point. Cecil wrote to the emperor to emphasise the English stance on these issues: no one in the realm could practise religion that was forbidden by law, the Austrians should pay for the archduke's household, and the terms of government would be the same as they had for Philip when he married Mary, with no place for Charles in the succession or in the country should the queen die without issue.[26]

The presence of Mary Stuart just across the border in Scotland made England keep negotiations with the emperor open despite these obstacles. Elizabeth was keen to keep the upper hand in their relationship. In addition to exploring the option of marrying into the Habsburg empire herself, she actively voiced her opinion about Mary's choice of husband. Elizabeth tried to narrow Mary's options, treating her as a younger sister or even daughter. She insisted on having the final word when it came to Mary's marriage to ensure it would be someone who would pose no threat to England and who would never support Mary's claim to Elizabeth's crown.

Mary was struggling to complete her own marriage arrangement. She was also facing trouble within her own kingdom as well, with John Knox and the Protestant lords working against her, and her former mother-in-law, Catherine de Medici, not willing to offer any support to help establish strong control in Scotland. Mary believed securing an advantageous marriage would solve all her problems. She was certain no one would dare challenge her so directly if she had a husband at her side. Her choices were diminishing with time. She had no wish to marry the unstable son of the Earl of Arran, and any of the Guise alternatives would cause immediate concern and resistance from Elizabeth or France. The chance of being able to marry someone in the same category as the king of France was dwindling to nothing.[27] Mary needed a husband, and she wanted to find someone who would help her maintain Scotland and gain another throne either now or in the future. In response to Elizabeth's efforts to control her choice of husband, Mary told Thomas Randolph, English ambassador to Mary's court, that Elizabeth should make a suggestion. Elizabeth had someone in mind.

It's difficult to assess the true feelings of any of the three people involved in Elizabeth's suggestion that Mary, Queen of Scots marry Robert Dudley, her long-time favourite. Did Mary consider it the undesired but necessary step that must be taken to be named Elizabeth's heir? Did Dudley realise that he would never be able to marry Elizabeth and that this was the way to create a path to becoming king of Scotland now and king of England upon Elizabeth's death? Did Elizabeth believe this sacrifice of her favourite was the best way to neutralise the threat of Mary and Catholic Europe and to keep both Dudley and Mary close and in her control? Was it an empty gesture on Elizabeth's part that was not taken seriously by anyone at all? Scholars disagree.

We see inklings of the plan in early 1563. De Quadra reported to Philip in late March 1563 that Mary's supporter William Maitland of Lethington had a discussion with Elizabeth. Maitland was known as a brilliant statesman and a wily operator, a 'practical politician' who consistently tried to make the best of whatever situation he found himself in. Elizabeth described him as the 'flower of the Scottish wits'. He was dedicated to helping Mary secure the English succession.[28] He met with Elizabeth and the subject of Mary's desire to marry was raised. Elizabeth said that she had the answer to Mary's question, and that if Mary wanted to marry safely and wisely, 'she would give her a husband who would ensure both': Robert Dudley. Elizabeth went on to tell Maitland that if she had any desire to marry, she would choose Dudley ahead of all the princes in the world, and that all these fine qualities would serve Mary well.[29]

The conversation reported by de Quadra indicated that Maitland was willing to play out the negotiation to see what Elizabeth had in mind. He replied that the suggestion indicated Elizabeth's great love for Mary, because Elizabeth clearly held Robert so dear. He told the English queen that Mary would never want to deprive Elizabeth of someone so important. Elizabeth, not to be put off, said she wished Robert Dudley had a more handsome brother she could offer to Mary, then went on to say that the earl of Warwick (Robert's brother Ambrose) was not so ugly and in fact was so liberal and magnanimous that he was also worthy of being the husband of any great princess. By this point, Maitland was becoming confused by Elizabeth's style of speech and was eager to end the conversation, so he suggested that as Mary was so young, perhaps Elizabeth could marry Dudley and have children by him and then, when God called Elizabeth home, Mary could inherit Elizabeth's kingdom and Dudley himself. In Quadra's words, 'so turning it to a joke he put an end to the conversation'.[30]

But the short conversation that Maitland wished to turn into a joke would not be so readily dismissed. At least not by Elizabeth.

The question of Mary's marriage continued to plague the English queen, even as negotiations for her own with the Archduke Charles went on. In the spring of 1564, Thomas Randolph presented Mary with a formal proposal that she marry Robert Dudley, who had been created Earl of Leicester. Elizabeth had previously sent instructions to Randolph to tell Mary that abiding by Elizabeth's wishes regarding marriage would be a key factor in determining if Mary would 'succeed us in this crown of England, if we shall depart this life without children'.[31] Randolph had told Cecil that Mary would 'never imbase [debase] herself so low as to marry in place inferior to herself, therefore to persuade her to marry any under the degree of a Prince (be he of England or elsewhere) can neither be honourable to herself not wisdom for any that is subject unto her to give advice in'.[32] Mary's refusal to marry anyone under the degree of a prince was a direct challenge to Elizabeth's request for the Scots queen not to unite with a foreign royal.

Elizabeth made it clear the choice she wished Mary to make. Randolph reported that 'After saying some what of your majesty's good will, signified in many ways, but never more than in this marriage, offering the choice of your majesty's subjects, "I named in special the Lord Roberte".' Mary said she needed time to think more about it. Mary pressed him, 'dothe your mestres in good erneste wyshe me to marrie my lord Roberte?' He said that was true. She asked if Elizabeth wished her to 'marrie her subject?' Randolph replied there was no worthier man in the kingdom than Dudley.[33] Randolph described the Scots Queen as being in a state of disbelief, with Elizabeth's affection for Dudley so well known.

Elizabeth may have suggested Dudley in part to buy herself time to navigate through her own marriage discussions. Plans for the marriage and Elizabeth's desire for the couple to live in England could only be accomplished after extensive discussions and negotiations.[34] As time went on, relations between the two queens soured as Mary continued her own quest for a marriage with a powerful prince. Elizabeth expressed some frustration about how to proceed with Mary. She wrote to Cecil, 'In such a manner of labyrinth am I placed by the answer that I am to give to the queen of Scotland that I do not know in what way I will be able to satisfy her, since I will not have given her any answer for all this time, nor do I know what I now should say.'[35]

Elizabeth was not the only queen frustrated by the impasse. While Elizabeth turned to Cecil, Mary turned to one of her most trusted agents and diplomats, Sir James Melville. She sent Melville to England to meet with Elizabeth and defend Mary's claim to the throne and right to be named heir. There was another part of Melville's assignment, the importance of which would become clear only after several months had passed. He was to deliver a message to the Countess of Lennox to gain permission for her son Henry to travel to Scotland.[36]

Melville spent nine days at Elizabeth's court in September of 1564, participating in a sort of verbal dance with the English queen. She invited him to her bedchamber, where he saw a table next to her opulent bed. The table contained paper and writing boxes. She showed him a small desk where she kept portrait miniatures. There was one of Mary, which Elizabeth told Melville she often looked at with delight. There was another labelled 'my lord's picture', which the queen unwrapped to display the image of Dudley. Melville asked if he could take it back to Scotland to Mary, but Elizabeth resisted saying she had only the one picture of him. Pointing out that she had the original, Melville pointed to Dudley, who was there along with Cecil, witnessing the scene. Elizabeth then kissed Mary's picture and reiterated her love for the Scots queen. Melville asked if Elizabeth might therefore send Mary either the portrait of Dudley or a large ruby, to which Elizabeth replied that soon enough Mary might have both, if she followed Elizabeth's counsel. She said she would send a diamond to her fellow queen as a token of her great affection.[37]

The next day, Elizabeth continued close conversations with Melville, asking him about his foreign service and requesting his advice and assessment about fashions abroad. She took great care in her own wardrobe, dressing in several different styles and asking which he preferred. After receiving his compliments on her gowns, she turned the questions more personal, asking him to compare her to Mary in terms of beauty, grace, and appeal. Melville managed to be as diplomatic as possible, assuring the English queen that each was the fairest in their own lands. When asked to compare their heights, Melville answered that Mary was taller than Elizabeth, prompting Elizabeth to reply that Mary was then too tall. To gain his recognition for what she believed was her superior skill as a musician, Elizabeth arranged for Melville to come upon her while she played the virginals as if she were alone. After hearing her, Melville agreed Elizabeth played more skilfully than Mary. And so it went on, Melville also telling Elizabeth that she was the better dancer.[38]

Melville's visit went well, but it did not resolve everything between the two queens or the two kingdoms. Maitland pushed to know exactly what Elizabeth would do about the succession, in terms of naming Mary as heir, if Mary agreed to marry Dudley. The English commissioners would not make a commitment, giving vague answers. This angered Maitland and the Earl of Moray, who wrote to Cecil that Mary would not marry an Englishman unless the succession was definitively settled on her. Cecil had realised by this time that Elizabeth may have made statements that led Mary to believe this could happen if she married Dudley, but that in fact Elizabeth was not prepared to name Mary as heir.[39] Cecil wrote that 'One thyng I think truly, that the Quenes majesty will never willingly consent with any creatur to so much of this request.'[40]

Mary and her ministers were unhappy with what they saw as Elizabeth having led them on. Cecil believed that if Elizabeth was able to create enough confusion and delay Mary's marriage, she could outwit the Scots. When Cecil decided to encourage Elizabeth to give permission for Henry Stuart, Lord Darnley, to travel to Scotland, he seemed to believe that Mary might want to marry Darnley. This would cast Mary in the role of petitioner, asking for Elizabeth's permission to marry, creating another opportunity for Elizabeth to come up with delay tactics and push Mary's marriage even further off.[41] If that's what he believed, he underestimated Mary's own frustration with the situation. She had become aware Elizabeth was offering Dudley as a way of maintaining control. Mary was suffering from health issues in the fall of 1564, and she felt politically vulnerable after the death of the Duke of Guise. She wanted a friend and found one in David Rizzio, a musician she elevated to the position of secretary. Mary trusted Rizzio, believing that those she raised up would be loyal to her – a mistake she would make more than once. Rizzio's promotion was troubling for the Protestant Lords, who took it as evidence she was making secret Catholic plots with European leaders.[42]

Against a background of Mary's losing popularity in Scotland, Darnley came to Scotland to meet the Queen of Scots in February 1565. One of the few men taller than Mary, Darnley seemed to her the 'best proportioned' man she had seen.[43] Elizabeth herself had anticipated an attraction, telling Melville months earlier that Mary might 'like better of yonder long lad'.[44] The long lad was indeed attractive to Mary, who had few options left. She was unwilling to marry Dudley without a guarantee of being named as Elizabeth's heir, and Philip II was no longer providing options. Darnley was attractive, had royal blood as a descendant of Margaret Tudor, and was right in front of her. When he became ill with measles or possibly an early sign of syphilis two months after they met, Mary risked her reputation by nursing him herself. She had determined to marry him, and she was not asking permission to do so. She no longer cared about pleasing Elizabeth or Cecil. Mary created Darnley Earl of Ross, and the die was cast.

Cecil and Randolph were stunned and appalled by Mary's actions. Cecil recognised the political implications of the match. As Darnley was also a possible heir to Elizabeth's throne, the marriage of the two created an alliance that could threaten to topple Elizabeth, her government, and her religion. The Darnley marriage wasn't just unpopular at the English court. Mary's lords were vocally opposed to the marriage. Her people hated him. Arran and Knox spoke out against him. Even Mary's friends and women expressed concern. Moray opposed the match and the likelihood of a Catholic resurgence.[45] But there was no stopping the Scots queen. Without the permission of Elizabeth, which she had sought for so long, and without a papal dispensation for marrying her cousin, Mary married Darnley at Holyrood Palace on 29 July 1565.

Mary's actions and marriages had been a challenge for Elizabeth since the first days of her reign. She and Francis II had claimed the throne of England. When Francis died and Mary returned to Scotland, the desire to find Elizabeth a foreign husband escalated because the potential of Mary and a powerful European Catholic prince represented a threat to the safety of Elizabeth, her hold on the throne, and the survival of Protestants in England. Mary's second marriage, to an English subject with a claim to the English throne, raised the stakes. Then, just two years later, everything changed again. The fallout of Mary's marriage to Darnley – which included the murder of Rizzio, the birth of Mary's son and heir, the murder of Darnley, another (possibly forced) marriage, another pregnancy, and the forced abdication of Mary herself – would create an even greater threat for Elizabeth and the Elizabethan religious settlement.

As Elizabeth's reign moved into the late 1560s and into the 1570s, her courtships would continue to be conducted with one eye toward the actions of Mary, Queen of Scots. Mary might be off the royal marriage market, but she still represented a threat to the English queen.

Had the time finally come for Elizabeth to seriously consider finding a husband of her own?

Chapter 8

Kenilworth and the Pageantry of Proposals

> Whereas your highness may be assured that heaven will smile, the earth will quake, men will clap their hands, and I will always continue an humble beseecher for the flourishing estate of your royal person.
>
> Part of Gascoigne's entertainment for Elizabeth

Both houses of parliament, Cecil and other privy council members, foreign ambassadors, and English nobles all wanted Elizabeth to marry. Through it all, Robert Dudley was ever-present, a figure in whose shadow much of the negotiation for the queen's hand took place. In the mid-1570s, he was about to take centre stage, quite literally.

As the queen's reign progressed, discussions about her marriage could be found in public arenas as well as at court. Several courtiers and groups devised entertainments to promote the idea of marriage and motherhood. Masques and pageants were designed to flatter the queen, gain her favour, and encourage her to take action. Political ambition was often at the heart of these entertainments. In this context, public plays operated in a special sphere. With the opening of the first public theatre in 1576, large crowds gathered to enjoy a spectacle. As they were not always performed at court or in the presence of the monarch or her government, public plays were heavily regulated and had to be approved by the queen's representative. By law, plays could not deal with questions such as religion or politics of the day. But other entertainments, such as masques performed for the queen at court or on progress, did find ways to enact the marriage question and make appeals to the queen to marry and provide an heir.

When Elizabeth first came to the throne, she used the classics, the pageantry, and poetry as tools to promote her claim to the throne. During her entry into London before the coronation, the queen made eleven stops along the way, observing five pageants and expressing affection towards her subjects.[1] Part of her enjoyment of these earliest pageants in her reign might have been related to the subject matter and goals. They were not yet focused on her marriage; instead, they were intended to praise Elizabeth and promote the legitimacy and promise of her reign. But before long, the theme shifted. The use of pageants, including debates between Juno and Diana crafted to urge Elizabeth to marry, can be found from early in the queen's reign to Dudley's grand production at Kenilworth in 1575.[2]

This was evident with the performance of *Gorboduc* shortly after Elizabeth came to the throne. Part of the new focus on marriage was linked to the man at the head of the holiday festivities, the same man who was the heart of the message of the play: the queen's English suitor Robert Dudley. By the time of the performance, Dudley's wife Amy had died, he had been cleared of any wrongdoing in her death, and he was presenting himself as the best candidate for her hand. The queen seemed delighted with his lavish attention and his obvious desire to be her husband. However, his quest had limited support and significant opposition. Key among Dudley's detractors was William Cecil. Dudley was aware he needed to overcome resistance to win the queen's hand, and *Gorboduc* can be seen as part of his plan.

Gorboduc, also known as 'The Tragedy of Ferrex and Porrox', was created by the members of the Inner Temple, Thomas Sackville and Thomas Norton. It was initially performed at the Christmas and New Year festivities of December 1561 to January 1562. *Gorboduc* was the first known English tragedy and the first drama composed in blank verse. Following the Christmas revels, the play was performed before the queen at Westminster on 18 January 1562 by members of the Inner Temple.

Gorboduc was a legendary king who decided to split the kingdom between his two sons, creating chaos and causing war and the death of the elder brother, Ferrex. The queen got involved and killed the younger son. The people, appalled by the actions of the rulers, rebelled and killed the king and queen. With an uncertain succession, the nobles were divided, and the country fell into civil war, causing the wise Eubulus to lament the destruction of a noble realm for 'want of an established heir'.[3] In the final moments of the play, Eubulus called upon God to 'restore / This noble crowne unto the lawfull heire: / For right will always live'.[4] The message to Elizabeth seems clear: there was danger in the lack of an established heir. She must marry and have a child to save the kingdom. The play also promoted the claim of an English husband for the queen, one that would avoid 'The heavie yoke of forreine governaunce'.[5] The entertainment is seen by many scholars as an attempt to call the queen to action and convince her to resolve the controversies surrounding 'her marriage plans (or lack of them) and the uncertainty of the succession'.[6]

Gorboduc was part of a larger celebration, with *The Prince of Pallaphilos* and *Beauty and Desire* performed in the evening. The second play also warned that disaster would follow attempts to resist the natural state of marriage. Dudley inserted himself into the pro-marriage theme, creating a classical genealogy, making himself a suitable husband for a queen. The focus on Dudley was made clear in the masque of *Pallaphilos* and alluded to in Gorboduc's call for the queen to avoid a foreign marriage. The message was clear: by marrying Dudley, the designated English choice, Elizabeth could save her kingdom.[7]

We don't know what Dudley's role was in creating the entertainments, but the fact he brought them from the Inner Temple performance to court indicates he believed they would support his chances with the queen. However, they did not. Elizabeth continued to put Dudley off and, in 1563, was in the process of reopening discussions with the Habsburgs about a marriage with the Archduke Charles. Over the next few years, as marriage negotiations went on, several dramatic productions were performed before the queen that focused on the benefits of matrimony. Several enacted a scenario where Diana, representing virginity, was defeated by Venus or Juno, the goddess of marriage.

For example, in March 1565, Guzman de Silva and the queen attended a production of a comedy where Juno argued for marriage and Diana for chastity and virginity. Jupiter ruled in favour of marriage.[8] Little more than a year later, in July 1566, a masque-oration was given at the wedding of Frances Radcliffe and Thomas Mildmay. Not surprisingly, given the context, the oration was a verse celebrating marriage over chastity.[9] In September of that year, while the queen was visiting Oxford, *Palamon and Arcyte* was performed before her in two parts. The play ended with the victory of Venus when Palamon is married to the votaress of Diana. The queen gave the author great thanks.[10]

The July oration is particularly interesting. Venus and Juno rewarded the bride for 'fulfilling her destiny of marriage'. Diana admitted that the bride 'was borne' for matrimony. Juno proclaimed the benefits of married life: 'for wedlocke I lyke best / it is the honorablest state / it passethe all the rest'. This language both echoed and disagreed with some of the ways Elizabeth had spoken about the single life as the state she preferred best and it being preferable for her above marriage. The queen did not seem to be offended by these productions and was described as laughing in appreciation and commending the actors and authors.[11]

After the negotiations with the Archduke Charles ended in the late 1560s, the marriage question was not in the forefront of public pageants for a few years. That set the stage for Robert Dudley's grand performance, staged over nineteen days in 1575 when the queen took a progress to his estate at Kenilworth.

The first castle at Kenilworth was built in the 1120s, and in the thirteenth century King John added stone walls to make the structure one of the strongest holds in his kingdom. John of Gaunt added a great hall and royal apartments in the fifteenth century, making the structure a royal residence. It became a favourite Lancastrian castle through the Wars of the Roses. Elizabeth granted it to Robert Dudley in 1563 as part of his creation as Earl of Leicester (and his being offered as an appropriate suitor for Mary, Queen of Scots). Dudley continued to enlarge and update the structure to make it large and grand enough to accommodate royal visits.

Elizabeth took several progresses during her reign. The journeys served several purposes. Logistically, they were a way to leave the heat and crowds of London and provide time for the royal residences there to be cleaned and refreshed. They also provided the queen the opportunity to show herself to the people of her realm beyond London, something she considered very important. Elizabeth traded heavily on her relationship with her people, and her journeys into parts of the country allowed her to be seen by large groups of people. She regularly travelled in open carriages or on horseback so she was visible and could hear cheers along the way. When she spent the night, she typically did so at homes of her favourites and greatest supporters. This was presented as a great honour and something to be desired, but in reality it was incredibly costly and sometimes destroyed the financial health of her 'lucky' hosts. In fact, after enjoying her stay with Sir Henry Lee in 1592, Elizabeth considered staying with him again during her 1602 progress. Horrified, Lee begged Robert Cecil to keep her away. He simply couldn't afford to house the queen and hundreds of her closest friends once more.[12]

Unlike Sir Henry Lee, Robert Dudley was eager for the queen to come as often as she liked. In 1575, he wanted to provide a welcome respite for Elizabeth, who was facing threats from the presence of Mary, Queen of Scots and Catholics at home and abroad. After Mary arrived in England in 1568 and the Pope excommunicated the queen in 1570, rebellions increased. In addition, priests trained in Rome were arriving in greater numbers. This caused rising worry in Elizabeth's court.

Other controversies were also simmering at this time. There had been fighting on the Scottish border, something that Tudor monarchs had been dealing with since the start of the dynasty. Things in Scotland had been relatively quiet in recent years, but now there was growing concern about Mary's supporters in Scotland. There was also concern about how to proceed in Ireland, where resistance to Tudor rule was leading to the potential for violence. In the midst of this, Dudley offered Elizabeth three weeks of fantasy and feasting. He tried to shut out all the troubles of the court, but of course they followed the queen and council everywhere.

When Elizabeth arrived at Kenilworth on 9 July 1575, she had already been on progress for six weeks. She would continue the progress after leaving Kenilworth, spending a total of nearly twenty weeks on the road. It would be the longest progress of her reign. The nearly three weeks she spent at Kenilworth was the longest stay of her reign. It was also the most elaborately designed attempt to please her. As a key member of the royal court, Dudley travelled regularly with Elizabeth. But here at Kenilworth he was her host, welcoming her to his home. This gave him precedence among other nobles: Ambrose Dudley, earl of Warwick; the lord chamberlain; Sir Francis Knollys and Sir James Croft, who were treasurer and comptroller of the household; the queen's two principal secretaries, Sir Thomas Smith and Sir Francis Walsingham; and of course, William Cecil, now Lord Burghley. Throughout the progress, privy council members would travel to where the queen was to conduct government business. In 1575, they were addressing such business as coordinating the sheriffs to prepare for defence of the Channel Islands against the French, authorising a French merchant to important wine and fine food, and discussing the problem of recusants with bishops.[13]

Government business was not the main focus of the queen's time at Kenilworth. Dudley seems to have had two goals: to convince the queen to marry him or to convince the queen to allow him to pursue his glory on the battlefield. Elizabeth was not the only one who had no heir to carry on the family glory. By 1575 only Ambrose and Robert were the only Dudley brothers left. After years of marriage, Ambrose had no children. That meant that it was up to Robert to continue the family line. He had hoped to marry the queen for more than a decade, but he realised time was running out. Around 1573, he wrote to a lady who was most likely his lover Douglas Sheffield. He explained that he could not marry her as that would endanger his place and favour with the queen. Still, he knew the possible cost of continuing to pursue his goal of marrying the queen after years of her refusing to agree.

Dudley wrote of his despair at not providing a Dudley heir. He acknowledged that, his brother not having had any children, 'it resteth so now in my self'. Not leaving a son to carry on the family name would be the end of his dynasty, and therefore he was desperate to have children. He wrote that there was 'nothing in the world' he would not give to 'be in hope of leaving some children behind me', continuing with the plaintive phrase 'being now the last of our howse'.[14] The duelling desires, to have a son and heir and to marry the queen, were brought into sharp focus when Dudley's mistress, Douglas Sheffield, gave birth to a son in 1574. Although the child was named 'Robert', he could not be acknowledged as Dudley's legitimate heir.[15] The need for an heir was pressing, and time was running out for Dudley to have children and create a legacy. This seemed to fuel his desire for glory, which culminated in the queen's visit to Kenilworth.

The entertainments performed for the queen on progresses were personal, designed to communicate praise and loyalty. It was also an opportunity to raise specific issues or to make specific requests. On progresses, these entertainments were performed before Elizabeth in private houses and sometimes used the home itself or the estate into the dramatic action. In addition, the hosts were often characters in the stories and the queen was often invited to participate as well. In the case of Dudley's 'Princely Pleasures' event, the entertainment demonstrated some growing ambiguity about the monarch's 'absolute authority'.[16] Dudley's resistance to the absolute power of the monarch put him at odds with the presumed focus of the queen's official visits.

Progresses gave the queen the opportunity to present herself as both majestic and human. She was and expected to be the focus of the spectacle. Typically, numerous people were involved with the pageants presented to the queen, with everyone from public officials to merchants and local residents having a part to play as well. The queen certainly understood her role in the process and participated in ways that demonstrated her virtues and love for her people. As rebellions increased, the progresses were also more focused on displaying the magnificence of the monarchy.[17] So Elizabeth came to Kenilworth with high expectations.

At Kenilworth, the queen entered a fantasy world created just for her. There were diversions such as music, dancing, tilting, and hunting – all activities Dudley knew the queen enjoyed. There were elaborate meals that featured the best food and drink he could provide. In fact, it's estimated that guests drank around forty barrels of beer and sixteen barrels of wine each day.[18] Elizabeth was greeted by a sybil, clothed in white silk and accompanied by trumpeters, a lighted floating island, and her long-time favourite. The entire castle was remodelled and enlarged for the 1575 festivities,[19] becoming an extended stage. Dudley had reportedly spent £60,000 in building costs alone.[20] There was nothing subtle about Robert Dudley, in his person, his dress, or his home. He reigned supreme at Kenilworth.[21] So, with the stage set and Dudley established as a star, perhaps even more important than the queen herself, the festivities began.

Elizabeth arrived at Kenilworth on Saturday, 9 July at 8.00 in the evening, according to Langham's account. She processed through a series of gates, where she was greeted by poetry and pageantry. Characters praised her along the way, evoking classical tales and the legend of King Arthur. Dudley presented a welcome ceremony for the queen that cast her as a visitor, as if she were entering a world that he controlled.[22] This created tension right from the start. When the Lady of the Lake told the queen she had held possession of the lake since King Arthur's day and was now desirous to give it to the queen, Elizabeth was reported to have said that she thought it was hers already.[23] After all, she had granted Kenilworth to Dudley, and she could take it back. In Elizabeth's mind, there was never a question about who was the star of the show. Dudley created and funded a magnificent experience for his queen to promote his own worthiness as her partner or her warrior. Given his claim of knowing her better than any man alive, he should have realised the danger in giving himself equal or superior billing. Or perhaps he did, recognising that for him the time had come to play all his cards at once in an attempt to win the game of love.

After the initial welcome, the queen then passed over a bridge and continued toward the castle, moving through a series of posts decorated with cages of birds, fruit, wine, speciality food, silver, and musical instruments. She came to the castle gate, where a poem described the gods and their gifts to the queen. She then moved into the inner court, where she alighted from her horse and was guided to her chamber. A show of fireworks and great sounds of guns rang out to announce the queen's arrival.[24]

The focus on the Arthurian legend, evident from the opening of the stay, was an important component of the festivities for Dudley. During the 1570s and into the 1580s, the legend of King Arthur and his knights was a powerful 'nationalist mythology' that informed performances among the nobility and in public pageants. The undercurrent of imperial ambitions was gaining ground during this period, something that Dudley incorporated into his attempt to invent a new version of Elizabeth's England.[25]

The next day, the queen and court attended church services, likely in the private chapel at the castle. Later in the day there were fireworks 'upon the water'.[26] On Monday the queen went hunting, and in the forest as she returned she met a savage man, dressed in ivy, who had a conversation with Jupiter about the welcome of Saturday and the presence of the court. To the question 'And who gave all those gifts?' Echo answered 'Dudley', placing the host in the centre of the dialogue. The savage man then met the queen and knelt before her, kneeling and praising her glory and her fame.[27] Dudley gave George Gascoigne, a famous Elizabethan poet, a significant role throughout the event – he devised and wrote three entertainments, including this scene. Dudley relied on Gascoigne heavily for the entertainments for the Kenilworth stay. Both men shared appreciation of the power of pageants and a commitment to English intervention in the Netherlands. Gascoigne later printed an account of the event that includes all the pageants, including the ones not performed. Dudley is given a near-princely status in Gascoigne's account,[28] demonstrating the poet's support of Dudley's efforts at self-promotion.

A second account of the progress written by Robert Langham takes us through each day of the queen's stay. This is different from Gascoigne's, which focuses on particular pageants. That's not the only difference in the two accounts. Gascoigne selects moments and entertainments to record, print, and publicise, emphasising the changing and political relationship between the queen and the man who is her suitor and privy councillor. In Gascoigne's account, Dudley is in control of the world. The 'Princely Pleasures' is a record that is also an advertisement for Dudley and for Gascoigne himself, the creator and actor as well as recorder of Dudley's event. Langham, on the other hand, presents a record that is cast as a letter to a friend. It includes details that reveal another view of events at Kenilworth, sometimes using an impatient tone as he describes the elaborate nature of Dudley's efforts. It 'pokes fun at the display of egos' that are fully on display before the queen.[29]

Langham also presents Elizabeth as more powerful than her host. He includes details such as the queen 'touching for the king's evil', a tradition by which the monarch healed those suffering from scrofula by laying their hands on them. This was something Elizabeth had practiced throughout her reign to reinforce her power as a spiritual leader force as well as a political one. This act demonstrated the 'accustomed mercy and charity' of the queen, and nine people were reported to have been cured.[30] Elizabeth also knighted five men on 18 July at Kenilworth. Langham's account mentions this and lists the men: Sir Thomas Cecil, Burghley's son; Sir Henry Cobham of Kent, soon to be special ambassador to Spain; Sir Thomas Stanhope, Sheriff of Nottinghamshire; Sir Arthur Basset, Sheriff of Devon; and Sir Thomas Tresham of Northamptonshire.[31] Elizabeth's authority is recognised and recorded by Langham, giving her a voice that Gascoigne's account denies her.[32]

What Langham included and Gascoigne left out makes it clear that the two recorders of what happened at Kenilworth had different goals. Langham's day-by-day account includes only what happened at Kenilworth, specifically what pageants and entertainments were performed. Gascoigne's account includes the pageants and entertainments that were devised but not performed. Gascoigne presented a version of Kenilworth as Dudley envisioned it, with the earl as triumphant. In reality, Elizabeth exercised control and seems to have at times either instructed an entertainment not to be performed or have expressed opinions that convinced Dudley to cancel the performance to avoid offending her. However, this version was only seen by those who attended the events. The printed version, which included some of the entertainments not desired by the queen, had a much wider audience, which gave Dudley a prominent voice in his quest for greater influence with the queen and her council.[33]

The time at Kenilworth was filled with days of music and dancing, more hunting, bearbaiting, acrobats, and fireworks – all displaying the wealth and glory of the host. Dudley also used his surroundings to promote himself as suitor and warrior in service of his queen. While Elizabeth was there, he unveiled two sets of life-sized portraits he had commissioned of himself and the queen. Dudley used portraits to further his efforts at self-promotion, commissioning more of himself than any other courtier of the time.[34] The two pairs of portraits of Dudley and Elizabeth were life-sized and dominated Dudley's large picture collection. They were intended to be a key element of the Kenilworth event.[35]

One pair of the portraits survives. They are by an unknown artist. Dudley is wearing crimson velvet, and Elizabeth is wearing a white jewel-encrusted doublet that Dudley had given to her as a New Year's gift that year.[36] The structure of the portraits is similar, with both of them resting their right arms on an elaborate chair as an indication of their wealth and status. They are not presented facing each other, something reserved for married couples and apparently too far even for Dudley. Still, they are complementary and are described as hanging together at Kenilworth. The pair do not depict a typical portrait of a queen and a courtier. The link to Dudley's desire to marry the queen is unmistakable.

The other pair was created by Federico Zuccaro, the famous Italian painter whom Dudley himself brought to England in spring 1575. Unfortunately, the portraits do not survive, but Zuccaro's drawings do and they give us a sense of the portraits themselves. Dudley is shown in armour, reflective of his alternate hope at Kenilworth – to convince the queen into taking military action in the Netherlands with him in a leading role. Dudley had European ambitions, and these were on display in the portrait as well as in the entertainments. He was a soldier and a representative of militant Protestantism. The queen was portrayed in a way that complimented her personally and politically. The columns around her are symbols of constancy. There is a dog, a common symbol of fidelity, perched on top of one of the columns. The queen was portrayed wearing ermine, representing royalty and purity.[37]

Dudley's military interests were also associated with the overall notion of empire building, something very much on the minds of those at court. The ongoing troubles with Ireland provided an opportunity for ambitious men for 'extending power bases and client networks, and providing economic opportunity for younger sons and others'. In presenting himself as a warrior, Dudley was aligning himself with the Protestant faction he believed he should lead. In addition to the politics associated with Ireland, it was also a religious hotspot: as a Catholic nation, it provided a potential landing place for Spanish troops attempting to invade England. It was not just fighting against Spain that was at stake, it was also competing with Spain for land in the establishment of empire. Ireland was the first attempt at colonisation, so it represented to Elizabeth and her council for a possible pattern for the future.[38] Dudley was aware of all of this, and it informed the way he presented himself throughout the progress and in the entertainments.

The portraits of the queen and Dudley were an important part of the overall experience of the stay at Kenilworth, as were the entertainments. This was the first evidence of portraiture being a deliberate part of a host's offering to celebrate the queen's visit. The trend was continued in later visits, such as with the Ditchley portrait, almost certainly commissioned in conjunction with the queen's visit to Sir Henry Lee in 1592. But Dudley was alone in his efforts to inject himself and his own narrative into the display of the queen. He did so with the paired portraits, and he attempted to do so in the pageantry displayed at Kenilworth. However, his entertainments did not all proceed as he planned.

On Wednesday, 20 July, Langham recorded preparations for the queen's entertainment, including 'a fair Pavilion and other provision according thither sent and prepared'.[39] The entertainment for that day was intended to be one Gascoigne had devised, a masque of Zabeta, one of Diana's best-loved nymphs who had been lost for seventeen years.[40] The queen had been on the throne for seventeen years. Juno had taken Zabeta under her protection and made her a queen.[41] But worthy queenship had a requirement: 'How necesserie were / for worthy Queenes to wed.'[42] Elizabeth had often aligned herself with the legend of Diana, but in this production Diana was lacking. Her father Jove turned against her, and Diana supported the marriage of Zabeta. The message to the queen was clear; 'Dudley's authors ultimately give male authority the last word, and the word is that Elizabeth must marry.'[43] Significantly, this play was not performed.

Gascoigne explains the lack of performance this way: 'There was prepared a show to have been presented before her Majesty … being prepared and ready (every actor in his garment) two or three days together, yet never came to execution, the cause whereof I cannot attribute to any other thing than to lack of opportunity and seasonable weather.'[44] It seems unlikely that weather was the primary cause for this play not being performed for Elizabeth. Langham reported that, 'This day also was thear such earnest talk and appointment of removing, that I gave over my noting, and harkened after my hors[e].'[45] No mention of bad weather; instead, reports of the queen and company leaving early. It's possible Elizabeth was told of the plot and became angry and wanted to leave, or that she was angry about something else and Dudley decided this play would not be well received.[46] Some historians believe Elizabeth herself censored the play.[47]

There is also a chance that the pageant was not performed because the queen was distracted by news from London. Walsingham had been in contact with James Douglas, Earl of Morton and the Regent in Scotland about the border controversy. He reported to Elizabeth that Morton disputed the English version of the events and went on to enlarge upon other problems the Scots were having with the English. Elizabeth was angry at the Regent and seemed to be considering the possibility of going to war. As part of the pageantry at Kenilworth was encouraging the queen to be more aggressive, this might have influenced her (though not in the way Dudley intended).[48] Walsingham, who was trying to resolve the issue, wrote to complain that the court at Kenilworth thought of nothing but 'banquetting and pasttime' except for the interruption associated with 'fear of a breach with Scotland'.[49]

Despite his failure to have this entertainment seen by the queen, Dudley continued his quest for the rest of her visit. Over the next several days, there was a tournament, in which Dudley wore armour that had been made in the royal workshops at Greenwich, likely specially for this occasion.[50] There was also hunting, a pastime Elizabeth enjoyed. Entertainments focused on the Arthurian legend, something sure to please the queen as her grandfather Henry VII had made much of his Welsh heritage and ties to the legendary king. If Henry VII was Arthur's heir, so was Elizabeth. But Dudley inserted himself here as well, as the keeper of the palace that included the 'Lady of the Lake'.[51] In his presentation, Kenilworth's glory came from Dudley, even though by law he held it for the crown.[52] Dudley appropriated part of the legend, the castle, and the glory – this view suggested the power was his, not the queen's.

On 27 July, the queen left Kenilworth. Langham's account simply said, 'Her Highness tarried at Killingworth till ... Wednesday ... being the 27 of this July.'[53] Gascoigne's account is much more elaborate, as he was tasked by Dudley with preparing something for her departure. His words 'The Queenes Majestie hasting her departure from thence'[54] indicating her leave-taking was earlier than expected. Gascoigne appeared as Sylvanus, stating the wishes of all that the queen would decide 'for ever to abide in this country'.[55] He continued to escort her, speaking words of praise and pleading, until Deep Desire emerges from a holly bush, imploring the queen to stay. The lengthy verse included these petitions:

> Vouchsafe, O comely queene,
> yet longer to remaine,
> Or still to dwell amongst us here!
> O Queene commaunde againe
> This Castle and the Knight,
> which keeps the same for you;
> These woods, these waves, these foules, these fishes
> these deere which are your due!
> Live here, good Queene, live here;
> you are amongst you friends;
> Their comfort comes when you approach,
> and when you part it ends.[56]

The queen left a pleading Dudley behind her. Langham summed up the visit with the focus on the queen: never 'was Kenelworth more nobled then by his Lordship's receiving hir Highnes heer now'.[57] For Dudley, the tide would turn. The queen's time at Kenilworth would never be equalled in length, expense, or extravagance of any other progress. But, ultimately, she did not choose to 'live here'.

There are two significant ways this progress stands out from others during Elizabeth's reign: Dudley's art collection and the entertainments he devised for the queen. Both seem intended to promote his message of being worthy to be a husband for a queen or a leader of an army. He was staking a claim for his own immortality, and he must have realised that he was taking a chance to present himself in competition with the queen for attention in such a public way. Dudley's choices demonstrate he recognised his own time limits for achieving glory and his unwillingness to go on forever as the queen's suitor without the reward of becoming her husband. He wanted marriage or military, and he was asking her to choose.

After Kenilworth, Elizabeth's likelihood of marrying and bearing children diminished. To counter this, the pageants began to focus on preference for virginity. Kenilworth represented not only a turning point in Elizabeth's relationship with Dudley, but also the perception of her ability to produce an heir of her body and the way her image was portrayed. She had always been a virgin queen, but rather than pageants pleading with her to marry, they now begin to celebrate her as the Virgin Queen, a symbol of proudly independent Protestant England.

Some of the depictions of the queen as an eternal virgin came at the time Elizabeth was considering her final chance at marriage, pondering the offer from a woman who had tried three times to become the English queen's mother-in-law, Catherine de Medici.

Chapter 9

'On Monsieur's Departure' and French Connections

Some gentler passion slid into my mind,
For I am soft and made of melting snow.
Or be more cruel, love, and so be kind.
Let me float or sink, be high or low;
Or let me live with some more sweet content,
Or die, and so forget what love e'er meant.

Elizabeth I, c. 1582

The years between 1558 and 1560 brought enormous and lasting change not only to England, but to all of her neighbours in Europe. As the health of Mary I declined in England, other leaders were preparing to deal with the end of the Anglo-Spanish alliance, which had held such promise for Catholic Europe in political and religious terms. In September 1558, Charles V died. As Holy Roman Emperor, Charles had cast a long shadow over Europe for years. His death was not the only significant shift in power. Over the next several months, England, Denmark, Portugal, and France would experience the deaths of their leaders. By the time 1560 dawned, there had been enormous shifts in the power structures of Europe's powerful nations. One shift was generational – at age 33, Philip of Spain was the oldest monarch in Europe. There was also gender change, with Elizabeth I becoming the second crowned regnant queen of England. Mary, Queen of Scots was also queen consort of France for a short time before returning to Scotland to take up her rule for the first time since she had left her native country at age 6. And with the deaths of her husband Henri II and her son Francis II, Catherine de Medici became the de facto ruler of France. There were religious reverberations of all these changes: there was now a Catholic queen in Protestant Scotland, and England was once more separated from Rome.

It was in this changing and volatile atmosphere that Elizabeth carried out her long and complicated, as well as very public, courtships.

From the time she was an infant, Elizabeth's potential role as a bride was a topic of political debate. France played a key role right from the start, as Francis I proposed his son Charles as a husband for the infant princess. To prove her worthiness and worth as a potential royal bride, Henry VIII had Elizabeth displayed naked before the French ambassadors to prove there were 'no impediments' to her betrothal, meaning they believed she could have children. Her ability to bear children was a key factor in her worth as a prospective bride even as a baby. The issue of the queen's physical health and her fertility was of paramount importance, 'for the security of the kingdom rested upon her ability to produce an heir to continue the Tudor dynasty'.[1] The notion of Elizabeth's fertility came to the forefront with a French suitor once more in the mid-1560s.

It was not the son but the grandson of Francis I who was considered a possible mate for Elizabeth in the first decade of her reign. When Elizabeth came to the throne, she inherited the war with Spain started by Mary I and her husband Philip. That conflict was resolved, but others continued with France, fed in part by Elizabeth's determination to recover Calais. The Edict of Amboise in 1563 provided a temporary end to French religious fighting, and the Treaty of Troyes the following year demonstrated England's failure to regain Calais. It also may have led Catherine de Medici to believe Elizabeth could be an effective ally. Catherine was ruling for the young King Charles IX of France. Having spent many years as the dutiful wife of Henri II while he publicly preferred his mistress Diane de Poitiers, and then nearly two years as the queen dowager while the charismatic Mary, Queen of Scots, charmed the French as wife of Francis II, Catherine was ready to exercise power. She declined Mary's wish to marry the new French king, effectively sending Mary back to Scotland. Now she was looking to find an appropriate husband for her royal son.

Catherine had her eye on Elizabeth of England. She made inquiries of the English ambassador, Sir Thomas Smith, about the likelihood of Elizabeth marrying Dudley then began to explore the possibility of a marriage with Charles. In early 1564, she began promoting her 13-year-old son as a husband for the 30-year-old queen. She sent Paul de Foix, the French ambassador to Elizabeth's court, to sound out the English. He began with praising Elizabeth, assuring her 'how much you are admired for your greatness by my French masters'. Elizabeth was pleased but tried to avoid a direct discussion. De Foix managed to state, 'The queen mother's grace would be increased if we would see the king accompanied by a great and virtuous queen such as yourself.' He also referred to a conversation with Cecil, who reportedly thought it a suitable match. Elizabeth demurred, however, stating her objection to be the age difference.[2] A few months after that conversation, Throckmorton wrote to Elizabeth that when he had met with Charles IX and his mother, they had tried to steer the conversation to the question of marriage with Elizabeth and expressed their regret that she did not seem interested.[3]

These were tumultuous years for Elizabeth and those around her. Mary, Queen of Scots was on the international marriage market. Elizabeth and her councillors had reopened talks about marriage with Archduke Charles. Religious and political rebellions in Scotland had erupted, and the Protestant earl of Moray had fled and was taking refuge in England. Dudley was continuing to press his suit with Elizabeth, and in 1564 she created him Earl of Leicester and proposed him as a husband for Mary, Queen of Scots. As all this was unfolding, Catherine de Medici was working to promote an alliance between France and England, highlighted by the marriage of Elizabeth and Charles IX. When Mary defied Elizabeth's wishes and married her cousin Henry Stewart in July of 1565, the union of two potential claimants to the English throne created new concerns.

Mary, Queen of Scots became pregnant quickly, but her marriage fell apart shortly thereafter. Darnley demanded to be crowned king, something Mary knew the lords would never accept. His behaviour drove his wife to spend time with others, particularly David Rizzio. Jealous and willing to give full rein to his worst instincts, in March 1566 Darnley led a group of lords into the queen's apartments and murdered Rizzio, also threatening the pregnant queen. Shocked and dismayed, Mary displayed courage and decisiveness as she convinced Darnley to return to her side and, with the aid of the earl of Bothwell, returned to control. Mary gave birth to her son in June of that year. The presence of a male heir was an immediate threat to Elizabeth, who continued to refuse to marry and have children or to name an heir.

Discussions about marriage between Elizabeth and the French king continued through all of this. In 1566, French ambassador Jacques Bochetel de la Foret raised questions about Elizabeth's ability to have children. Elizabeth's refusal to marry had given rise to various rumours about her being unable to have intercourse or bear children because of a physical condition. Of course, there were just as many rumours about her having slept with Dudley, Hatton, and other courtiers and having secretly given birth to many children. Attacking a woman's virtue and ability to achieve the lofty status of motherhood was a common way to destroy her reputation and her worth, and this was no different with the queen. La Foret met with one of Elizabeth's physicians to 'ascertain whether his royal mistress would be a suitable wife for the young French king'. An age difference of fifteen years was a consideration and something the queen herself had raised as an obstacle. The physician assured la Foret that as the queen was only 32, he would personally answer for her being able to have ten children.[4] This seems overly ambitious for the times, when women typically ceased having children in their mid-30s. In addition, Elizabeth was known to have irregular periods. Still, the official medical assessment was that she could certainly have children, her physician adding, 'no one knows her temperament better than I do'.[5] Even with this assurance, however, the marriage did not move forward smoothly.

Elizabeth was under enormous pressure to marry. Parliament continued to petition her to marry or name an heir, a request she responded to with anger: 'It is monstrous that the feet should direct the head.'[6] Still, they continued to push her. Elizabeth, even when standing alone in that all-male group of parliament and council members, stood firm. She would not commit to marry – 'at least not now, and certainly not when compelled to do so by ordinary men'.[7]

The chaos in Scotland spilled into England in dramatic ways in the next two years. Mary's marriage to Darnley culminated in his violent death in February 1567. A graphic image created for William Cecil shows Darnley lying outside the house with his baby son, crying out, 'Judge and avenge my cause o Lord.'[8] Bothwell was immediately suspected in the murder, and because of her relationship with him, Mary was implicated as well. Her marriage to Bothwell turned the lords completely against her, and in June she was captured and forced to abdicate her throne on behalf of her young son. She was imprisoned in Loch Leven Castle and managed to escape a year later. Desperate for support, she fled to England and demanded an audience with Elizabeth.

Catherine de Medici, formerly Mary's mother-in-law and attempting to take the same role with Elizabeth, reached out to the English queen on Mary's behalf. She asked Elizabeth to shelter and support Mary, but noticeably offered no French support. At the same time, Catherine continued to 'court' Elizabeth on behalf of her son, stressing that no one cared as much for Elizabeth and her well-being as Catherine herself. Catherine sent Bertrand de Salignac, la Mothe de Fenelon to ensure peace between the two countries and to promote a marriage between Elizabeth and one of Catherine's sons.[9] Fenelon arrived with letters from Charles IX regarding ongoing issues about Englishmen detailed in France, with Elizabeth providing assurances of England's restitution.[10] But his other task would prove more difficult. He began by flattering the English queen, then pointing out that the best way to preserve her best qualities would be through her posterity. Elizabeth objected that the king of France would not wish a wife who looked so old and that Catherine herself might wish for a younger daughter-in-law. Elizabeth ended the conversation, and before long Charles IX married Elisabeth of Austria.[11]

A shrewd politician, Catherine was loath to abandon the chance of a union with England. She had other sons, and she was ready to promote the case of the king's younger brother, Henri of Anjou. She was eager for a marriage between Henri, reputed to be her favourite son, and the queen of England. She already had one son who was a king – why not two? Catherine had been limited for years by her marriage to a man who openly preferred his mistress; now she was flexing political muscles and showing off her power. In addition, she believed a marriage between the Protestant queen and her son could pacify the Huguenots, who were growing in power in France.[12] Catherine saw marriage between her son and Elizabeth as a way to increase her own power and influence in France and abroad.

Elizabeth was now willing to consider a French marriage, having ended negotiations with Archduke Charles in 1569. The political and religious landscapes were shifting, and Elizabeth was facing greater dangers. With Mary, Queen of Scots in England, Elizabeth's lack of named heir made this danger even greater – if Elizabeth died, there was no Protestant lined up to replace her. With Catholic Europe threatening, the continuation of Protestantism rested almost entirely on the safety of Elizabeth. Her longest-serving advisor William Cecil wrote to Walsingham in 1570, 'I am not able to discern what is best, but surely I see no continuance of her quietness without a marriage.'[13]

Catherine and Fenelon used Elizabeth's vulnerability to promote the marriage between Elizabeth and Henri, Cecil and some members of the English council, apparently as well as Elizabeth herself to some degree, were eager for the marriage as well. The problem initially was French King Charles IX, who was angry at Elizabeth for her treatment of Mary, Queen of Scots. The Guise family, still powerful in France, were unhappy to see their kinswoman held captive in England, so they approached Anjou and raised the option of his marrying Mary instead of Elizabeth. Younger and reportedly more beautiful than her English cousin, Mary was an appealing choice. But Catherine was not to be outdone by her sons and certainly not by the hated Guise family, and she convinced Henri to pursue the match with Elizabeth.[14]

In 1571, Fenelon came to the English court to discuss the possibility of the marriage. He said he understood she had regret about not thinking enough about her posterity and assured her about the magnificence of the French royal house. The queen agreed, saying she knew the duke was from a fine family. Her concerns were that his family had a reputation for honouring their wives instead of loving them, perhaps a thinly veiled jab at Catherine herself, whose husband had honoured her as queen and mother of his children but had publicly loved someone else. Elizabeth stated she would not marry a man who would look at her only as queen and not love her as a woman. When Fenelon hinted that perhaps the hesitations were coming from members of her council, Elizabeth responded firmly that as a sovereign queen, she did not depend upon the approval of her council. This was a way of emphasizing that as sovereign, her status was highers than Catherine's as Dowager. Believing she had the upper hand, Elizabeth allowed negotiations to move forward, with Anjou agreeing to formally court the English queen.[15]

As was so often the case with Elizabeth, there was an impasse with the prospective husband's religion. Even though Catherine de Medici might view the religious differences between Henri of Anjou and Elizabeth to be an advantage as she attempted to navigate a difficult relationship with French Huguenots, Elizabeth and Henri were committed to maintaining their own faith. Religious differences had been a key factor in ending negotiations with Archduke Charles. As talks went on, it became clear this could become the sticking point for the French marriage as well.

Both courts tried to work through the issue of how an alliance would affect the religious practice of Elizabeth and Henri of Anjou. Elizabeth pressed Walsingham, her ambassador to the French court, to create a solution that might resolve the issue. At the same time, the English queen was determined that her husband could not flout English law and practise the Catholic religion while in England. It was Elizabeth continuing her practice of 'answers answerless': 'confusing her suitor by not giving clear indication of what she truly wanted'.[16] It was typical of Elizabeth, and probably not surprising to anyone, that despite the recognition of the dangers she faced and the possibility that marriage would alleviate some of them, she ultimately weighed the idea of marriage and found it wanting. She wrote to Catherine de Medici that her conscience would not allow her to proceed unless her requests were accepted.[17] She reiterated this sentiment, writing to Walsingham in September that she could not permit Henri of Anjou to 'exercise the [Catholic] form of Religion in England, that is prohibited by the Laws of our Realm' and goes on to emphasise 'Surely we cannot, not may not give him any authority in facts of such Rites as are prohibited by our Laws.'[18]

As always, Elizabeth understood the necessity of maintaining the goodwill of her suitors even after the suit had ended. As negotiations foundered over the sticking point of religion, as well as Elizabeth's usual requirement that she be able to meet her suitor in person before making a decision about marriage, she took steps to maintain positive relations with the French rulers. She wrote to Henri of Anjou, assuring him that the difficulties in carrying out the marriage were not due to any lack of goodwill on her part, but because her devotion to her kingdom required that she acted in a way that would preserve it. She assured him that she had acted with sincerity throughout the discussion. She also wrote to Catherine herself in a similar way, expressing her goodwill and love toward the queen and toward her son.[19]

In France, Catherine had been willing to work with Gaspard II de Coligny, a French nobleman and admiral who converted to Protestantism during the reign of Francis II and became a leader of the Huguenots during the reign of Charles IX. He had hoped a marriage between Elizabeth and Anjou would lend a level of protection to the Huguenots, something Charles IX was willing to accept. In 1572, Coligny was working with English ambassador Sir Thomas Smith in hopes of creating a league or alliance that could promote a peaceful promotion of Christendom, making space for the old religion and the new. The

Treaty of Blois, signed in April 1572, would be strengthened by a marriage between Elizabeth and Catherine de Medici's third offer: her youngest son, Hercule-Francois.

The French royal family recycled names and titles during this period. Hercule-Francois became known as Francois after the death of his brother Francois in 1560. In 1572, when he became a possible husband for Elizabeth, he was Duke of Alencon (a title previously held by his brother Henri). He became Duke of Anjou in 1574, when his brother the Duke of Anjou became Henri III of France. Hercule-Francois is frequently referred to as 'Anjou' in discussions of his relationship with Elizabeth. I'll refer to him as Hercule-Francois and then as 'Anjou' when he assumes that title. Whatever we call him – Hercule-Francois, Duke of Alencon and Anjou, or Elizabeth's 'Frog' – he ended up being one of the most significant suitors the English queen had.

Catherine de Medici thought she could reduce the tension between Catholics and Huguenots with a marriage between her youngest son and Elizabeth. Hercule-Francois was a Catholic but had consistently shown understanding and support for Huguenots. In addition to pursuing the marriage with Elizabeth, Catherine took another step by arranging a marriage between her daughter Margaret of Valois and Henry of Navarre. Henry was the son of Jeanne d'Albret, a leader of the Huguenots and an important supporter of the Peace of Saint-Germain-en-Laye, which ended the third religious war in France. Catherine and Jeanne arranged the marriage between their children. Jeanne d'Albret died on 9 June 1572, just a few months before the wedding. Plans for the marriage went ahead. There was hope that the wedding between Margaret and Henry represented a manifestation of religious toleration. But everything went wrong.

The wedding provided fuel to the religious fire. As Huguenots came to Paris to celebrate the wedding, Catholic preachers began to warn of the influx of 'heretics' who posed danger to the physical and moral safety of the city. Catholics in Paris had a hard summer in 1572, and many were hungry and angry at the government. Two Catholic bishops refused to be involved with the royal marriage at all. The Cardinal of

Bourbon eventually agreed to preside at the wedding, but only if he was recognised simply as the groom's uncle, not as a priest.

The wedding took place on 18 August 1572. Mobs gathered outside Notre Dame to harass the Protestants who withdrew from the marriage ceremony during the mass threatening to force them inside. In the celebrations that followed, King Charles IX's younger brother and heir, Henri, created pageants and tournaments that ended with the humiliation of Huguenots as Protestants were portrayed as prisoners or infidels. Less than a week after the wedding, things came to a head when Admiral Coligny, an important Protestant hero, was shot.

The impetus behind and blame for the attempted assassination of Coligny continues to be a matter of debate. Some believe Catherine herself was behind it, believing the Protestants were becoming a threat to her son's reign. She persuaded Charles IX the threat remained because Coligny had survived, and the king himself unleashed the Catholic response that led to the slaughter of thousands of Huguenots in Paris and beyond.[20] Some even believe Catherine encouraged or ordered the slaughter of the Protestants.[21] More recently, historian Dr Estelle Paranque painted Catherine de Medici and Charles IX as meeting with the injured Coligny and promising to find and punish the would-be assassin.[22] Whoever planned the initial attack, the results were catastrophic for the Huguenots in Paris and throughout France.

For days, deadly riots continued in Paris. A payment was made to city workmen for burying more than 1,000 bodies that had been thrown into the Seine. In the middle of the bloodshed was Francis Walsingham, Elizabeth's resident ambassador in France. Outside the doors of his official residence, the city he knew so well turned into a horror, with the streets and the Seine running with blood. Walsingham never really got over the scene because it enacted his worst fear – violent, dedicated attempts to assassinate Protestants and wipe out Protestantism. Charles IX wrote to the French ambassador in London on 27 August that he had sent guards to protect Walsingham's house. The next day, Walsingham sent a 'bearer' with an oral account of the horrors he had witnessed, being hesitant to commit anything to writing. As the violence in Paris subsided over the next month, there were still eruptions and Walsingham would not leave his home without a large escort. He sent his family home to England as soon as he felt it was safe.[23]

Walsingham had already been committed to his religion and his queen. After witnessing the massacre on St Bartholomew's Day, he became determined to do anything necessary to prevent something similar happening in England. Not on his watch. He would protect the Protestant queen he served and the Protestant faith he believed in at all costs. Walsingham's experience shaped his relentless pursuit of Mary, Queen of Scots and her Catholic supporters in England through the 1570s and 1580s. It was also part of his resistance to the marriage between Elizabeth and any of the French princes offered to her. While it was true that the youngest son, Hercule-Francois, was less of a zealot for the Catholic cause than his brother, and while Catherine de Medici made significant overtures to England for an amicable agreement that would promote religious tolerance, Walsingham could not bring himself to support the idea of Elizabeth marrying a Catholic. His voice would be a steady and persuasive one during the years that followed.

Elizabeth was also horrified by the events in France. With the slaughter of thousands of Huguenots in Paris and around France, she felt more pressure to support Protestants abroad. At the end of August, Antonio de Guaras, Philip II's ambassador to Elizabeth, wrote to the Duke of Parma that 'an incredible event has happened in Paris', going on to report that 8,000 Huguenots had been killed. He added, 'if it be true, the queen and council will be equally alarmed', before stating his own feelings: 'God grant that it may be true and that these rebel heretics have met with this bad end.' The pleasure of European Catholic leaders with the murder of Protestants in France must have reminded Elizabeth and her council of her vulnerability. De Guaras assumed that if reports of the massacre were true, 'the league between these people and the French will come to nothing'.[24] Elizabeth refused to even meet with the French ambassador for a few days, but eventually saw him. When Fenelon was admitted to the queen's presence, he found her and her court dressed in mourning. He assured her he was also sad about the 'accident' in France and that Charles IX had acted as well as he could have.[25]

When Elizabeth became ill at this point, the council feared it might be smallpox again.[26] This reignited fears about the succession. There was also ongoing discussion about an alliance with France and the possibility of Catherine de Medici coming to England to meet with Elizabeth.[27] There were also new rumours about the queen's sexual indiscretions, specifically with Robert Dudley and Christopher Hatton. These rumours were eagerly spread by Catholics such as Kenelm Berney, who was arrested for his involvement in a plot to kill William Cecil and depose Elizabeth. The Archbishop of Canterbury became alarmed when many seemed to believe the rumours, opening the possibility that disputes over the slander could cause civil wars in England similar to those in France. He warned Cecil of his fear that Catholic would rise against Protestant, a Catholic regime would be installed, and Elizabeth murdered or executed.[28] After the events in France, civil war seemed a real possibility. With English Catholics being trained in Jesuit seminaries, Cecil, Walsingham, and other councillors feared increased foreign support for English Catholic sympathisers and rebellions.

Against the background of these rumours and worries about the safety of Elizabeth and the Protestant church, the possibility of marriage between Elizabeth and the French prince seemed a path to security. The murder of the Protestants, and Elizabeth's support of French Huguenots in their efforts to rebel against their Catholic monarchs, posed political problems for Elizabeth's marriage to Hercule-Francois for some time. Toward the end of 1574, however, the possibility of a marriage between Elizabeth and the youngest son of Catherine de Medici was being seen in a new light. In May 1574, Charles IX died, and his brother Henri became Henri III of France. As a fourth son, Henri had probably not expected to inherit the throne and had been elected King of Poland and Duke of Lithuania in 1573. He was not in France when his brother died, so once again Catherine took up the position of Regent. It was a short-term arrangement. Although only

22 years old, Henri was the only one of Catherine's children to take the throne as an adult with no need of assistance. This changed Catherine's position. Charles IX always relied heavily on his mother. Henri III respected his mother and her views, but he had already established himself as a ruler and as a warrior, and he came to the French throne with his own ideas.

With his older brother as king, Hercule-Francois was now heir to the French throne. In 1576, he was made Duke of Anjou. The French religious wars continued, and Henri III and Catherine de Medici were concerned about Anjou's potential support of the Huguenots. Even before the death of Charles IX, while religious wars in France and tensions with England were ongoing, Catherine continued to write to Elizabeth and encourage the English queen to marry her son. Before Fenelon, the French ambassador with whom Elizabeth had developed a good working relationship, left England in the late 1570s at the end of his term of service. Before he returned to France, he assured Catherine that Elizabeth would give a firm answer in a few days.[29] But as usual, Elizabeth did not provide anything definitive. She wished to keep the French in play as she navigated through the perils facing her. Once she left Kenilworth in 1575 and made clear she would not marry Dudley, her chances for marriage became narrower. As the 1570s ended, Elizabeth entered into what would be her final marriage negotiation, an extended back and forth with the new Duke of Anjou, her 'Frog'.

In 1579, Anjou sent Jean de Simier to England to negotiate a marriage with the English queen. Anjou was focused on the wars in the Netherlands, which were not going well. His troops were deserting him, and his brother was not interested in supporting the venture financially. Anjou saw Elizabeth as his best option for gaining support in the war and rebuilding his credibility with William of Orange.[30] His choice of Simier was a good one. Described by Camden as 'a choice courtier, a man thoroughly versed in love-fancies, pleasant conceits, and court dalliances', Simier made a favourable impression on the queen. She received him so graciously that Dudley was angry.[31] His success raised the hopes of Catherine de Medici, who had never given up on the hope of seeing another son on a European throne and gaining an alliance with Elizabeth and England.

In offering her sons to marry Elizabeth, Catherine was also offering herself. Although Henri was not as publicly reliant on his mother as his brother Charles had been, in England there was little doubt who was the power behind the throne. In his secret correspondence, Cecil used the cipher 'tout' (meaning 'all') when referring to Catherine and 'rien' (meaning 'none') when referring to the French king himself. Catherine wished to be a mother figure to the English queen, and she sent her own envoy, Monsieur de Roquetaillade, to carry letters from Catherine to Elizabeth. Elizabeth was flattered and expressed appreciation to Catherine.

The English court was becoming more concerned about Philip's ambitions to spread his power in Portugal and the Netherlands, something that threatened England and the English queen. In addition, the ongoing arrival of Jesuit priests and troubling presence of Mary, Queen of Scots, represented what could be an irresistible temptation for Philip to invade England. Elizabeth knew that French support would be necessary to hold off Spain and other Catholic nations. However, she was not about to jump into marriage. Her personal approach was, as always, to extend negotiations as long as possible. She insisted once again that before she even proceed seriously with the talks, Anjou must visit England so they could meet in person. There were rumours that the duke had been seriously scarred by smallpox and that he was not as handsome or well-built as his brother. As eager as she was for the negotiations to proceed, Catherine had reservations, as did Henri III. For months, the French king had told his brother not to go to England until he had assurance that he would be named king if he married the English queen.[32] Catherine agreed they should resist the queen's invitation until conditions in the marriage contract were agreed upon.[33]

By spring 1579, Elizabeth's actions convinced her council that the queen was seriously considering marrying. Even Dudley thought so, writing to William Davison lamenting that he feared that if Anjou came to England and Elizabeth liked him, 'she will have him'. The council met in March and spent weeks discussing the possibility of the marriage, considering it in terms of the succession, the queen's health, domestic implications, and impact on foreign relations. The council was split over the marriage.[34]

Cecil was in favour of the marriage. His practical nature saw the political advantages, and, in his opinion, these outweighed the objections. After all, it was possible the queen could still conceive and give the nation an heir, something Cecil had been fighting for since Elizabeth came to the throne. He understood it would have been far preferable if she had married earlier, but even now children were a possibility that should be pursued. He also believed, as did many at the time, that marriage would improve the queen's health.[35] He thought the queen's marriage into the French royal family was the 'only realistic and safe remedy' for the nation as it faced religious and political dangers on every side. Cecil believed that the possible Catholic alliance against England would spell an almost certain disaster. If Anjou did not marry Elizabeth, he might form an alliance with Spain. Supporting the marriage would solidify Cecil's standing with Elizabeth as well.[36] He convinced many on the council to take his side.

Walsingham led opposition to the Catholic marriage. He had not forgotten the massacre in France and was firmly convinced that marriage between his Protestant queen and a Catholic, even one who had demonstrated some accommodation of the Huguenots, would be a disaster. There was also resistance to any foreign power having a strong say in England's political future. The memory of war with France, which was often laid at the feet of Queen Mary's marriage to the Spanish king, still lingered. In addition, although it was not something to be discussed openly, the likelihood of the queen bearing a child at this point was questionable because of her age. Elizabeth was in her mid-40s and past the age when most women of the time were able to give birth. Even if she did conceive and have a child, her age increased the danger of death in childbirth. Several on the council shared Walsingham's resistance, including Dudley. Of course, Elizabeth's favourite was also worried about losing his unique status at the queen's side. Even without marrying her, Dudley had managed to remain close to Elizabeth and have greater access to her than most of the other courtiers. That would almost certainly change if she married.

Despite his devotion to the queen, Dudley had not limited his affections to Elizabeth. His affair with Douglas Sheffield lasted from around 1570 through 1574, when she gave birth to his son. He never married her because he was unwilling to risk his favour with the queen. After the queen's refusal at Kenilworth, Dudley rekindled an earlier flirtation with Lettice Knollys, daughter of Catherine Carey Knollys, Elizabeth's first cousin and one of her closest friends. Catherine had become a senior Lady of the Bedchamber shortly after Elizabeth came to the throne, and she served the queen until her death in 1569. Lettice joined the queen's household with her mother as a maid of the privy chamber. She married Walter Devereux in 1560 and continued to serve the queen. Devereux, who became Earl of Essex, died in Ireland in September 1576. Their son Robert became Earl of Essex. (Stay tuned for more about him in Chapter 11!) After Devereux's death, Lettice and Dudley were married secretly in September 1578. They had so far managed to keep the marriage secret from the queen for months, and they were determined to continue to do so.

Dudley probably felt that staying close to the queen would help him keep his marriage a secret. He joined Walsingham in opposing the marriage, expressing his fears about the danger facing Elizabeth if she proceeded with the Anjou marriage.[37] Recognising that the marriage could only succeed if Dudley supported it, Anjou set out to establish a relationship with the earl. Anjou offered Dudley Spanish horses and arranged extravagant banquets for him and the other resistant councillors. This had some effect on the council, but Dudley himself was unmoved. He swore that nothing could get him to support the marriage. Unfortunately for Dudley, Simier discovered Dudley's secret marriage. Believing that was the only way to eliminate the obstacle, he took the news to the queen.[38] Elizabeth was, predictably, furious about the marriage and deception and sent Dudley and Lettice from court. She would forgive come to Dudley and have him back, but she would never forgive Lettice.

Perhaps this perceived 'betrayal' from her long-time trusted favourite pushed Elizabeth along in her desire to meet Anjou, whom she now referred to as her 'Frog'. In August 1579, he quietly left France and sailed for England, arriving at Greenwich on 17 August. Elizabeth was determined the visit should remain a secret, as there was growing dissatisfaction with the public about the marriage. Anjou travelled in disguise with a small retinue, but such a secret was impossible to keep. The Spanish ambassador, Bernardino de Mendoza, wrote in detail to Philip of Spain about the visit. As early as 20 August, there was news Anjou had arrived, and Mendoza requested an audience with the queen to remind her of Spain's unhappiness about the marriage. He told Philip the people were unhappy about Anjou and that the queen was angry about the speculation about the visit and formally ordered that no one talk about it. The council members denied Anjou was there and stayed away from court so they wouldn't see or hear him. A few days later, Mendoza wrote that the queen and Anjou were delighted with each other and 'she has let out to some of her courtiers saying that she was pleased to have known him, was much taken with his good parts, and admired him more than any man'. Dudley was upset and 'the people in general seem to threaten revolution about it'. Mendoza concluded that Dudley and others said that parliament 'would have something to say as to whether the queen married or not'.[39]

While Elizabeth was charmed by the French prince and by Simier as well, her people were not. Popular resistance to the marriage grew. Pamphlets and ballads resisting the marriage simmered during 1579 and into the 1580s. In response to her nickname of 'Frog' for Anjou, legend has it that the folksong 'Froggie Went a Courting' began as a ballad mocking the queen's possible marriage. More direct opposition came from a tract written by John Stubbs entitled *The Discoverie of a Gaping Gulf whereinto England is like to be swallowed by another French marriage, if the Lord forbit not the banes, by letter her Majestie to see the sin and punishment thereof.* The tract was inspired by religious and political opposition to the marriage and accused the queen of putting her personal desires above the needs of her nation. Anjou was the serpent who was poised to seduce 'our Eve', creating the danger of losing paradise. Stubbs described himself as the queen's true and loving servant, but that was not how Elizabeth saw it.

The queen responded with fury, banning the book and ordering the Lord Mayor of London to burn all copies. Stubbs was arrested and condemned to losing his hand. This didn't silence opposition.[40] Resistance to the marriage continued, possibly encouraged by Stubbs himself, who after having his right hand cut off, raised his hat with his left and called out, 'God save the queen.' Other messages of opposition were printed and spread. In addition, Dudley's preacher presented the queen a petition and asked her to read it. When she realised it contained more arguments against her marriage, she was angry, gave orders that the chaplain be arrested, and demanded that Dudley not leave his house. Still, there was much talk and 'every day in the streets defamatory libels were circulated' against Anjou and the marriage.[41] Anjou left England late in August, with Elizabeth unsure about what to do.[42]

In April 1580, Simier arrived in France with an assignment to continue negotiations for the marriage. Catherine de Medici was communicating with Elizabeth on her own, assuring the English queen her greatest desire was to 'see the good resolution of the marriage between you and my son'. Most of Europe knew how eager Catherine was that the marriage go forward. In fact, some said that it was Catherine who was Elizabeth's most determined and loyal suitor.[43] Elizabeth seemed less sure of what outcome she wanted in terms of the marriage, but she did seem to want to do what she always did – keep negotiations 'in a deliberately managed state of limbo as she sought to maintain an alliance with France'.[44] In France, Catherine was determined to win as well, sending letters to Elizabeth encouraging her to move forward.[45] All this was not enough to convince the English queen. Anjou decided he had to go back to England. He was the first of Elizabeth's foreign suitors to visit her and court her in person, let alone make a second visit. This time he meant to stay.

Marriage talks continued. France sent Marchaumont as a special envoy, and Fenelon accompanied him to meet with Walsingham and Cecil. Walsingham said the marriage with Anjou would raise hopes of English Catholics and inspire them to rebel, and Marchaumont countered that the marriage would appease the Catholic dissidents. Cecil had the last word, saying the marriage was not settled because the questions of the contract were not resolved. The French were fuming but continued planning for Anjou's visit. He arrived in November and went to Richmond.[46] On 22 November, with Dudley and Walsingham attending her, the queen appeared with Anjou. The French ambassador said the French king wished to know the queen's mind regarding the marriage. The queen stated, 'you may write this to the king: the duke of [Anjou] shall be my husband', kissing him on the lips and giving him a ring. The French were overjoyed, according to Mendoza's report to Philip II.

It's interesting to see how Mendoza continues his letter. He describes Elizabeth sending a message to Cecil, who replies, 'Blessed be the Lord that this business has at last reached a point where the queen on her part has done all she can: it is for the country now alone to carry it out.' The people in London considered the marriage as good as accomplished. But Mendoza was not convinced: 'I am unable to look upon the matter as by any means concluded.' He had watched Elizabeth in action and believed if she had wanted to marry Anjou she would have already done so. Instead, by 'personally pledging herself in this way, she binds him to her', setting Anjou against his brother, and leaving the eventual decision to the terms of the contract.[47]

Some English councillors also doubted Elizabeth would go through with the marriage. They were right. Having spent the night thinking about all the implications, perhaps hearing from her ladies about the reasons not to marry, or maybe having been planning to do this all along, Elizabeth took back her promise to marry Anjou. The terms she demanded for the marriage to go forward – including the return of

Calais and French support against Mary, Queen of Scots – were ones Elizabeth knew would not be accepted.[48] Anjou continued to press, but she had finally made up her mind. In February of 1582, Anjou left England. Elizabeth's official courtships had come to an end.

The poem 'On Monsieur's Departure' is attributed to Elizabeth, even though no manuscript copy survives from her time:

> I grieve and dare not show my discontent;
> I love, and yet am forced to seem to hate;
> I do, yet dare not say I ever meant;
> I seem stark mute, but inwardly do prate.
> I am, and not: I freeze and yet am burned,
> Since from myself another self I turned.
> My care is like my shadow in the sun –
> Follows my flying, flies when I pursue it,
> Stands, and lies by me, doth what I have done;
> His too familiar care doth make me rue it.
> No means I find to rid him from my breast,
> Till by the end of things it be suppressed.
> Some gentler passion slide into my mind,
> For I am soft, and made of melting snow
> Or be more cruel, Love, and so be kind.
> Let me float or sink, be high or low.
> Or let me live with some more sweet content,
> Or die, and so forget what love e'er meant.[49]

The poem seems to express the queen's feelings as not only the individual Duke of Anjou, her Frog, leaves England, but also her chances of marrying come to an end.

Although the alliance between an English queen and a French prince would always be political, this relationship also developed into something personal for Elizabeth. Perhaps more than anyone other than Robert Dudley, Anjou was someone Elizabeth felt affection for and seemed to enjoy spending time with. Robert Dudley was the through line of Elizabeth's courtship, knowing her from the time they were children and remaining close to her until he died. Anjou was Elizabeth's final chance at marriage, and their courtship lasted twelve years and helped create her emergence as the Virgin Queen. That would be the image under which her final 'courtships' would be conducted.

Chapter 10

Courtly Love – Changing the Rules of the Game

Word for word, that is justice,
One for one, two for two.
They are gracious so to converse,
Respond yourself graciously –
With fine words!

Margaret of Austria

In 1573, a woman living in Elizabeth's England received a letter that contained this language:

> The great wisdom I find in your letters, with your Country counsels are very notable, but the last word is worth the bible. Truth, truth, truth, Ever may it dwell with you. I will ever deserve it. My spirit and soul (I feel) agreeth with my body and life, that to serve you is a heaven, but to lack you is more than hell's torment unto them. My heart is full of woe. Pardon (for God's sake) my tedious writing. It doth much diminish (for the time) my great griefs. I will wash away the faults of these letters with the drops from your poor Lydds and so inclose them. Would God I were with you for one hour. My wits are overwrought with thoughts. I find myself amazed. Bear with me, my most dear sweet Lady. Passion overcometh me. I can write no more. Love me; for I love you.[1]

It seems like an earnest letter from a lover or husband to his sweetheart. In fact, it is from Sir Christopher Hatton to Queen Elizabeth. The language of praise and love echoes the form and nature of courtly love, a construct Elizabeth relied on throughout her reign. After the closing of negotiations with the Duke of Anjou, Elizabeth shifted into a phase where marriage and children were no longer part of her future. But the language used by her courtiers continued to include excesses of praise and apparently heartfelt declarations of love. As a woman who spent more than forty years in a role most believed should be the domain of a man, Elizabeth had to exercise a unique kind of power and authority that law and custom denied her. She relied in part on the tradition and legends of courtly love to preside over the hearts and minds of her courtiers and the actions of policies of her council as well.

But what, really, is 'courtly love'?

Words with Many Meanings

The first specific use of the term 'courtly love' comes in an article written by Gaston Paris in 1883 describing the love between Lancelot and Guinevere in Chretien de Troyes's *Conte de la Charette*. According to Paris, the term comprised four elements: (1) the love was secret and forbidden; (2) the male lover was insecure, and the beloved was elevated and possibly disdainful; (3) the lover earned the lady's affection by proving himself in a series of challenges; and (4) the love was subject to rules and regulations. Paris does allude to the earlier example of the troubadours in the twelfth century, but he doesn't specify if that earlier version was 'real' courtly love.[2]

The idea of courtly love in the time of the troubadours is caught up with the multiple legends surrounding Eleanor of Aquitaine. In many ways, Eleanor defied the notions of womanhood, instigating the divorce from her first husband, the king of France, and selecting her second husband, who would become the king of England. Having been crowned queen consort of both France and then England, Eleanor provided Henry II with a houseful of sons and then supported those sons when they rose up against their father. Henry II forgave his sons their rebellion, but he did not forgive his wife, and Eleanor spent sixteen years in prison. When her favourite son became King Richard I, she was released from prison and immediately went to work promoting his reign and legacy. She travelled through Europe, securing Richard's release after he was captured following his fight in the Crusades. When Richard died, Eleanor supported her son John's claim to the throne, fighting on his behalf against her nephew Arthur. She outlived both her husbands, many of her children, and nearly all her contemporaries before dying in 1204 at age 82.

In addition to all the fascination of what Eleanor actually achieved in her lifetime, there are extraordinary legends surrounding what she most likely did not. Henry II is often described as a patron of the arts, and the Plantagenets enjoyed the ways art enriched life. However, it is Eleanor whose presence in the English court brought the appreciation of poetry and music as the granddaughter of the great troubadour William IX of Aquitaine. According to Amy Kelly, Eleanor helped lead England into the enlightened lifestyle of the continent and became the focus of poetry and love songs in the English court.[3] The cultural flavour of the French-born queen grew in England as Eleanor continued to travel back and forth between the two countries.

In 1170, Eleanor arrived in Poitiers to take possession of the area and install her son Richard as duke and herself as mistress, ready to dispense her own patronage. Her first daughter Marie, born while she was married to Louis VII of France, joined her there. Poets and artists were drawn to this court at Poitiers, set apart from the piety of Louis's court in Paris and the ambitions of Henry II's court in England. Eleanor and Marie, according to the legend, gathered books about love and created an elegant society that included assemblies in the queen's hall full of troubadours, poetry, and music. This notion of courts of love, over which the queen and her daughter presided, became a legend.[4] Although most historians now dismiss any idea of the reality of these courts of love, the legend continues. Literary conferences held in the twentieth century focused on Eleanor's involvement in the courts of love, and one collection of papers stated firmly, 'courtly love is real'.[5]

The ideals of courtly love, linked with the legends of King Arthur and chivalric knights battling evil in honour of their ladies fair, did take hold in parts of Europe over the following centuries. The story crafted by Chretien de Troyes in the twelfth century continued to spread and appeal to men and women, and the ideal version of love he created infused subsequent retellings of Arthur's story, notably that of Thomas Malory in the 1460s. In the later years of the fifteenth century and well into the sixteenth, the notion of Arthur's legend and courtly love would help shape England's newest dynasty, the Tudors. Henry VII, a man from Wales, tapped into the Arthurian legend to strengthen his own story and claim to the throne. He used the Welsh red dragon as an emblem before he settled on the red rose, and he arranged to have his first child born at Winchester, a place associated with the mythic king. Henry VII was richly rewarded for his belief in his association with the legend – when the child arrived it was a boy, and the king named him Arthur.

After Arthur's early death, Henry VII was succeeded by his second son, who became Henry VIII. The second Tudor king warmly embraced the association with gallant knights, acting out his role through his love of jousting and defeating opponents while wearing the badge of a lady. Early on, he was content to wear the colours of his wife, Katherine of Aragon, but as time passed and Katherine failed (in his view) to provide him with a son, Henry began to wear the tokens of other ladies. He also wore badges with statements about his devotion to a woman, such as 'Declare I dare not' at the Shrovetide joust of early 1526. The woman who had caught the king's eye at that point was no stranger to the notion of courtly love.

The Courtly Legacy of Anne Boleyn

Anne Boleyn received an extraordinary upbringing in two of the most extravagant and elegant courts of Europe in the early sixteenth century: Burgundy and France. Margaret of Austria, the Dowager Duchess of Savoy after the death of her husband, had been impressed with the ambassador from the English court, Thomas Boleyn. At his request, she agreed to find a place in her household for his second daughter.

Anne Boleyn left England in 1513 and travelled to Margaret's favourite palace, Mechelen, to take her place as one of the archduchess's eighteen maids of honour. There are ongoing debates about exactly when Anne was born, with 1501 being the current favourite, with others favouring years up to 1507. The 1501 date would make Anne at most about 12 years old when she arrived at the sophisticated court. Despite her youth, she impressed Margaret, who wrote to Anne's father that she was 'confident of being able to deal with her in a way which will give you satisfaction so that on your return here the two of us will need to intermediary other than she. I find her so bright and pleasant for her young age that I am more beholden to you for sending her to me than you are to me.'[6]

In Margaret's court, Anne studied diligently to learn French. She understood the purpose of her time at Margaret's court, writing to her father:

> Sir, I understand by your letter that you desire that I shall be a worthy woman when I come to the Court and you inform me that the Queen will take the trouble to converse with me, which rejoices me to think of talking with a person so wise and worthy. This will make me have greater desire to continue speaking French well and also spell, especially because you have enjoined it on me, and with my own hand I inform you that I will observe it the best I can.[7]

In addition to French, Anne learned the skills that were so valued at court, including dancing and playing musical instruments. As a member of the household, Anne was expected to be a credit to the archduchess and to gracefully entertain the numerous foreign dignitaries who visited the court.

Margaret of Austria was strict with her ladies, expecting the highest levels of deportment and conversation at all times. It was here that Anne learned the power of language associated with courtly entertainment, courtly politics, and courtly love. Margaret herself was skilled in the language and uses of courtly love, and she required that her ladies participate in the playful banter according to strict conventions. Margaret described her expectations and gave counsel to her ladies in poetry, writing:

> Trust in those who offer you service,
> And, in the end, my maidens,
> You will find yourselves in the ranks of those
> Who have been deceived.
> They, for their sweet speeches, choose
> Words softer than the softest of virgins;
> Trust in them?
> In their hearts they nurture
> Much cunning in order to deceive,
> And once they have their way thus,
> Everything is forgotten.
> Trust in them?

Margaret's caution is clear, as is her instruction in how to respond to unwanted or untrustworthy advances:

> Fine words are the coin to pay back
> Those presumptuous minions
> Who ape the lover
> By fine looks and such like.
> Not for a moment but instantly
> Give to them their pay –
> Fine words!
> Word for word, that is justice,
> One for one, two for two.
> They are gracious so to converse,
> Respond yourself graciously –
> With fine words![8]

For Anne Boleyn, the words of courtly love ran throughout her relationship with Henry VIII. Early in their relationship, the besotted king courted his lady love with a series of letters. Although the letters are not dated, they cover the period from the early days of courtship around 1526. The letters themselves display the king's growing affection, as Henry VIII wrote each one by hand rather than dictating them (the king hated to write letters himself). He also used hearts and monograms to personalise the letters, linking their initials and names. In fact, sometimes they seem more like the private doodling of a teenager than the letters of the king of England. His language in some cases sounds like the excessive flattery of courtly love: 'on my part the pain of absence is already too great for me', 'having been for a whole year stricken with the dart of love', and 'my heart and I surrender ourselves into your hands, beseeching you to hold us commending to your favour, and that by absence your affection to us may not be lessened: for it were a great pity to increase our pain, of which absence produces enough and more than I could ever have thought could be felt'.[9]

Henry's expressions of love go beyond what Margaret of Austria had counselled Anne, however, as Henry was seeking full satisfaction. His letters were erotic in places, as when he asked Anne to think of him while eating the flesh of a deer he sent her. He insisted she tell him how she felt about him. And he frequently asked, early on, for her to become his mistress in the physical sense. However, Anne refused to become the king's mistress. Although we don't have her letters back to the king, we can be sure she used courtly 'words, fine words' as the archduchess had taught her, to navigate the long courtship, at once keeping the king's desire steady while denying him the full satisfaction he asked for. Eventually, in what was an extraordinary decision at the time, Henry decided to set aside his first marriage without the pope's approval, to establish (or, in his version, re-establish) the Church in England, and to declare himself Supreme Head of the Church of England. All these steps were taken, at least in part, to pave the way to marriage to his sweetheart.

The courtly love that had served Anne so well turned against her at the end. Less than three years after her secret marriage to Henry VIII and her glorious coronation as queen of England, Anne had given the king only one living child: a daughter, Elizabeth. Henry felt betrayed by the lack of a son, and he blamed Anne. After a final failed pregnancy in early 1536, Anne realised the sands were shifting beneath her feet. The king was publicly courting Jane Seymour, and powerful men at court were supporting Jane. Thomas Cromwell gave his own rooms to Jane's brother Edward, allowing Jane and the king to meet easily. Anne must have felt desperate to have made the mistake of engaging in a dangerous conversation with Henry Norris, a favourite courtier of hers and the king's. Challenging Norris about his hesitation to marry, Anne stated that he looked for 'dead man's shoes' and went on to say that if the king were to die, Norris would wish to marry Anne. This erupted into an argument, with Norris realising immediately that speaking about the king's death, even in such a non-threatening way, was treason. More than that, there were witnesses.

The notion that Norris would love and express a desire to worship and serve the queen fit into the construct of courtly love. But for Anne to take the lead in the conversation and speak about the king's death shattered the parameters. She scrambled to right the error, having Norris go to her almoner and state she was a 'good woman'.[10] But as Cromwell arrested and interrogated Mark Smeaton, who as a musician was frequently in the queen's chamber and seemed to have a fantasy of a real relationship with her, he pushed the movement against Anne to the point of no return. At the May Day joust, the pinnacle of courtly love played out by healthy and attractive young men taking sport before the queen and the injured king. Henry could no longer participate in the joust and was likely jealous of the men he was watching, and when he received a note he abruptly walked away from Anne's side. She would never see him again.

After her arrest, the 'potentially lethal slipperiness of the language of courtly love' continued to condemn her and the men accused with her. As terror took over, Anne's words in the Tower became unguarded.

She recounted a conversation with Francis Weston where she chided him for not marrying Mary Shelton and suggested Weston might be in love with her.[11] Again, being in love with the queen was an acceptable pretence in the world of courtly love, but Henry had turned ferociously against his wife. Anne Boleyn was now an object of danger instead of desire. Anne's words were reported, and Weston was arrested. Caught in this web, his death was as pre-determined as that of the others.

Anne Boleyn's fall was swift and violent. From her arrest on 2 May, it would be less than three weeks before she and five men, including her brother, were beheaded at the king's command. Henry was directly involved in the details of Anne's execution, giving William Kingston, the constable of the Tower, specific instructions how and where to carry out the beheading of his once-beloved wife. The king might have been driven by some bit of regret in his decision to allow Anne to be beheaded instead of burned and to be executed within the confines of the Tower, where fewer people could see her demise.[12] He also called for an expert executioner from Calais, sparing Anne from execution by the axe, which often took multiple blows. Although this might also have been some kind of merciful act, I believe it was more about appearance, as the first execution of a queen was already a blow to Henry's image, and to have a queen's life end in butchery at the block would not fit his perception of himself as a chivalric knight and king.

Anne's life at court was shaped by courtly love. She employed it with great effect to achieve her grand dream of becoming queen of England. But in the end, her careless misuse of those 'fine words' led to her death. The power of words was a lesson her daughter would need to learn well.

Elizabeth and Courtly Love

Although her mother died before she turned 3 years old, Elizabeth inherited attributes from Anne Boleyn: her narrow face, her dark eyes, her facility with language, her quick wit. In addition, I believe, Elizabeth inherited her use of the language and trappings of courtly love.

Shortly after Mary I was crowned queen of England, her great supporter Simon Renard wrote to Charles V that Elizabeth had 'characteristics in which she resembled her mother'.[13] Of course, Renard, a consistent enemy of Elizabeth, meant negative traits and reasoned that Elizabeth was likely to cause as much trouble as her mother had. Still, he was correct in recognising that there were ways Elizabeth was like Anne Boleyn. For one thing, 'she was determined to be mistress of her own destiny'. Like her mother, Elizabeth did not conform to social conventions.[14] Anne Boleyn had been determined to marry the king rather than be his mistress; Elizabeth ultimately decided not to marry. Although it is difficult to know how seriously she was in her early statements, Elizabeth regularly stated she preferred being single and preferred her single state. In an address to parliament in 1575, she stated, 'I would not forsake that single state to match myself with the greatest monarch.'[15]

That did not mean that Elizabeth avoided the company of men. Instead, she maintained friendly and flirtatious relationships with suitors and courtiers alike throughout her reign. As a queen and as a woman, she represented a prize that kings, dukes, and others believed was worth pursuing. As her courtier and admirer Sir Christopher said, 'the queen did fish for men's souls and had so sweet a bait, that no one could escape her network'.[16] Elizabeth often relied on the language and methods of courtly love to navigate complicated roles with courtiers and councillors alike.

Elizabeth used a version of courtly love where the male lover swears his undying love to an unattainable lady. Although the language used can be suggestive or include hints of eroticism, the possibility of a sexual relationship is out of bounds. The queen used this construct with suitors and with council members; in other words, with her body personal and with her body politic. As Elizabeth's reign went on, she played various roles in the world of 'the court' and 'courtship' continued. This was complicated with a queen on the throne.

Part of the was complicated related to the language that was used. Earlier, people had associated ideas about 'court' and 'courtship' with 'being at court or behaving as a courtier'. Court was coming to be associated strongly with the king (for hundreds of years, it had always been a king, and most people thought that was the way it should be). When Castiglione created his *The Book of the Courtier* in 1528, the notion of 'being at court' meant advising the king, providing wise and tactful advice. Court meant a centralised source of power, incorporating those around the king. Words such as 'courting' and 'courtship' meant 'behaving as a courtier'. Over time, 'courting' came to mean as 'persuading' and 'wooing' – including wooing a woman. Two ideas, that of persuasion associated with power and persuasion associated with sex, came to intersect in the notion of courtship. This was especially true in the reign of Elizabeth I. Throughout Elizabeth's reign, the word 'courtship' came to represent the peculiarities of government and those of romance.[17]

As a female monarch, the governing body was housed in a physical body that was expected to be weaker than and reliant on the body of a man. In Elizabeth's case, she used a tradition that existed outside of the political world to exercise power and control over a male group of councillors. Men could not be expected to take orders from a woman – such a thought was against nature, against God's law, and against the accepted law of the land. Instead, they sought to serve a lady fair to whom they wrote and spoke to in the language of love. Men clustered around the queen, eager to do her bidding. Although that structure doesn't seem to make space for someone like William Cecil, who was Elizabeth's greatest statesman and political supporter, it did cast him as a bureaucrat, 'the archetypal (and, in the courtly story, slightly contemptible) clerk always opposed to the knight'.[18] And courtiers sometimes relied on a 'politicised language of love and an eroticized language of politics'. Counselling, as well as wooing, relied on appearing to be sincere when addressing the queen. Courtly language gave privy councillors like Cecil and other men serving the queen 'a means of getting their way'.[19]

In Henry VIII's day, the privy council could meet in the privy chamber, sharing time with the king while drinking, playing games, and talking politics in an intimate setting. This was not possible with the queen. In addition, the king took pains to present himself as a potent and sexual figure, sharing bawdy talk with the men around him. Henry's obsession with displaying what he considered his masculine prowess is especially evident in the portraits he commissioned, with the upside-down triangle created by his broad shoulders and relatively narrow waist overlapping with the triangle created by his legs apart and narrow waist overlapping and calling attention to the exaggerated codpiece at the centre. Henry VIII made the 'Superman pose' famous years before scientists claimed it increased confidence. Confidence and sexuality were connected.

When the centre of the councillors and the centre of court life was not a king but a queen, everything changed. In the Elizabethan court, the queen was at the centre of her government as 'court' and, as that government begged her to take a husband, she was at the centre of romantic 'courtship' as well. Her reign saw the results of an ongoing separation between the 'Domus Regie Magnificencie' and the 'Domus Providencie'. The former came to represent political and public space and activity, and the latter more personal and less public activity. Even so, the queen's body was considered to be a matter of state, her marriage a matter of national security, and her 'courtship' was at the centre of 'court' debates. The personal and public intersected in Elizabeth's reign, as evidenced by some of her favourites who came to hold positions of political power.

In the Christmas and New Year celebrations of 1575, George Gascoigne gave the queen a lavish manuscript of 'The Tale of Hermetes the Heremyte', translated into four languages. The story, which Elizabeth had heard at Woodstock the previous summer, was about three lovers who were saved from separation by the miraculous presence of the queen. This was a strong example of the complications of courtship: being a courtier and seeking political advancement and pursuing a relationship with a woman. There can be a sense of this being a type of game or system where the goal is to reassure the prince (politics) or mistress (personal) of steadfast and dutiful service.[20] Elizabeth's subjects and most of her fellow monarchs, with the exception of the also female Mary Queen of Scots, felt ambivalent at best about having a woman at the head of government. The lack of clarity created confusion and at the same time opportunities to consider how best to create a relationship with the queen.

Elizabeth's court explored and reimagined questions and confusion about the meaning of 'courtship', 'courtier', and 'courting'. There were multiple interpretations – being at court meant being in the presence of the queen and her council, being a courtier meant at once pledging allegiance to and flattering the queen and possibly conducting political business, the act of courting included writing texts (letters, plays, pageants, poetry) and speaking words that praised the queen's beauty and femininity as well as her right to rule the men around her and at the same time working in the business of the country. All this was simmering throughout Elizabeth's reign, as members of her council vied with foreign royals and their representatives for her attention and favour. Some attention was associated with a potential marriage, but throughout her so-called 'marriageable' years, the queen continued to allow the possibility to go only so far, constantly confusing foreign suitors by giving favour to her English favourites and denying her favourites (Dudley in particular) his ultimate goal of marriage by continuing to consider foreign offers.

Through it all, the queen was also playing the role of the lady fair, subject of the adoration of all in her kingdom. This emphasis on her femaleness raised concerns in a realm and society and world that assumed the centre of government business ought to be male. There were anxieties about a queen ruling a male-dominated society and court. Handsome and charismatic men such as Dudley and Hatton had the ability to charm the queen in the early years of her reign, and both also played key roles in the government. This pattern continued even after the real chance of marriage was over. Elizabeth flirted with the Earl of Essex and Walter Ralegh during the final years of her reign, and they flirted with her. The tradition and trappings of 'courtly love' exemplified what went on throughout Elizabeth's entire reign, from the early attentions of Dudley and Philip II to the final relationships with Essex and Ralegh: a 'tension between individual desire' expressed by men with a personal relationship with the queen and the demands of society and government.[21]

Although Elizabeth described herself as being on a stage and unable to hide from the eyes around her, in these situations it was the men who were performing, setting themselves on a stage of sorts before the queen. The successful courtiers learned and perfected the art of courtship, using language to navigate the personal and political components of the Elizabethan world. A reliance on language was part of the courtly love tradition – not unlike Anne Boleyn receiving instruction to command the use of 'fine words', Elizabeth and her courtiers, some of whom acted as suitors in various ways, used courtly language to carry on the simmering steps in the dance. And like the Volta, one of Elizabeth's favourite dances, the dance of courtly love also brushed up against eroticism and sexuality in carefully controlled ways that carried the danger of spilling over into the forbidden. After all, anything based on the myth of Arthur and his knights included the potent threat of immoral love.

Elizabeth and her court acted out their relationship in the space shared with harsh and all-too-real politics. The marriage dance with all Elizabeth's foreign suitors carried political weight and international implications in addition to any personal desire the queen might or might not have felt. The extended relationship with Anjou, the only foreign suitor to woo in person and one with whom the queen seemed to share genuine affection, came out of political expediency and was ultimately quashed by political concerns. English suitors were also political, as politicians like Cecil worked against the queen's marriage to Dudley because there was likely only room for one person at the queen's side – a husband or a politician.

It's no great surprise that Elizabethan authors would create poetry that extolled the celebration of love and comedic plays that so often end in marriage in this environment. Some of these can give us a way of seeing the court of Elizabeth in thinly veiled depictions. John Lyly's

Endymion, written in 1588, was seen as an allegory of Elizabeth's court, with Cynthia representing the queen herself. Cynthia was a paradox, both cruel and kind, both constant and unpredictable, a good model for the changeable queen. Endymion's relationship with Cynthia captured the complexities of the relationship between members of court and Elizabeth. Endymion's love was flattering but not sexual or erotic, and his desire was not to rule over Cynthia as a husband would rule over a wife. Likewise, the courtiers' love and desire existed without expectation or hope of sexual fulfilment. They flattered the queen in ways that may have seemed personal but did not in any way disrupt her political authority. Such behaviour became 'a convenient way of expressing political loyal and devotion in desexualized' ways.[22]

Elizabeth adapted the traditions of courtly love to her own end throughout her reign. She took on the attributes of the courtly lady, capricious, volatile, and utterly in charge of the situation and those around her. She was unattainable, not because she was married, as were the traditional courtly ladies, but because she was queen. The courtly lady was typically of higher rank than her suitors and thus able to grant favours and demand loyalty in return, and who was more able to grant favours and demand loyalty than the queen herself?

There was also a spiritual element to the courtly love story, as we see in Beatrice and Laura for Dante and Petrarch. Elizabeth filled this role as well, as she was God's anointed on the earth. Paying homage to the queen, a political necessity for success at court, became admirable and even spiritual. Elizabeth's own behaviour, her 'tactics' and her 'temperament' can be seen as 'more like artistry'.[23] Elizabeth used this relationship with religious connotations to adopt other methods to interact with her courtiers and people. As a courtly lady, she was set apart from other women, as were the biblical heroines such as Judith and Esther.[24] Eventually, she shifted her virgin status from virginal young and marriageable woman to venerable (she would never say old!) Virgin Queen, still able to be 'courted' and flattered and praised in this way.

One of the fascinating things about the way Elizabeth wielded the tool of courtly love is the way she used it to strike a balance between acting as a person who inspired devotion and desire and a person who ruled and exercised political power. With her favourites at court, she was able in many cases to strike an appropriate and effective balance between 'sex appeal and statesmanship'.[25] But there was a danger in this mingling of the personal and professional. Could a favourite have too much influence with a monarch? During Edward II's reign, for example, his rule was weakened by his over-reliance on men such as Piers Gaveston and Hugh Despenser. In Elizabeth's case, was it possible that a woman in particular could be led astray by the suggestions and manipulations of a strong male favourite? In a political space, the game of courtly love in Elizabeth's court had the potential for danger.

The use of courtly love is part of how Elizabeth was able to prevail against Mary, Queen of Scots. With so many leaders and nations behind the movement against Elizabeth, why couldn't the combined resources of Philip of Spain and the Pope and the Habsburgs and the French could not pierce the inner circle of the English queen? Had Elizabeth's relationship with Burghley and Walsingham and Leicester been based on just words (no matter how fine) or men trying to manipulate a weak woman for their own ends, an offer of money and position from the heart of European power might have tempted them. But the truth was that Elizabeth had also used words and wit to assemble a team of exceptional men and establish a relationship with them that went beyond political expediency. True, there were exceptions, but for the most part, Elizabeth's ability to attract the right talent and inspire loyalty was one of her greatest attributes. She used courtly love as part of a power that inspired a loyalty that could not be broken.

As 'Virgin Queen' in the final years of her reign, Elizabeth seems to have tapped into the multiple layers of meaning associated with the term, using virginity to mean strength and independence. Up to the final 'real' courtship with Anjou, Elizabeth had been potentially willing but ultimately unattainable, apparently by design. In other words, 'Elizabeth had played the courtly game more skilfully than any.' It had not always been easy. There had been numerous scurrilous rumours about her sexuality, her inability to have sex, her sexual depravity, her inability to have children, her numerous secret children, and more. Though it all, she maintained her stance as lady fair, at once virtuous and desirable. Courtly love is one way of understanding her longest relationship, that with Robert Dudley. Dudley wished for marriage and pressed repeatedly for it; when Elizabeth refused to marry him, he married someone else, making the queen feel betrayed. But ultimately, he returned to his position as the knight to her lady fair until his death.

Dudley's death created a void that continued to grow as other of Elizabeth's favourites and most loyal council members died. As they passed out of her court, a new group of courtiers emerged. This generation would push 'courtly worship to its greatest height' and by doing so would expose 'the hollowness of the reality – the unpalatable brew of compulsion and ambition that lay behind the fantasy'.[26] In these final years, the new version of courtly love would revolve around Elizabeth's final 'suitors', the Earl of Essex and Walter Ralegh.

Chapter 11

False Friends, Final Suitors, and Unforgiveable Betrayals

> I am Richard II, know ye not that?
>
> Elizabeth I to William Lambarde, August 1601 (John Nichols)

In 1572, William Cecil became particularly concerned about the potential influence a favourite courtier might have on the queen and the decisions she made. He decided to present a 'memorial' to Elizabeth addressing the subject. Adopting a flattering tone, Cecil assured Elizabeth that she was not someone who needed to be warned against the dangers of being influenced by a favourite because she was so wise. Even so, he went ahead and warned her, making specific recommendations regarding how to avoid even the appearance of this. Cecil knew that having favourites among the men at court could be a threat to the monarch's authority and the good of the nation if the queen's actions were influenced by an ambitious courtier. Cecil believed the monarch must be led by the unified advice of councillors and not the concerns of one person seeking to gain favour. A favourite might very well lack the skills and good resources of council members and was most often advising the monarch in his own self-interest.

In his document, Cecil included examples of previous monarchs whose favourites had led them astray. He was smart enough not to name anyone in the queen's household or government. Instead, he cited the example of Thomas Wolsey, whom he described as rising to power beyond his abilities. Wolsey offered Henry VIII flattery instead of truth, and ultimately did the king harm rather than good. Cecil was not the only one to express worry and even hostility toward favourites in Elizabeth's reign. It was also evident in the works of historians and artists of the day.[1] Poets, playwrights, and politicians warned the queen about the dangers that favourites could pose to her reign.

Throughout Elizabeth's reign, the backdrop of courtly love allowed men to say that they came to court because their love for the queen was so overpowering they could not live without her. They wrote elaborate letters, flattering the queen by describing their despair at being deprived of her presence. All kinds of courtiers participated in this, even though most of them were not in love with Elizabeth in a personal way. Even her second cousin, Robert Carey, was described by a friend as having left his post on the Scottish border to come to court because he could no longer endure separation from the queen and had come to London for the happiness to be found in seeing her and kissing her hand, and then speedily returned assignment.[2] The queen was surrounded by men praising and pampering her, paying a special kind of 'court' to her as their unattainable lady fair. Some wanted to go further; both Robert Dudley and the Duke of Anjou courted the queen in more traditional ways as well as those of courtly love, seeking to become her husband. For the majority, though, the compliments and adoration flowed to the queen, according to tradition without any expectation of return.

Of course, it was more complicated than that. The queen's favour was something worth securing; as her godson John Harrington wrote, 'when she smiled, it was pure sunshine that everyone did choose to bask in'.[3] Beyond the sunshine, there was often an even greater prize: influence and financial rewards. The queen handed out peerages, which were greatly desired, but she did so sparingly. The total number of peerages diminished during her reign, from fifty-seven when she came to the throne to fifty-five when she died. She also gave out grants and licences, which were the means of literally enriching those whom she favoured. This included personal favourites, like Dudley, who was entitled to revenue from the sweet wines that came into the country, and political supporters, like Robert Cecil, who was granted revenue from imported silks and satins.[4] The queen's favour could literally bring a man sunshine – in the form of political influence and financial success.

Throughout her reign, the distribution of Elizabeth's favours to particular men had caused frustration and chaos at court. Dudley enjoyed the queen's favour in consistent and public ways, which created factions and frustrations with the privy council and with foreign diplomats. Dudley was a spectre in any marriage negotiation, and his presence and physical closeness to the queen meant foreign suitors faced a significant hurdle. During the extended negotiations with the French over the Anjou marriage, the French representative Simier realised this and used his knowledge about Dudley's secret marriage to Lettice Knollys to drive a wedge between Elizabeth and her 'sweet Robin'. This was his best chance of success.[5] Elizabeth was furious with Dudley about his marriage, which she considered a personal betrayal. Even so, when she did not marry Anjou, Dudley returned to favour. It's not difficult to see why such a firm hold on the queen's affections and trust would trouble others seeking to play a significant role in her government.

As time went on, beginning in the 1580s, the court around Elizabeth began to shift in significant ways. As she approached her fiftieth birthday in 1583, Elizabeth was in the midst of a battle with Mary, Queen of Scots for control of her people's support and the crown. Mary's trial and execution were extremely difficult for Elizabeth, who was then plunged into war with Spain as her former brother-in-law and suitor Philip II launched his Armada to invade England and seize control of her throne. The victory over the Armada in 1588, one of the crowning glories of her public campaign, was followed immediately by a series of deaths that devastated the queen. Robert Dudley died in late 1588, sending the queen into a deep despair. Two years later, she lost her beloved Blanche Parry, who was Chief Gentlewoman of the Privy Chamber and had served Elizabeth from the time the queen was an infant. Francis Walsingham, the 'spymaster' who masterminded the campaign that captured Mary, Queen of Scots and secured the kingdom, also died in 1590. And William Cecil, who had been at her side ever since being the first minister Elizabeth appointed right after she learned she was queen, held a grand event at his home at Theobolds

House to mark his retirement from public life. The queen resisted his leaving, and he remained in a more limited capacity. He died in 1598.

These and other shifts in the make-up of court created opportunities for newcomers to 'court' Elizabeth, who was emerging as a new kind of 'Virgin Queen' – one who would remain single, one who drew strength from her virginity. The queen still demanded and had the ability to richly reward those who fought for and secured her favour through the tools of courtly love. In this new Elizabethan court, two men emerged who would be the queen's final courtly suitors: Walter Ralegh and Robert Devereux, Earl of Essex.

In the 1580s, Ralegh and Essex were players in a crowded field of favourites. Dudley remained at the queen's side through the worst of the Armada, and he walked next to her when she delivered her famous 'Tilbury' speech. In addition, Christopher Hatton was active in playing the game of courtly love with Elizabeth through the early 1580s. He was particularly irritated when Ralegh came into favour in 1582 and sent the queen carefully chosen gifts including a small bucket, which seemed to play on Ralegh's name (Walter) and the queen's nickname for him (Water). The accompanying letter included a reference to the unstable nature of water, something that likely delighted the queen. She responded with the gift of a dove, a biblical symbol of receding water, telling Hatton that Ralegh 'was no threat to his place in her affections'. Even so, Ralegh continued to grow in Elizabeth's esteem.

Part of Ralegh's ongoing appeal were the grand adventures he carried out on the queen's behalf. The queen granted him a charter to explore, and he did so by setting out to determine what was available in the 'new world'. In 1584, he sailed from England and upon arrival claimed the land on the east coast for the queen, naming it 'Virginia' in her honour. Early attempts at permanent settlements failed, including the famous Roanoke colony which mysteriously disappeared. Still, Ralegh continued his efforts and brought back his treasures to the queen. Although potatoes and tobacco were already known in Europe from Spanish explorers, Ralegh is credited with bringing them to England and certainly popularised them there.[6] Ralegh's dashing exploits endeared him to the queen, who was flattered by his claiming to do all of it in her honour. During Ralegh's success, a new favourite emerged: Robert Devereux, Earl of Essex.

Robert Devereux was bound to be a complicated player in Elizabeth's life even before he came to court. He was the son of Walter Devereux and Lettice Knollys, Elizabeth's second cousin. Lettice was also the daughter of Elizabeth's cousin and close friend, Catherine Carey Knollys. In fact, as some believed Catherine was the daughter of Henry VIII (her mother was his former mistress Mary Boleyn), so she might have been Elizabeth's half-sister and cousin. Either way, Elizabeth was very close to Catherine, and Lettice joined the queen's court at a young age. Even before Dudley's grand gesture proposal at Kenilworth, there were rumours about his having some kind of a relationship with the then-married Lettice. Some even suggested that Dudley was Robert Devereux's father rather than Walter, although this was unlikely. When Walter Devereux died in 1576, his son became a ward of William Cecil and grew up alongside Robert Cecil. Devereux, the new Earl of Essex, went to Trinity College and graduated in 1581.

Dudley secretly married Lettice in 1578. When Elizabeth found out, she seemed to prefer to pretend Lettice didn't exist. Keeping her out of sight was a handy way to continue the illusion that Dudley was hers alone (much as she had done when Dudley was married to Amy Robsart early in the reign). Dudley and Lettice had one son, Robert Dudley, Lord Denbigh. He died at age 3 in 1584, which devastated both of his parents. The couple had no more children together, and Robert Dudley took on the young Earl of Essex, his stepson, as a kind of heir. Dudley had Essex take over some of his duties and brought him to court in 1584. Dudley shaped Essex to take his place in the queen's affections, but the relationship between Essex and Elizabeth was very different. The queen and Dudley had shared a lifetime of experiences, knew the same people, and understood the court and what behaviour was expected. The two argued sometimes, and Elizabeth was furious about Dudley marrying Lettice, but their bond was indestructible. Essex came from an entirely different perspective. His youth and inexperience were amplified by unbridled ambition and an ease with putting his own desires about the service of queen and country. Essex's relationship was based on 'ritualized performance' rather than a real connection, as Dudley's had been.[7] As Dudley spent less time at court, Essex worked to secure the vacated place at Elizabeth's side.

After 1584, both Ralegh and Essex were at court. The next years would see high levels of drama and factions as the two competed for the favour and rewards of the queen. According to Dr Penry Williams, the royal court played four big roles in the political work of Elizabethan England. The first role was as the space for the dignified element of monarchy, the stage for the queen and the nobles to act out their power and influence, performing for the nation and for the rest of the world. The ceremonies of Elizabeth's government created and celebrated the image of Elizabeth as monarch. The second role was as the place where patronages of various kinds were distributed by the queen. Men came to court to seek leases, licences to trade, monopolies, titles, and other honours and opportunities. The court was the place where fortunes and futures were made or lost. The third role was the place where political rivalries play out, an arena of sorts where men fought over influence and stature. Members of the privy council were part of this, so we see years of Cecil versus Dudley and then Robert Cecil (after William Cecil managed to turn the reigns over to his son) versus Essex 'factions' debating each other and vying for pre-eminence. Fourth and finally, the court was the place where the central government of London was linked to the localities throughout the country.[8]

Walter Ralegh was an object of disdain and suspicion as his role grew at court. He was accused by his contemporaries of exercising inappropriate influence on the queen and turning her against others. In truth, the offices he held were appropriate given his military experience. These offices included warden of stannaries Lord Lieutenant of Cornwall, and Vice Admiral of the west. He was also elected to parliament for Devon. He certainly did more than entertain the queen at court – he served the realm 'in ways fitting for a man with a track record of success in military and naval affairs'.[9]

As time went on and the 'old guard' gave way to the new, court was certainly the place for gaining rewards. Ralegh and Essex were in direct competition for whatever Elizabeth was willing to give. This created more serious competition to come into the queen's presence. In 1594, there was specific effort taken to manage and control who could enter court space and access the queen or those closest to her. To 'restrain the great resort of unnecessary persons to court, the Lord Chamberlain is to appoint an usher and quarter waiter to join with one or two of the clerks of the household, to attend daily to view all persons that come to court for service of Her Majesty'. These men, called 'masters of requests', were given a room to receive and give answers to suitors and decide who would come to court. There was even instruction that back doors and gates were to be kept shut so no one could sneak in.[10] This effort might have helped some, but competition for favour continued to grow. Rowland Whyte wrote to Robert Sidney in 1597 that the competition for offices took up much of court happenings.[11]

In the late 1580s, Ralegh begged for the queen's assurance of her affection in a poetic form of courtly love, and Elizabeth replied in similar and comforting words. Ralegh's concerns about 'fortune' seem a reference to Essex, his primary rival at the time. In accordance with courtly love, their conversation was carried out in verse.[12]

From Walter Ralegh to Elizabeth:

> Fortune hath taken thee away, my love,
> My life's soul and my soul's heaven above;
> Fortune hath taken thee away, my princess;
> My only light and my true fancy's mistress.
> Fortune hath taken all away from me,
> Fortune hath taken all by taking thee
> Dead to all joy, I only live to woe,
> So fortune now becomes my mortal foe.
> In vain your eyes do waste your tears,
> In vain your sighs do smoke forth my despairs,
> In vain you search the earth and heaven above,

In vain you search, for fortune rules in love.
Thus now I leave my love in fortune's hands,
Thus now I leave my love in fortune's bands,
And only love the sorrows due to me;
Sorrow henceforth it shall my princess be.
I joy in this, that fortune conquers kings'
Fortune that rules on earth and earthly things
Hath taken my love in spite of Cupid's might;
So blind a dame did never Cupid right.
With wisdom's eyes had but blind Cupid seen,
Then had my love my love for ever been;
But love farewell; though fortune conquer thee,
No fortune base nor frail shall ever alter me.

The queen's reply to Ralegh:

Ah, silly Pug, wert thou so sore afraid?
Mourn not, my Wat, nor be thou so dismayed.
It passeth fickle Fortune's power and skill
To force my heart to think the any ill.
No Fortune base, thou sayest, shall alter thee?
And may to blind a witch so conquer me?
No, no, my Pug, though Fortune were not blind,
Assure thyself she could not rule my mind.
Fortune, I know, sometimes doth conquer kings,
And rules and reigns on earth and earthly things,
But never think Fortune can bear the sway
If virtue watch, and will her not obey.
Ne chose I thee by fickle Fortune's rede,
Ne she shall force me alter with such speed
But if to try this mistress' jest with thee.
Pull up thy heart, suppress thy brackish tears,
Torment thee not, but put away thy fears.
Dead to all joys and living unto woe,

Slain quite by her that ne'er gave wise men blow,
Revive again and live without all dread,
The less afraid, the better thou shalt speed.

Ralegh's devotion to his queen is reflected in art as well. A portrait of Ralegh painted in 1588 is one of the few contemporary portraits of him and is now in the National Portrait Gallery in London. It includes several emblems related to Elizabeth I. There are numerous pearls, and those on Ralegh's cloak form a 'sun-in-splendour', a frequently used heraldic device. The choice to be depicted with pearls was a way to connect to Elizabeth and her frequent use of the jewels in her outfits and portraits. The pearls were also symbolic of the queen as the moon goddess, with Ralegh as 'water', willingly controlled by the queen as the moon controls the tides. Ralegh also chose to be painted wearing black and white, Elizabeth's colours. The Latin on the left reads 'amor et virtue' (by love and virtue), echoing Ralegh's pledge to the queen.[13] This commissioned portrait was one way that Ralegh demonstrated his devotion to his mistress.

Essex's ambition and narcissism convinced him he was Dudley's rightful heir for the queen's affections. That was understandable given his closeness to Dudley and Dudley's public support. But Essex wanted more: he also wanted to succeed William Cecil, and be the queen's premier military commander and minister of state. His efforts to establish himself as the clear choice in both roles were complicated by his deep resentment of the need to follow the queen's orders. He did not believe a woman's ideas and wishes should take precedence over his own.[14] Shortly before William Cecil's illness finally ended his life in 1589, he wrote to his son Robert, counselling him to 'serve God by serving the queen, for all other service is indeed bondage to the devil'.[15] Cecil had served the queen loyally since becoming her first minister, and even before then during Mary I's reign. He might have disagreed and even argued with Elizabeth, but his loyalty was never in doubt. Elizabeth was devastated by the thought of losing him, and reportedly visited him and even fed him herself in his final days. He wanted his son to succeed him in her service, and Robert Cecil threw himself into the task.

Essex took deliberate steps to solidify his standing with the queen. In 1595, he presented a lavish pageant that focused on a debate between the lover of desire and self-love. The construct of desire and courtship was still a staple of court entertainment. Philautia, representing self-love, warned the queen against the words of lovers and counselled the queen to surround herself with men of duty to serve her. In contrast Erophilus, the part played by Essex, argued in favour of romantic love and even hinting at sexuality and eroticism. Flattering more than dutiful, Essex used the language of courtship to reassure the queen of his devotion. The entertainment explored the use of role playing that the queen and her courtiers relied heavily on in the final years of her reign.[16] Essex wanted more, lobbying for the key role in government Cecil had exercised. He lost that hope when the queen appointed Robert Cecil as her secretary in July 1596. In truth, Essex was never suited to such a role. But he did eventually take precedence over Ralegh in the more personal role as courtly lover.

Ralegh continued to gain favours and rewards from Elizabeth, including Durham House and Sherbourne. He was also appointed Captain of the Yeomen of the Guard. But as a young and ambitious man, he wanted his own legacy and life. Sometime before 1591, Ralegh became involved with Elizabeth (or Bess) Throckmorton, one of Elizabeth's favourite ladies-in-waiting. They managed to keep their relationship a secret, even when Bess became pregnant. The two were married in 1591 before the child was born. After the baby was born, Bess quickly returned to her service at court. It was another year before Elizabeth discovered the marriage, and when she did, she was predictably furious. The deception of two people so close to her made the betrayal all the more painful for the queen. She ordered Ralegh and Bess imprisoned in the Tower in June 1592. Ralegh was released and allowed to go on expeditions, after which he was sent back to the Tower. He was eventually released and became a member of parliament. Bess was also released but was not welcome back at court.

Eager to restore his favour with the queen, Ralegh used poetry again to reach out to her after his disgrace. His lengthy 'The Ocean's Love to Cynthia' was likely written around 1600, after his banishment. The poem played on the same shared language between the two, with the ocean representing 'Water' and Cynthia the goddess of the moon. It was never published, so the exact date is not known. The lengthy piece might not be complete, as it does not come to a clear resolution. These verses in particular are references to Elizabeth and his desire to regain and maintain her favour:

> O hopeful love my object and invention!
> O true desire the spur of my conceit!
> O worthiest spirit, my mind's impulsion!
> O eyes transpersant, my affection's bait!
> O princely form, my fancy's adamant!
> Divine conceit, my paines acceptane!
> O all in one, O heaven on earth transparent!
> The seat of joys and loves abundance!
> …
> Her regal looks my vigorous sighs suppressed;
> Small drops of joys sweeten'd great worlds of woes;
> One gladsome day a thousand cares redressed;
> Whom love defends, what fortune overthrows?
> …
> To seek new worlds for gold, for praise, for glory,
> To try desire, to try love sever'd far,
> When I was gone, she sent her memory,
> More strong than were ten thousand ships of war,
> To call me back, to leave great honour's thought,
> To leave my friends, my fortune, my attempt,
> To leave the purpose I so long had sought,
> And hold both cares and comforts in contempt.
> …
> Thus home I draw, as death's long night draws on;

Yet every foot, old thoughts turn back mine eyes:
Constraint me guides, as old age draws a stone
Against the hill, which over-weighty lies
For feeble arms or wasted strength to move;
My steps are backward, gazing on my loss;
My mind's affection and my soul's sole love,
Not mixt with fancy's chaff or fortune's dross,
To God I leave it, who first gave it me,
And I her gave, as she return'd again,
As it was hers; so let His mercies be
Of my last comforts the essential mean,
But be it so or not, the effects are past;
Her love hath end, my woe must ever last.

It was years before Ralegh regained full favour with the queen. As a result, he travelled frequently and was seldom at court. With Ralegh out of favour, Elizabeth was more willing to recognise Essex as her chief favourite. His looks and confidence charmed her, and his flattery was especially appreciated as she aged. When the earl indulged his adventurer spirits by going on an expedition to Cadiz in 1596, the queen wrote to him, saying she would petition God for his safety and that she wished she could be at his side. He relied on courtly words in his reply, praising the queen's beauty and pledging his devotion. At least, that was his public face. Privately, he was mocking his mistress, laughing at her behind her back.[17] Like his stepfather, he wanted more than courtly exchanges with the queen. But while Dudley wanted Elizabeth herself, Essex wanted glory. In this quest, he was his own worst enemy.

Essex railed against the rule of a woman, especially when it curbed his ambition. In 1598, the queen reportedly refused one of his requests, and he responded by angrily turning his back on her. This was a significant breach of etiquette that the queen could not let stand in a public gathering. She was angry enough to strike back and box the earl's ears. At this point, those who were there described Essex reaching for his sword. To be armed in the presence of the queen would have been disastrous for Essex, so he was lucky that another courtier immediately stopped him. Essex stormed off, shouting that he would not have tolerated such an insult even from Henry VIII, implying Henry was a more powerful monarch than Elizabeth. The queen forgave him, but this turned out to be a mistake, as Essex's wild and impulsive anger would continue to threaten her reputation and power.

After this outburst, Essex never regained his full favour with the queen. Although Elizabeth enjoyed the attention and flamboyant praise, the queen was not in love with Essex. She always maintained the upper hand in any relationship. Elizabeth thrived on the public adoration expressed by a younger man, and it helped her continue her image as a still-vibrant queen who would remain on the throne for years. She enjoyed and benefitted in her way from their relationship, just as he gained a fortune and political status from it. But ultimately the queen set the rules for her games of courtly love. When Essex broke them, he paid the price.

As he pushed against the bounds of courtly love and behaviour at court, Essex looked for an opportunity to gain greater glory. The problems in Ireland gave Essex his chance to become recognised as a warrior on the international stage. Hugh O'Neill, Earl of Tyrone, had spent much of his youth in England and had been loyal to Elizabeth for several years. After a few of his early rebellions, the queen sought reconciliation. In 1598, Tyrone abandoned loyalty to English rule and encouraged all four provinces to revolt against the crown. Elizabeth was determined to bring him to heel, and she agreed to send Essex to do the job.[18]

Essex was given every chance of success. The queen provided 1,400 horsemen and 16,000 foot soldiers, with promises of further reinforcements every three months. It was one of the largest forces sent out of England during Elizabeth's reign. He was provided munitions, and a new treasurer-at-war was appointed to make sure troops were promptly paid (making them more likely to continue to fight). He was even made Lord Lieutenant in 1599. But he still wasn't satisfied. He criticised previous commanders for not crushing Tyrone earlier, and once he was in Ireland was hesitant to confront Tyrone himself. He spent weeks marching about, arranging for ceremonial grand entries into already loyal towns, and creating new knights. His army dwindled as some men were lost in inconsequential squabbles and many more died of illness. Blaming Ralegh for sabotaging his mission and his standing with the queen, Essex complained about lack of support. Furious, Elizabeth insisted that he confront Tyrone immediately. Instead, he continued to waste time. When he finally encountered Tyrone, it in was a meeting, not a battle, and the two agreed upon a truce. Essex wrote to the queen offering few details about the agreement, having decided that a personal visit was the only way he could restore his reputation and standing with Elizabeth.[19]

Despite the queen's order that he remain in Ireland, Essex sailed for home. In late September, he came to Nonsuch Palace and burst in upon the queen without waiting to be announced. Elizabeth had once described herself as 'no morning woman', and this was one reason why. The queen was not prepared to receive anyone at that early hour. At age 65, Elizabeth now required a considerable amount of time to create a public face and body to meet the world. It took at least an hour or more to create the royal image each day. The amount of make-up, yards of expensive and showy fabrics, and ropes of pearls and other jewels that were part of the image the queen portrayed to the world were not all about vanity on her part. Elizabeth was well aware that she had no heir, and that the safety and security of her people and her nation depended on her continuing to project an image of vitality and good health to demonstrate the strength of the country. For years, the assumption had been 'strong king, strong country', and Elizabeth was not about to let this slip in her reign. Therefore, no one was allowed in her bedchamber at this hour. The intrusion was stunning. It's said Essex didn't initially recognise the elderly woman sitting on the bed with wisps of grey hair around her face. He was looking for the queen.

The queen was at her most vulnerable, stripped of the trappings she relied on to conceal her humanity from the world. Despite her shock at the earl's wild behaviour on his part as he flung himself on the floor in front of her when he finally recognised her, the queen maintained her composure and asked him to return in an hour.[20] Essex left and did return an hour later for a conference. At that point, he behaved appropriately while in the presence of the queen. But privately, he ridiculed her intelligence and appearance, saying that she was an old woman with a mind no less crooked than her carcass.[21]

Essex realised the queen was angry and his power to charm her wasn't working. Elizabeth accused him of insubordination and called for the privy council to interrogate him. Essex might have thought he could still turn things around, but he was wrong. Elizabeth never agreed to see him again. The privy council charged Essex with six offences, including leaving Ireland against orders and entering the queen's chambers without permission, and he was taken to York House. Although the queen softened in her firm stance against Essex in December when he was reported to be ill, she did not agree to see him. Essex was eventually allowed to return to Essex House, and in June 1600 a special royal commission heard his case. Essex refuted the charge he had been disloyal, but he agreed he had been guilty of disobedience and confessed some errors. He was hopeful Elizabeth's anger would not last and was encouraged when she directed that he be allowed liberty. Still, he was banned from court. This tipped Essex from sorrow and repentance to rage and rebellion.[22]

Another blow came in September 1600 when the queen refused to renew his monopoly on sweet wines, his greatest source of income. Facing bankruptcy, Essex looked for someone to blame and decided to take the position that Robert Cecil was out to get him. Essex was known to have developed a relationship with King James VI of Scotland, Elizabeth's most likely successor at this point. Worried that this might come back to haunt him, Essex claimed that Cecil, Ralegh, and others were afraid of a reign featuring James as king with Essex as councillor. Essex went so far as to say they were determined to turn the country over to the Spanish Infanta when Elizabeth died. In fact, Cecil and the others were not attempting to put Isabella on the English throne, but they were eager to find evidence against Essex. Essex decided his best option was to take actions against others and invited friends and supporters to come meet him at Essex House.

In early February 1601, Essex was summoned to come before the council and explain why his friends were gathering at Essex House in such great numbers. The Essex supporters began to fortify the house in fear of arrest. When Cecil sent lords to persuade Essex to come before the council, the earl's supporters seized them.[23] Essex's supporters, perhaps at his instruction or with his support, also paid members of the Lord Chamberlain's men to put on a public performance of Shakespeare's *Richard II*. This play was problematic, as it included the king being deposed after he was determined to be an unsuccessful ruler. Elizabeth reacted strongly against the play, and by law the scene of the deposition was not allowed to be performed. By sponsoring a performance of this play that included the forbidden scene, Essex and his supporters were possibly attempting to rally support for the overthrow of the queen and her government.

About 200 men accompanying Essex surged out of Essex House, crying, 'To the court.' Believing the public would rise up in his support and that the Sheriff of London would provide him a thousand men, Essex was confident of success. Almost no one jumped in to follow the cause. Essex lurched on, desperate to create energy and gather followers, but by the time he reached the Sheriff's house, he realised the cause was likely lost. Even the Sheriff, after he let Essex in, went out the back door to join the queen's supporters.[24] At this point, Essex's followers retreated to Essex House, where they were besieged. Essex and the earl of Southampton, his most stalwart supporter, swore they would never surrender but in fact did so that evening. Both men were tried and found guilty. Southampton begged for mercy, while Essex declared that life was an ongoing torment to him.[25]

What was Essex's real goal? Was he trying to overthrow the queen and her government or trying to attack Robert Cecil and possibly Walter Ralegh? Did he really believe that members of the council were willing to turn crown and country over to a Catholic Spanish princess, or was that a scare tactic designed to stir up support? With Essex, it's impossible to know for sure. The rebellion was bound to fail, almost comically disorganised – it was even rumoured that they stopped to eat along the route. Still, for Elizabeth it represented an ultimate betrayal. She had allowed Essex into her inner circle, had given him public favour and high military positions. She had enjoyed and possibly believed his flattery and protestations of love. Despite her reservations and suspicions, she had let him in, and he had betrayed her in the most unimaginable way possible – he had tried to turn the city of London against her, and he had reached for her crown.

The game of courtly love allowed an ageing queen to retain her place at the centre of the love and adoration of some of the most dashing, handsome, charismatic, talented members of the court. Sir Walter Ralegh and the Earl of Essex represented bright lights at court, and for a time their words lit up the queen. But ultimately Ralegh betrayed his queen by marrying one of her favourite ladies-in-waiting. He lied about it for months. He was allowed back at court, but the trust was gone. Essex had tried to step into the place of Elizabeth's great love and best friend, his stepfather. He represented a younger version, with a promise of the feelings she had lost when Dudley died. But Essex betrayed her in personal and political ways. She mourned his loss, but she went forward and signed his death warrant without hesitation. When a messenger brought the news of the earl's death, Elizabeth was playing the virginals in the privy chamber. Everyone became silent after hearing the news, including the queen. She waited a few moments, and then 'after a time she began to play again'.[26] She had survived, and she was still the queen.

Ultimately, there would be only one suitor whose love Queen Elizabeth was always able to count on, the one suitor that she wooed herself as well as being wooed by. The husband she had claimed from the beginning of her reign. Her country.

Chapter 12

'Bound Unto a Husband, Which is the Kingdom of England'

> And therewith she drew the ring from her finger, and shewed it, wherewith at her coronation she had in set form of words given her self in marriage to her kingdom.
>
> William Camden, *Annals of the Reign of Queen Elizabeth*

As Princess of England, Elizabeth was considered a potential bride for a foreign prince from the time she was an infant. Her desires and wishes were not part of the equation that would select the most appropriate husband for her. As was the case with most royal princesses, her father and the men at court would determine which marriage would provide the greatest service for the king, the royal council, and the country. As a queen, Elizabeth was considered a potential bride for a foreign king, prince, or duke and a mother of a future king. Many assumed her desires and wishes, although they might be taken into consideration, would not be the most important factors in the selection of the most appropriate husband. Men in her privy council and parliament counselled the queen to marry from the beginning of her reign. It was her sacred duty to enter into a marriage that would allow her to be guided in the affairs of state and to provide the nation the security of a peaceful succession.

These requirements were not unique to Elizabeth or to Mary I, the other crowned Tudor regnant queen. Both were expected to marry and adhere to legal, religious, and cultural expectations for women. Mary took the throne in July 1553 and married Philip of Spain in July 1554. During the first year of her reign, the question of the queen's marriage was a frequent topic of political discourse, and her choice of husband was one of the factors leading Thomas Wyatt the younger and his companions to stage a rebellion. Mary's choice was not made on the advice of her English council, but it was made according to the wishes and counsel of Charles V and his agent, Simon Renard. It can certainly be said that men chose her husband.

Even though she always declared a willingness and even an eagerness to wed, Mary was aware of her own position and presented herself to her people as their queen and ruler. In so doing, she combined the unique position she held as monarch with a more acceptable position as wife and mother. She delivered a speech in the midst of the Wyatt rebellion that called on her people to support her by emphasising her relationship with them:

> Now loving subjects, [who] I am, you right well know. I am your queen, to whom at my coronation when I was wedded to the realm, and to the laws of the same (the spousal ring whereof I have on my finger, which never hitherto was, nor hereafter shall be left off) ye promised your allegiance and obedience unto me … And this further I say unto you in the word of a prince, I cannot tell how naturally a mother loveth her children, for I was never the mother of any; but certainly a prince and governor may as naturally and earnestly love subjects as the mother doth her child. Then assure yourselves that I being your sovereign and quene do as earnestly and tenderly love and favour you.[1]

She, like Elizabeth, had grown up as a princess whose marriage was assumed to be a matter of state, not of the heart. She, like Elizabeth, saw the matter of her marriage take on even greater political importance when she became queen. It represented the expectation of her people, her council, and all of Europe.

By describing herself as the wife of her kingdom, 'wedded to the realm', and pointing to the ring on her finger, Mary reminded those who might be considering rebellion that she was bound to them in religious and legal terms. She went on to describe her maternal feelings for her people as well, because even though she did not (yet, she hoped) have children of her own, she was certain that a ruler might 'as naturally and earnestly love subjects as the mother doth her child'. According to these two patterns, as a wife and as a mother, Mary was bound to love and serve her people. She desired their love and support in return.

The speech was a rousing success, and the rebellion was put down. Mary had, in a moment of crisis, appealed to the emotional nature of her people and to their beliefs in the ideals of womanhood and motherhood. She cast herself as a representative of each. She was not yet a wife or a mother in fact, but in spirit she was both to her people.

Elizabeth would learn from and build upon this foundation created by her half-sister. By the time Elizabeth came to the throne, Mary's unpopular marriage had marred her relationship with her subjects. She had convinced herself twice she was with child, but it came to nothing and she did not have a child to succeed her. Although Elizabeth's succession was uncomplicated and smooth, it was not desired by everyone. After five years of female rule, those close to the heart of government were eager to settle the succession quickly. Elizabeth was the final of Henry VIII's children, so the Tudor line would end if she did not provide an heir. When she took the throne, she was 25 years old, a proper age to become a wife and mother. There were plenty of childbearing years ahead, plenty of time to have a son.

That Elizabeth might not wish to marry was not a consideration. All women wished to marry. And even if she was hesitant, her duty as queen required it. It probably never occurred to anyone that Elizabeth I would never marry. Did Elizabeth ever really want to marry? Was she ever tempted to share her life, her country, and her whole self with a man? Did she only stop at various points because her council could not agree on a particular candidate? Or did she mean it when she said, possibly as early as when she was 8 and certainly during the reign of Mary I and then repeatedly during her own reign, that she was determined to continue in her single state? These are questions we continue to debate.

Perhaps Elizabeth gave us the greatest clue. There was one partner to whom she was wooer as well as wooed. One partner whose goodwill she continually sought, to whom she regularly pledged her undying devotion. One partner she seemed to consider her greatest and most reliable suitor, the one whose love she always sought and on whom she consistently showered her love: England, her nation and her people. In various ways, Elizabeth was married to England, her greatest love.

The queen travelled a long road to her final destination, one she had projected early on, from her first speech to parliament: 'And in the end this shall be for me sufficient: that a marble stone shall declare that a queen, having reigned such a time, lived and died a virgin.'[2] It was a road she paved with requests for her people's love.

From the moment she became queen, Elizabeth knew the value of cultivating her people's support. During her coronation procession, she showered praised and affection on her people. An anonymous source described her entrance into London:

> Our most dread sovereign Lady Elizabeth, by the Grace of God Queen of England, France, and Ireland, defendour of the faith, marched from the Tower to pass through the city of London toward Westminster, richly furnished and most honourably accompanied, as well with gentlemen, bars, and other nobility of this realm, as also with a notable train of goodly and beautiful ladies, richly appointed. And entering the city was of the people received marvelously entirely, as appeared by the assembly, prayers, wishes, welcomings, cries, tender words, and all other signs, which argue a wonderful earnest love of most obedient subjects toward their sovereign. And on the other side her grace by holding up her hands, and merry countenance to such as stood far off, and most tender and tengle language to those that stood nigh to her grace, did declare herself no less thankful to receive her people's good will, than they lovingly offered it unto her. To all that wished her grace well, she gave hearty thanks, and to such as bad God save her grace, she said again God save them all, and thanked them with all her heart. So that on either side there was nothing but gladness, nothing but prayer.[3]

This speech was published ten days after the coronation procession and was designed to assure the queen's subjects that she reciprocated their love while maintaining her regal qualities and standing. The printing press allowed Elizabeth's supporters to spread a specific version of the queen and her procession to an audience far beyond those who had crowded the London streets to watch her go by. It also promoted the new regime's agenda and reminded people of Elizabeth's belief in their support.[4] Elizabeth was involved in the details and pageantry of her coronation procession and it was no accident both the procession and the printed record of it would promote her connection to her people.[5] The goal was to help people around the country understand God had brought Elizabeth to the throne and how the 'love of God and love of people promised indeed a wonderful reign to come'.[6]

The queen's responses to gifts given to her along her coronation procession gave her an opportunity to woo her people. When she was given a satin purse filled with gold, she replied:

> I thank my Lord Mayor, his brethren, and you all. And whereas your request is that I should continue your good Lady and Queen, be ye assured that I will be as good unto you as ever queen was unto her people. No will in me can lack, neither, do I trust, shall there lack any power. And persuade yourselves that for the safety and quietness of you all, I will not spare if need be to spend my blood. God thank you all.

The crowd expressed great appreciation for her words.[7]

The notion of a reciprocal relationship between monarch and subject was not unique to Elizabeth. It was not as frequently invoked in medieval political discourse. Some of the Tudors made the most of projecting a specifically 'loving' relationship between monarch and people. Henry VIII's reign had examples of the king expressing his love for his people, but he was primarily concerned that his loving subjects were faithful and obedient to him. Edward VI's accession proclamation included the king's assurance to his loving subjects that he would be a gracious and benign sovereign lord. Mary I's accession proclamation mentioned her appreciation for true and faithful subjects. Elizabeth's accession proclamation promised her subjects no less love than her predecessors had shown and stated confidently she did not doubt their commitment to be true and loving subjects in return.[8]

Elizabeth's accession was greeted with a level of enthusiasm, at least in London, that was remarked upon by foreign ambassadors. 'The whole of London turned out and received her with great acclamations,' reported ambassador Feria to Philip of Spain.[9] He used the word love to explain how her people had protected her during Mary's reign, saying that 'if the love which the people bore her had not been so great', her half-sister's government would have put her to death. He was saying her people's love had saved her.[10] Elizabeth agreed with Feria about her people's love being necessary, and she deliberately courted and cultivated that love. It's reported that her coronation procession took longer than anticipated because she frequently stopped to hear what people were saying to her. Foreign visitors were shocked that she spoke so willingly to people of all ranks of society. But the queen knew the support of all the people was the essential component of her ability to rule. She was, in that sense, a suitor to the people of England.

Elizabeth, like Mary, used her coronation ring as a symbol of her marriage to her nation. Since at least the thirteenth century, the coronation ceremony in England has included the placing of a ring on the fourth finger of the left hand – the finger traditionally associated with the wedding ring. Sometimes called the 'wedding ring of England', this ring often contained a ruby. In a ceremony such as Elizabeth's, the ring would be placed on the queen's finger after she was anointed with holy oil as part of the investiture. This would have been followed by the placing of the crown on her head.[11] Elizabeth used this experience to fall back on at different times in her reign, beginning at her first parliament. When Elizabeth declared early on that she was already married to England, that she preferred to remain in her unmarried state, and her preference that her tomb include the words she lived and died a virgin, few took her seriously. Most thought she was just young and inexperienced.[12]

In her first parliament, the queen was faced with a request that she quickly marry and produce an heir. Marriage and motherhood were set out by her government as the path for Elizabeth to take. On 6 February 1559, the Speaker of the House of Commons told Elizabeth I that the only prayer of her country was that she marry and have children. It was just days into the first parliament of the queen's reign, and Thomas Gargrave claimed to be representing the wishes of the nation.

In one version of Queen Elizabeth I's answer to the petition of the House of Commons that she marry, the queen is quoted as saying, 'To conclude, I am already bound unto an husband, which is the kingdom of England, and that may suffice you.'[13] The source for this statement comes from William Camden's History: 'I have already joined myself in marriage to an husband, namely, the kingdom of England.'[14] Camden's version of Elizabeth's initial speech includes her statement about being married to England, but other versions do not include that statement. Cecil had asked Camden to write a history that preserved and promoted Elizabeth's honour, so it was meant to be a flattering look back rather than necessarily an accurate historic account. Cecil's papers do not include the reference to the queen being married to her country.[15]

This is not the only time Elizabeth described herself as being married to England, nor is Elizabeth the only monarch to consider herself married to her country. However, as Elizabeth continued to avoid marriage, her perception and descriptions of herself as married to England take on a special significance. In the parliamentary art collection, there is a painting created in 1911 called *The Commons Petitioning Elizabeth I to Marry* by Joseph Solomon. The subtitle is 'With the ring I was wedded to the realm', a refrain Elizabeth used. In the painting, Elizabeth is holding a ring and showing it to the members of parliament who surround her. This work, created centuries after the event, points to the lasting notion that Elizabeth at time projected the image of herself married to her country.

Elizabeth's commitment to connecting herself to her nation through marriage is reflected in the language she uses when addressing her subjects. 'One distinctive feature of the reign of Elizabeth Tudor was the panache with which she wooed her English subjects.'[16] This wooing had important political purposes and implications. Elizabeth always carefully considered the audience and context in which she expressed ideas. She used a wide range of ways to deliver her messages, including reaching large audiences with printed tracts and proclamations. The relationship between monarch and subjects, with respect to the subjects' allegiance, evolved over the Tudor dynasty, and by Elizabeth's reign many subjects felt direct and personal obligation to the crown.

The introduction of the language of love into political discourage and Elizabeth's 'wooing' of her subjects was an essential part of this.[17] She began with her coronation procession, the official publication of which was distributed widely. Near the end of the document, after vivid descriptions of pageants celebrating the queen and her reign, more loving language is included:

> As at her first entrance she as it were declared herself prepared to pass through a city that most entirely loved her, so she at her last departing, as it were, bound herself by promise to continue good lady and governour to that city which by outward declaration did open their love, to their so loving and noble prince in such wise, as she herself wondered.[18]

Elizabeth told the lord keeper to tell parliament that she would be careful of them and desired that they should be careful of her. She continued to assert this 'mutual care and careful reciprocity throughout her reign'.[19]

From the beginning, Elizabeth used direct personal communication with loyal advisors as well.[20] During the first half of her reign, Elizabeth was actively engaged in marriage negotiations, which amplified a woman's voice in political discourse. By the final years of her reign, with marriage talks abandoned and Elizabeth presenting herself as an eternal virgin, dramas of courtship by poets and playwrights thrived with lively debates about the nature of marriage. Although Elizabeth herself was no longer the centre of marriage discussions, the queen 'politics of courtships had merged with a wider social and literary conversation about courtship, marriage, and women'.[21] Elizabeth's reliance on the language of courtly love, and her expectation that those around her use that language as well, enabled the queen to continue a courtship relationship with her people until the final days of her reign.

Elizabeth frequently expressed her love, but she also reminded her parliament that it must be received appropriately. She reminded them it was 'unmeet' to 'draw my love to your liking or frame my will to your fantasies'.[22] Her love was not to be taken for granted or manipulated.

Part of Elizabeth seeking to gain and maintain the love of her people was her serving not only as the nation's wife but as its mother. As parliament and her council begged her to become mother of an heir, Elizabeth replied that as a virgin she could be a good mother to her country, replacing Gargrave's biological notion of motherhood with her own version – a public persona based on a metaphor that allowed her access to power as a female ruler.[23] Elizabeth was not the first to link a women's reign to motherhood – her half-sister Mary had done so. Mary had qualified her statement by imagining what it would feel like to be a mother, while Elizabeth stated that as queen, she actually was one.

It seems traditional motherhood held little appeal for Elizabeth. She apparently didn't expect to love her children, believing that if she had them, she would see them as rivals. She explained to an ambassador from Scotland, 'Princes cannot like their children, those that should succeed unto them.'[24] In fact, in her response to her first parliament's petition that she marry and have children, she speculated that God might prefer that she remain single and provide a different way to have an heir to succeed her, saying that such a person might be 'peradventure more beneficial to the realm than any such offspring as may come of me'.[25]

The role of mother was a complicated one, particularly in a time where a royal woman's success was determined in large part by her ability to have a son. Elizabeth had experienced this first-hand. Both she and her half-sister Mary were deemed inadequate to be heirs by their father the king; both of their mothers were set aside because of their inability to produce a male child. Mary's marriage to Philip had been considered a failure by many because she had not produced a male heir. Elizabeth heard repeated pleas from her government that she marry, and those pleas often included the desired outcome of such a marriage: a male heir. Not providing a son was seen as a disaster for Elizabeth, as it had been for women close to her.

The final weeks of pregnancy were spent in a period of seclusion, with the woman withdrawing from public. A queen in seclusion, cut off from access to her court and council, could easily result in a loss of political power. Having a child could be physically dangerous, often taking the life of the mother and the child. And even if both mother and child lived, a royal mother remained separated from society for a period of purification or churching, giving even more time to any who wished to threaten her status. Even after all of that, having a son could be dangerous for a sovereign queen, providing a rival to the mother's throne. The presence of her son made Mary, Queen of Scots more vulnerable to her lords, and they were quick to replace her with a male infant when her behaviour offended them.

Elizabeth created her own version of a powerful maternal identify, but this did not prevent her male parliament and council from trying to exert their rights over here, much as husbands and fathers would.[26] When the Commons tried again to make the succession issue the primary subject of discussion, they appealed to the maternal role the queen had claimed, using it against her. They asked that 'your most gracious and motherly care for them' and said to get that motherly care, they 'have summoned this parliament principally for stablishing some certain limitation of th'imperial crown of your realm, for preservation of your subjects from certain and utter destruction if the same should not be provided for in your life'. Her subjects were petitioning their mother to provide for their safety and prevent their utter destruction by providing for the succession. They tie their own lives to Elizabeth's safety, linking her safety to the succession:

> These things, as your majesty hath upon your own danger most graciously considered for our comfort and safety, so we your most humble subjects, knowing the preservation of ourselves and all our posterity to depend upon the safety of your majesty's most royal person, have most carefully and diligently considered how the want of heirs of your body, and of certain limitation of succession after you, is most perilous to your highness, whom God long preserve among us.[27]

Elizabeth's reply acknowledged their concerns, explaining that she knew full well she was mortal and also knew that God had entrusted her with this great office, and knew He expected her to carry it out well, 'for of them to whom much is committed, much is required'.[28] She assured them she did not resent or mislike their bringing up the subject of the succession, realising it was part of the great care they had for her. However, she was 'determined in this so great and weighty a matter to defer mine answer till some other time' when she would be able to think more clearly about it. This is another example of her 'answers answerless', where she stated how clearly she understood their request and their need, how much she appreciated their concerns, and how she would address the matter some other time. She also returned to the theme of motherhood they had raised, adding 'And so I assure you all that though after my death you may have many stepdames, yet shall you never have any a more mother than I mean to be unto you all.'[29]

By avoiding the vagaries of biological motherhood, Elizabeth also avoided the potential embarrassment Mary had experienced when she had been unable to produce a child, the disastrous outcome for her mother when she had failed to produce a son, and the fatal result of pregnancy she had witnessed in two of her stepmothers, Jane Seymour and Katherine Parr.[30] Elizabeth was able to position herself as a mother to her realm in a metaphorical sense, promising to care for her subjects as a mother would care for her children. At the same time, she distanced herself from biological motherhood, avoiding the physical, social, and religious limitations that were associated with motherhood at the time. 'By transforming motherhood into a self-descriptive metaphor, Elizabeth escaped practical and cultural constraints while retaining the political benefits of an emergent maternal authority. Her figurative motherhood naturalized the anomaly of female rule and defined the bonds joining subject to queen as those of loving mutual responsibility.'[31]

From the beginning of her reign until around 1563, Elizabeth explicitly used the notion that she was 'mother of her country' in her speeches. She adopted a symbolic and political maternal stance, using this as one way to legitimise her authority as a female prince. One benefit of portraying herself as a mother is that it enabled Elizabeth to preserve her independence, something always important to the queen, while using the powerful images of wife and mother to describe her relationship with her country.[32]

Producing a son was the only way to continue a family line. This was the primary responsibility of all noble and royal women. Elizabeth was the final Tudor when she came to the throne, and the only way for the dynasty to continue would be through her children. Having a child would promote the peaceful transfer of power from her to her successor. It could also provide her a sense of security during her lifetime and reign, as the Tudors could not be overthrown by eliminating Elizabeth because her child would be ready to succeed her. Having a child would also put to rest the rumours that had been swirling at court, through the country, and abroad since Elizabeth had taken the throne that she was physically inadequate, less than a real woman, unable to bear children.

At the same time, there were also rumours that she had borne several illegitimate children to a variety of men. Sometimes these opposing rumours were even spread by the same people. It seems absurd, but it actually underscores the point – by refusing to take on the traditional role of wife and mother, Elizabeth set herself outside of what could be expected of her as a woman. In their discomfort, others tried to harm the queen by spreading tales that demonstrated how unnatural she was in terms of motherhood, either unable to bear children at all or unwilling to bear them in an honourable marriage.

Elizabeth imagined a unique relationship with her subjects as their virgin mother. She linked this to her standing as an anointed monarch and manifestation of God's will for England. In this way, she claimed a 'distinctive form of feminine personal government'. Her people, whom she loved as a mother would, 'were children expected to accept the limitations of their subordinate status with perfect submission'.[33]

The queen's way of speaking about her relationship with her people influenced public discourse. In early autumn of 1567, Henry Denham obtained a licence to print a book entitled *A Mery Metynge of Maydens in London*. Soon after, Thomas Hacket received permission to print a reply pamphlet.[34] The maydens' letter was part of a lively social debate and its language is similar to that of the queen. The maydens challenge the traditional patriarchal structure. They also state that the relationship between servant and mistress/master should be mutually supportive, profiting both parties. Their language about mutual cherishing 'mirrors Elizabeth's penchant for declaring her loving relationship to her loving people'. It seems that Elizabeth agreed that a household would thrive when the mistress and the serving women made the effort to 'understand, love, and respect each other'. Elizabeth felt the same about her role as monarch and her nation.[35]

Edmund Tilney published *A brief and pleasant discourse of duties in Marriage, called the Flower of Friendship* in 1568. Not surprisingly, this dialogue about marriage was dedicated to the queen. It was partly political in intent, as Tilney was seeking patronage from the queen or the Howards. Tilney showed himself to be supportive of Elizabeth as a female sovereign, refuting those who didn't accept her right to be head of the church or who argued that no woman should rule. His dialogue not only redefined a view of marriage to encourage a husband to win his wife's affection by treating her 'with loving care', it also provided a model 'for amicable, mutually rewarding relations between a female monarch and her husband, or a female monarch and her male subjects'. Elizabeth's council members and others had discovered the way to win her favour was not by correcting her or challenging her authority, but by respecting her and behaving with love.[36] Tilney was addressing the marriage question, and reinforced the queen's language as she expressed mutual love, care, and respect between herself as queen and her subjects.

'Over the course of her reign, Elizabeth focused on sustaining her proclaimed (political) love for her people as an integral part of her strategy for security.'[37] Elizabeth used love language to describe her maternal relationship with her subjects as an intimate and personal bond. In 1586, she spoke to parliament, describing all God's blessings upon her and her reign, including the preservation of her life. She went on, 'I do not thank God for that nor for all the rest so much as for this: that after twenty-eight years' reign I do not perceive any diminution of my subjects' good love and affection towards me. This is the thing I most joy in and that wherein I take my greatest comfort, and without which I would not desire to live.'[38] Later that month, she said,

> And now, as touching you, I must needs say and confess that there was never prince more bound to his people than I am to you all. I can but acknowledge our great love and exceeding care of me to be such as I shall never be able to require, having but one life, except I had as many lives as you all. But I will never forget it while I shall breathe.[39]

Two speeches late in Elizabeth's reign are compelling examples of her ongoing desire to woo her people.

The words the queen delivered at Tilbury in 1588 during the standoff with Philip's Armada are among the best-known of her reign. As well as stating firmly that she had 'the heart and stomach of a king, and a king of England too', to inspire her troops to fight, she made a commitment to give her all along with them. It was an echo of her statement to those who presented her with a purse at her coronation procession that if needed she would not hesitate to spend her blood in her people's defence. At Tilbury, she made the same promise, but this time during an actual military threat. She opened by explaining that although her being there made some worried for her safety, 'I assure you I do not desire to live to distrust my faithful and loving people.' Their queen was not afraid; it was tyrants who should fear because of the strength of the mutual love of the queen and her people. In the face of danger, the queen promised to 'live and die amongst you all' pledging her life in defence of her people. She said she was willing to 'lay down for my God, and for my kingdom, and my people, my honour and blood, even in the dust'.[40]

Of course, there was never any possibility that the queen would lead her troops into battle. But her speech, a contemporary record of which is in the British Library, is a carefully constructed expression of the queen's desired relationship with her people. She was counting on them to keep her safe. This was especially important in the 1570s and 1580s, as English Catholics had been encouraged by the pope to rise up in rebellion and put a Catholic monarch on the throne. Elizabeth was expressing her confidence in their love for her and promising to love and protect them in return. The queen's belief in her people was generally well placed. Yes, some of her subjects sought to return the country to Catholicism, some supported Mary, Queen of Scots, and some housed illegal priests and enemies. But the majority of the people did support Elizabeth, and she maintained her throne.

The years after the Armada glory were unhappy for Elizabeth. She lost Robert Dudley shortly after the victory, and over the next few years she lost beloved ladies-in-waiting and cherished councillors. She outlived friends and enemies, and her final favourite, as the Earl of Essex betrayed her. Still, she continued to court her people to the end. The truth was, it was still necessary for the queen to court her people and remind them and her enemies of the people's love for her. On the surface, after the Armada victory in 1588, Elizabeth's reign seemed more secure than ever. Mary, Queen of Scots, a long-time threat, was gone. The Spanish war continued, but it never loomed as ominous as it had in 1588. The iconography of Elizabeth as Virgin Queen, embodied in the *Armada Portrait* which presented the queen and the nation as unassailable, was firmly established. However, a closer look reveals that things were falling apart, right at the centre court – in the queen's own household.

In the final decade of her reign, one of Elizabeth's greatest challenges came not from foreign or religious threats but from the behaviour of her court. A monarch was expected to maintain the highest standards at court, and this was especially important for a queen. Women were considered to be more susceptible to the desires of the flesh, so a woman ruler was operating at a disadvantage already. For Elizabeth, despite her own positive feelings about her mother, she was haunted by Anne Boleyn's scandalous downfall and the campaign to present her as sexually voracious like her mother. Elizabeth had been sensitive to the dangers of physical desire since the days when she was 14 years old and the mention of Thomas Seymour had caused her to blush. She had desired Robert Dudley, but she tempered her feelings to keep her crown secure. She sacrificed her desires for duty. As she entered her final years, she found that those who surrounded her were unwilling to make the same sacrifices. The queen was no stranger to this: 'The strain between duty and desire was one that Elizabeth had known personally all too well, and in the queen's view, succumbing to emotion over obligation was not only a shameful weakness but also a threatening one.'[41] The sexual misdemeanours of the queen's court included unmarried women becoming pregnant, married men seducing other men's wives, and her own women and favourites like Ralegh and Essex secretly marrying. This created an image of an ageing woman who could scarcely control her own household, let alone the country.

Elizabeth took sexual indiscretions very seriously from early in her reign, and she punished those involved. She did advance marriages she believed were suitable, but if she had other plans for one member of the couple or didn't think them well matched or just didn't want a particularly close person to marry, she made her feelings clear. Often, the couples had no choice but to hide their love and their marriage. When Elizabeth found out, as she eventually did, her anger often sent one or both parties to prison. Elizabeth's behaviour was not unusual among monarchs; Philip of Spain had required his chief military commander to remain unmarried. When he married secretly, those who had helped the couple were arrested.[42] A ruler's lack of control over marriage in the court was believed to threaten future success and peace. In the final years of Elizabeth's reign, her own household threatened the queen's reputation. In 1591, Elizabeth's lack of control was on full display as half of the queen's maids of honour were dismissed for scandalous behaviour.[43]

Essex was at the heart of many of the scandals of the 1590s. He managed to maintain the queen's favour during much of that time. Relying on playing courtly love games with the queen, men like Essex and Ralegh distracted Elizabeth from their behaviour with other women with grand gestures of loyalty and excessive flattery. Elizabeth lost faith in Ralegh when he betrayed her by marrying. Essex betrayed her by giving into his desires for other women and his desire for greater power. Faced with Essex's rebellion and the loss of this last favourite, Elizabeth once more felt the strain between desire and duty. After all, Essex was her last connection with Dudley. Still, Essex was executed by her command in February 1601. Betrayed and alone, Elizabeth turned once more to her most consistent source of love: her people.

In her last speech to parliament, which has come to be known as her 'Golden Speech', Elizabeth made her final statement of love to her people. She recognised that her greatest fear was coming true: her councillors were turning from her to the rising sun, James of Scotland, who was to be the next king. She knew members of parliament were upset about the issue of royal monopolies, one of the ways the queen had rewarded loyalty to a few favourites. The practice was raising prices, and parliament wanted it stopped. The Ireland campaign was very expensive and seemed impossible to conclude to everyone's satisfaction. To reclaim her councillors' attention and affection, the queen decided to speak to parliament. Making a personal address would make the queen vulnerable, but she was not one to miss a chance to use her words to work her magic.

One of the challenges with this and any of the queen's speeches is that we don't know for certain exactly what she said. There are records, but they often don't agree. Elizabeth tended to write out a speech, make on the spot changes during delivery, and then approve a text for publication and distribution – meaning there are several versions of every speech, even when we have a draft in the queen's hand.[44] For this speech, looking at the different versions helps us to construct a sense of what the queen said and how she delivered her message. This speech represents the culmination of her efforts to present herself as ruler of her people, to ask for and generously receive their love, and to pledge her love in return.

Through her reign, Elizabeth's speeches are often reminiscent of dialogues based on giving messages to her subjects and receiving messages from them. Many speeches, especially in the final years of her reign, are about love.[45] The version of her final speech to parliament is held at the National Archives and was described as being 'taken verbatim in writing by A.B. as neere as he could possibly set it downe'. It included phrases such as:

> Mr Speaker, we perceive by you, whom we did constitute the mouth of our Lower House, how with even consent they are fallen into the due consideration of the precious gift of thankfulness, most usually least esteemed, where it is best deserved. And therefore we charge you tell them how acceptable such sacrifice is worthily received of a loving king.
>
> …
>
> And as nothing is more dear unto us than the loving consideration of our subjects' hearts…
>
> …
>
> We think ourselves most fortunately born under such a star, as we have been enabled by God's power to have saved you under our reign from foreign foes, from tyrants' rule, and from your own ruin; and do confess that we pass not so much to be a queen as to be a queen of such subjects for whom (God is witness, without boast or vaunt) we would willingly lose our life ere see such to perish.
>
> …

Thus we commend us to your constant faith, and yourselves to your best fortunes.[46]

The version held at the Bodleian Library in Oxford comes from the journal of Hayward Townshend, MP for Bishop's Castle, Shropshire, who was in attendance at the meeting. He reported that after the queen delivered the remarks that include the statements above, she stood and said more. In addition to details about monopolies and grants, the queen continued to emphasise the mutual love that existed between her and her people:

> I take it exceedingly gratefully from them, because it gives us to know that no respects or interests had moved them other than the minds they bear to suffer no diminution of our honour and our subjects' love unto us, the zeal of which affection tending to ease my people and knit their hearts unto me, I embrace with a princely care. For above all earthly treasures I esteem my people's love, more than which I desire not to merit.
>
> …
>
> For myself, I was never so much enticed with the glorious name of a king or royal authority of a queen as delighted that God hath made me His instrument to maintain His truth and glory, and to defend this kingdom (as I said) from peril, dishonour, tyranny, and oppression. There will never queen sit in my seat with more zeal to my country, care for my subjects, and that will sooner with willingness venture her life for your good and safety, than myself. For it is not my desire to live nor reign longer than my life and reign shall be for your good. And though you have had and may have many princes more mighty and wise sitting in this seat yet you never had or shall have any that will be more careful and loving.[47]

The other significant version of this speech is the one held at Huntington Library in California. It was found among the papers of Sir Thomas Egerton, lord keeper of the Great Seal and Master of the Rolls during the last years of Elizabeth's reign. It contained similar sentiments:

> The zeal of which affection tending to ease my people and knit their hearts unto us, I embrace with a princely care. For above all

> earthly treasure, I esteem my people's love, more than which I desire not to merit. And God that gave me here to sit, and set me over you, knows that I never respected myself, but as your good was concerned in me. Yet what dangers, what practices, what perils I have passed. Some (if not all) of you know. But it is God that hath delivered. And in my governing, this I have ever had the grace to use – to set the Last Judgment Day before mine eyes and so to rule as I shall be judged, and to answer before a higher Judge, to whose judgment seat I do appeal that never thought was cherished in my heart that tended not to my people's good.
>
> …
>
> And though you have had and may have many mightier and wiser princes sitting in this seat, yet you never had nor shall have any that will love you better.[48]

Her message emphasised the queen's love, put her love above all over monarchs who have come before or will come after, and (I believe) included an unspoken request: 'I love you best, now you love me best too.'

In this last address to parliament, and by extension to her people, the queen addressed the matters at hand but focused on her constant message, the one that started at the beginning of her reign: she loved her people and relied on their love for her. 'To the very end she remained in full control of her situation, allowing no man to rule her, and, by her own special brand of magic, keeping the goodwill of all her husbands – the people of England.'[49] When Elizabeth began her reign, Feria stated that everything depended on the husband she chose. Instead, everything depended on Elizabeth herself. She chose a partner: her people. In a life and reign marked by disappointment, tragedy, and betrayal, the lasting relationship and the one true partner Elizabeth had was England.

Notes

Chapter 1

1. Hunt, *Drama Coronation*, p. 51.
2. Lipscomb, 'Thomas Seymour'.
3. Somerset, p. 18.
4. Elizabeth I, CW, p. 28.
5. Lipscomb, 'Thomas Seymour'.
6. Solly.
7. Elizabeth I, CW, p. 17, note 3.
8. TNA PRO, State Papers Domestic, Edward VI 10/2 fol.84c.
9. Elizabeth I, CW, pp. 17–19.
10. Ibid.
11. Elizabeth I, CW, p. 26.
12. Lipscomb, 'Thomas Seymour'.
13. Doran, *Monarchy*, p. 14 and Somerset, pp. 23–24.
14. Castor, 'Unfathomable'.
15. Somerset, p. 24.
16. Lipscomb, 'Thomas Seymour'.
17. Somerset, p. 24.
18. Ibid.
19. Ibid.
20. Lipscomb, 'Thomas Seymour'.
21. Mumby, pp. 69–70.
22. CSP Spain, 28 Nov.
23. Doran, *Monarchy*, p. 16.
24. CSP Spain, 17 Dec. 1553.
25. Doran, *Monarchy*, p. 18.

Chapter 2

1. Kantorowicz, p. 7.
2. Ibid.
3. TNA SP12/1 f. 12.
4. Levin, *The Reign*, p. 242.
5. Levin, 'Mary I'.
6. Weil, p. 90.
7. Neale, vol. 1, p. 136.
8. Axton, p. 12.
9. Ibid.
10. Ibid., p. 14.
11. Ibid., p. 16.
12. Plowden, *Commentaries*, pp. 212–213.
13. Axton, p. 17.
14. Neale, vol. 2, p. 119.
15. BL Harley 6798, f.87.
16. Weil, p. 93.
17. Levin, *Heart and Stomach*, p. 131.
18. CSP Spain IV, 131.
19. Levin, *Heart and Stomach*, p. 140.
20. Ibid., p. 143.
21. Camden, *Elizabeth*, p. 416.
22. BL Harley 6798, f.87.
23. Levin, p. 145.
24. Green, p. 421.
25. Ibid., pp. 422–423.
26. Loomis, p. 12.
27. CSP Venice, 12 Apr. 1603.
28. Loomis, pp. 24–26.
29. Manningham, p. 148.
30. Nichols, p. 613.
31. Loomis, p. 98.
32. Ibid., pp. 98–99.
33. Nichols, p. 613.
34. Loomis, pp. 98–100.
35. Ibid., p. 100.
36. Ibid., pp. 109–110.
37. Frye, p. 24.

Chapter 3

1. Neale, p. 15.
2. SOR, vol 3, pp. 471, 673, 955.
3. Levine, 'Parliamentary Title', p. 122.
4. Holinshed, *Chronicles*, p. 1066.
5. Richards, p. 903–904.

6. Levine, 'Parliamentary Title', p. 126.
7. CSP, Spain 28 Nov. 1553.
8. SOR, vol. 4, p. 358.
9. Levine, 'Parliamentary Title', p. 123.
10. Heisch, *Rhetoric*, p. 33.
11. Neale, vol. 1, pp. 41–47.
12. CSP Venice, Feb. 1559.
13. Levin, *Reign*, p. 51.
14. Camden, pp. 25–26.
15. Ibid.
16. Camden, pp. 26–27.
17. Elizabeth I, CW, pp. 57–58.
18. Neale, p. 50.
19. Bell, *Voice*, p. 49.
20. Somerset, p. 153.
21. Levin, *Reign*, p. 51.
22. Elizabeth I, CW, p. 73.
23. Ibid., p. 74.
24. Ibid., p. 82.
25. Ibid., pp. 85–86.
26. BL Landsdowne MS 94/15.
27. Bell, p. 107.
28. Levin, *Reign*, p. 52.
29. Neale, vol. 1, p. 131.
30. Ibid., p. 136.
31. Bell, p. 111.
32. Elizabeth, CW, pp. 92–93.
33. Bell, p. 111.
34. Elizabeth I, CW, p. 95.
35. Ibid., p. 96.
36. Bell, p. 113.
37. Elizabeth I, CW, pp. 97–98.
38. CSP Foreign, 14 Jul. 1561.
39. Neale, p. 144.
40. Somerset, p. 97.
41. Elizabeth I, CW, pp. 95–96, 101.
42. Neale, vol. 1, pp. 163–164.
43. Ibid., p. 170.
44. BL, MS Cotton Charter IV.38.
45. Neale, vol. 1, pp. 175–176.
46. CSP Spain, 5 Jan. 1567.
47. Bell, p. 115.

Chapter 4

1. CSP Spain, 21 Nov. 1558.
2. Whitelock, *Queen's Bed*, p. 8.
3. CSP Spain, 21 Nov. 1558.
4. McLaren, pp. 259–260.
5. Ibid., p. 267.
6. Ibid., p. 274.
7. CSP Foreign, 31 Aug. 1559.
8. CSP Scotland, 19 Jun. 1560.
9. Ibid., 3 Aug. 1560.
10. Act of Uniformity, 1559.
11. Watkins, *Marriage a la Mode*, p. 89.
12. Ibid., p. 88.
13. Taylor-Smither, 'Psychological', p. 61.
14. Levin, *Reign*, p. 75.
15. Somerset, p. 107.
16. CSP Spain, 21 Nov. 1558.
17. Ibid., 14 Dec. 1558.
18. Ibid., 10 Jan. 1559.
19. Ibid.
20. Somerset, p. 109.
21. CSP Spain, 12 Feb. 1559.
22. Ibid., 19 Mar. 1559.
23. Somerset, p. 108.
24. Levin, *Reign*, p. 74.
25. Somerset, p. 90.
26. CSP Foreign, 1 Oct 1559.
27. Levin, *Reign*, p. 6.
28. Somerset, p. 118.
29. CSP Foreign 1 Oct. 1559.
30. Levin, *Reign*, p. 74.
31. SCP Foreign, 1 Oct. 1559.
32. Levin, *Reign*, p. 74.
33. TNA SP 10/11 f.74.
34. Levin, *Reign*, p. 74.
35. CSP Spain, 4 Apr. 1559.
36. Levine, p. 76.
37. Somerset, p. 109.
38. Ibid., p. 118.
39. CSP Spain, 30 May 1559.
40. Levin, *Heart and Stomach*, p. 49.
41. Somerset, pp. 180–181.
42. CSP Spain, 23 Jul. 1565.
43. Ibid.
44. Levin, *Heart and Stomach*, p. 51.
45. Ibid., 52.

Chapter 5

1. CSP Venice, 6 Feb. 1559.
2. Ibid., 8 Jan. 1559.
3. Somerset, p. 110.

4. Levin, *Reign*, p. 75.
5. CSP Venice, 6 Feb. 1559.
6. Levin, *Reign*, p. 75.
7. CSP Spain, 10 May 1559.
8. Ibid., 30 May 1559.
9. Somerset, p. 110.
10. Levin, *Reign*, p. 75.
11. www.historyofparliamentonline.org
12. Hibbert, p. 158.
13. CSP Spain, 23 Jul. 1565.
14. Ibid., 5 Nov. 1565.
15. Whitelock, p. 106.
16. Naunton, p. 44.
17. Nicolas, p. 5.
18. BL, 'The Book of the Courtier'.
19. Waddington, p. 105.
20. Doran, Circle, p. 144.
21. Levin, *Reign*, p. 85.
22. Doran, *Circle*, p. 144.
23. Waddington, p. 109.
24. Levin, *Reign*, p. 85.
25. Whitelock, p. 150.
26. Nicolas, *Memoirs*, p. 23.
27. Irish, *Review*, p. 362.
28. Paul, *History Extra.*
29. Borman, 'Great Love'.
30. Doran, *Circle*, p. 113.
31. Ibid.
32. Castor, p. 47.
33. Whitelock, p. 37.
34. Borman, 'Great Love'.
35. CSP Spain, 29 Oct. 1559.
36. Ibid., 13 Nov. 1559.
37. Ibid., 11 Sep. 1560.
38. Metraux, *How Did.*
39. Doran, *Circle*, p. 113.
40. Doran, *Monarchy*, p. 42.
41. Metraux, *How Did.*
42. TNA KB 9/1073/f.80.
43. Metraux, *How Did.*
44. Herman.
45. CSP Spain, 22 Jan. 1561.
46. Somerset, p. 132.
47. CSP Foreign, 10 Oct. 1560.
48. Borman, 'Great Love'.
49. CSP Foreign, 15 Jan. 1561.
50. Somerset, p. 134.
51. CSP Spain, 23 Feb. 1561.
52. Somerset, p. 135.
53. CSP Spain, 17 Mar. 1561.
54. Somerset, p. 135.
55. CSP Foreign, 6 May 1561.
56. Ibid., 8 May 1561.
57. Naunton, *Elizabeth's Favourites*, p. 9.

Chapter 6

1. Elizabeth I, CW, pp. 198–200.
2. Bell, p. 2.
3. Heisch, pp. 31–33.
4. Neale, vol. 2, p. 432.
5. Heisch, p. 34.
6. Ross, p. 59.
7. Bell, p. 4.
8. Heisch, p. 31.
9. Elizabeth I, CW, p. 59.
10. King, pp. 34–36.
11. BL Lansdowne MS 94.
12. Elizabeth I, CW, pp. 57–58.
13. Ibid., p. 58.
14. Ibid., p. 59.
15. Neale, vol. 1, p. 49.
16. Levin, *Heart and Stomach*, p. 44.
17. Hibbert, pp. 116–117.
18. Gawronski, p. iii; Ross, p. 76.
19. Bell, p. 5.
20. Gawronski, p. 1.
21. CSP Spain, 14 Dec. 1558.
22. CSP Spain, 12 Feb. 1559.
23. Ibid., 29 Feb. 1550.
24. Ibid., 19 Mar. 1559.
25. Ibid., 11 Apr. 1559.
26. Gawronski, p. 4.
27. CSP Spain, 27 Jul. 1559.
28. Ibid., 14 Oct. 1559.
29. Ibid., 16 Oct. 1559.
30. Ibid., 21 Jan. 1560.
31. Ibid., 3 Feb. 1560.
32. Gawronski, pp. 11–12.
33. CSP Spain, 19 Feb. 1560.
34. Levin, *Heart and Stomach*, p. 45.
35. Neale, vol. 1, p. 142.
36. *Much Ado About Nothing*, II.1, 447.
37. Bell, p. 8.

38. Ibid., p. 5.
39. Ibid., pp. 27–28.

Chapter 7

1. Williams, pp. 23–25.
2. Ibid., p. 88.
3. CSP Spain, 10 Jan. 1559.
4. Ibid., 8 May 1559.
5. Ibid., 30 May 1559.
6. Ibid., 2 Oct. 1559.
7. Ibid., 20 Oct. 1559.
8. Ibid., 5 Nov. 1559.
9. Ibid., 13 Nov. 1559.
10. CSP Foreign, 31 Dec. 1560.
11. Williams, p. 101.
12. Ibid., pp. 113–114.
13. Ibid., pp. 115–117.
14. CSP Scotland, 16 Mar. 1563.
15. Ibid., 30 Apr. 1563.
16. Williams, p. 136.
17. Doran, *Monarchy*, p. 73.
18. Bassett, p. 107.
19. Doran, *Monarchy*, pp. 73–74.
20. CSP Spain, 27 Mar. 1565.
21. Doran, *Monarchy*, p. 74.
22. CSP Spain, 26 Apr. 1565.
23. Levin, *Heart and Stomach*, p. 51.
24. Doran, *Monarchy*, p. 80.
25. CSP Spain, 23 Jul. 1565.
26. Doran, *Monarchy*, p. 81.
27. Williams, pp. 137–139.
28. Duncan, pp. 151–153.
29. CSP Spain, 28 Mar. 1563.
30. Ibid.
31. CSP Scotland, 20 Aug. 1563.
32. Ibid., 21 Feb. 1564.
33. Ibid., 30 Mar. 1564.
34. Somerset, p. 163.
35. Elizabeth I, CW, p. 115.
36. Whitelock, p. 83.
37. Ibid., p. 85.
38. Dunn, pp. 271–272.
39. Somerset, p. 167.
40. CSP, Scotland, 16 Dec. 1564.
41. Somerset, p. 168.
42. Williams, p. 143.
43. Ibid., p. 144.
44. Wormald, p. 147.
45. Williams, p. 146.

Chapter 8

1. DeMolen, p. 212.
2. Hackett, p. 15.
3. Rider.
4. *Gorboduc*, lines 1773–1775.
5. *Gorboduc*, line 1689.
6. James and Walker, p. 109.
7. Doran, 'Juno', pp. 261–262.
8. Ibid., p. 264.
9. Nichols, *Progresses*, vol. 1, p. 212.
10. Doran, 'Juno', p. 264.
11. Ibid., p. 265.
12. Meares.
13. Tinniswood, pp. 15–16.
14. Read, p. 25.
15. Paul, p. 313.
16. Nash, pp. 81–82.
17. Sharpe, pp. 320, 430.
18. Goldring, *History Extra*.
19. Morris, p. 241.
20. Goldring, *History Extra*.
21. Paul, p. 305.
22. Frye, p. 63.
23. Gristwood, p. 242.
24. Colthorpe, pp. 23–25; the Folger's Day by Day account gives a detailed description of each day of the progress, summarising Langham's and Gascoigne's contemporary accounts.
25. Ellis, p. 4.
26. Nichols, vol. 1, p. 494.
27. Colthorpe, p. 27.
28. Goldring, Kenilworth, pp. 368–370.
29. Frye, pp. 63–65.
30. Colthorpe, p. 29.
31. Nichols, vol. 1, p. 459.
32. Frye, p. 65.
33. Ibid., p. 92.
34. Siobhan and Collins, p. 82.
35. Goldring, 'Portraiture', p. 164.
36. Goldring, *History Extra*.

37. Goldring, 'Portraiture', p. 180.
38. Ellis, p. 15.
39. Colthorpe, p. 31.
40. Nichols, vol. 1, p. 502.
41. Nash, p. 95.
42. Nichols, vol. 1, p. 514.
43. Nash, p. 95.
44. Folger, p. 31.
45. Nichols, vol. 1, p. 459.
46. Nash, p. 96.
47. Goldring, 'Portraiture', p. 172; Frye, p. 92.
48. Ellis, p. 11.
49. CSP Domestic, 29 Jul. 1575.
50. Folger, p. 32.
51. Nash, p. 98.
52. Frye, p. 69.
53. Colthorpe, p. 34.
54. Nichols, vol. 1, p. 515.
55. Colthorpe, p. 34.
56. Nichols, p. 522.
57. Ibid., p. 481.

Chapter 9

1. Borman, *Private Lives*, p. 287.
2. Paranque, pp. 130–131.
3. CSP Foreign, 14 Apr. 1564.
4. Borman, *Private Lives*, p. 290.
5. Jenkins, p. 129.
6. Elizabeth I, CW, p. 98.
7. Paranque, p. 138.
8. TNA MPF 1/366/1.
9. Paranque, pp. 143–144.
10. CSP Foreign, Jul. 1569.
11. Paranque, pp. 144–145.
12. Robinson, p. 51.
13. Digges, p. 55.
14. Robinson, p. 51.
15. Paranque, p. 153.
16. Ibid., p 155.
17. CSP Foreign, 6 Jun. 1571.
18. Digges, p. 65.
19. CSP Foreign, 2 Sep. 1571.
20. Somerset, p. 272.
21. Levin, *Heart and Stomach*, p. 59.
22. Paranque, p. 170.
23. Budiansky, pp. 15–16.
24. CSP Spain, 30 Aug. 1572.
25. Whitelock, p. 145.
26. CSP Spain, 12 Oct 1572.
27. Ibid., 12 Oct. 1572.
28. Whitehead, p. 149.
29. Paranque, p. 180.
30. Doran, *Monarchy*, p. 154.
31. Camden, *History*, 227.
32. CSP Venice, 26 Oct. 1558.
33. Doran, *Monarchy*, p. 156.
34. Ibid., pp. 156–157.
35. Whitehead, pp. 174–175.
36. Doran, *Monarchy*, pp. 158–159.
37. Whitehead, p. 175.
38. Paranque, p. 187.
39. CSP Spain, Aug. 1579.
40. Whitehead, p. 181.
41. CSP Venice, 4 Dec. 1579.
42. Whitehead, p. 182.
43. Paranque, pp. 191–192.
44. Whitehead, p. 183.
45. Paranque, 194.
46. Ibid., pp. 195–197.
47. CSP Spain, 24 Nov. 1581.
48. Paranque, pp. 198–199.
49. Elizabeth I, CW, pp. 302–303.

Chapter 10

1. Nicholas, p. 26.
2. Moore, p. 622.
3. Kelly, pp. 98–100.
4. Ibid., pp. 158–165.
5. Moore, p. 631.
6. Ives, p. 19.
7. Boleyn in Norton, pp. 33–34.
8. Ives, pp. 21–22.
9. Henry VIII, *Freedonia*, pp. ii–vii.
10. Ives, p. 325.
11. Heale, p. 299.
12. Borman, *Anne & Elizabeth*, p. 87.
13. CSP Spain, 28 Nov. 1553.
14. Borman, *Anne & Elizabeth*, p. 184.
15. Elizabeth I, CW, p. 170.
16. Harrington, pp. 136–137.
17. Bates, p. vi.

18. Gristwood, *Tudors in Love*, p. 303.
19. Bates., p. vii.
20. Ibid., pp. 1–2.
21. Ibid., p. 19.
22. Ibid., pp. 88–89.
23. Gristwood, *Tudors in Love*, p. 316.
24. Ibid., p. 300.
25. Ibid., p. 327.
26. Ibid., pp. 348–349.

Chapter 11

1. Doran, *Elizabeth and Favourites*, pp. 157–158.
2. Somerset, p. 331.
3. Folger, p. 8.
4. Somerset, pp. 331–333.
5. Doran, *Circle*, p. 160.
6. www.rmg.co.uk.
7. Castor, *Insecurity*, p. 86.
8. Penry, pp. 259–265.
9. Doran, *Favourites*, p. 167.
10. CSP Domestic, Feb. 17, 1594.
11. Penry, p. 263.
12. Elizabeth I, CW, pp. 307–309.
13. www.npg.org.uk.
14. Castor, *Insecurity*, pp. 88–89.
15. Alford, *Politicians*.
16. Bates, *Rhetoric*, pp. 76–83.
17. Borman, *Private Lives*, p. 365.
18. Cavendish.
19. Somerset, *Elizabeth*, pp. 531–543.
20. Castor, *Insecurity*, p. 92.
21. Borman, *Private Lives*, p. 365.
22. Whitelock, *Queen's Bed*, pp. 317–318.
23. Doran, *Circle*, p. 198.
24. Whitelock, *Queen's Bed*, p. 321.
25. Doran, *Favourites*, p. 189.
26. Whitelock, *Queen's Bed*, p. 321.

Chapter 12

1. Holinshed, p. 16.
2. Elizabeth I, CW, p. 58.
3. 'The Passage'.
4. Richards, p. 146.
5. Borman, *Anne & Elizabeth*, p. 151.
6. Richards, p. 152.
7. Hilton, pp. 121–122.
8. Richards, pp. 135–139.
9. CSP Spain, 25 Nov. 1558.
10. CSP Venice, 30 May 1559.
11. www.rct.uk.
12. Plowden, p. 83.
13. Elizabeth I, CW, p. 59.
14. Camden, *History Elizabeth*, p. 27.
15. King, pp. 35–36.
16. Richards, p. 133.
17. Ibid., pp. 133–134.
18. 'Passage'; language modernised.
19. Bell, p. 122.
20. Ibid., p. 50.
21. Ibid., p. 142.
22. Elizabeth, CW, p. 57.
23. Coch, 423–424.
24. Somerset, pp. 96–97.
25. Neale, vol. 1, p. 49.
26. Coch, p. 448.
27. Elizabeth I, CW, p. 73–74.
28. TNA 12/27 f. 143r-144v and alluding to Luke 12:48 in the Great Bible.
29. The manuscript copy in the British Library reads 'a more natural mother'; CW, p. 72, note 7.
30. Levin, *Heart and Stomach*, p. 65.
31. Coch, p. 425.
32. Leah Marcus in Coch, p. 424.
33. Coch, p. 446.
34. Fehrenbach, p. 285.
35. Bell, pp. 122–123.
36. Ibid., pp. 132–134.
37. Richards, p. 16.
38. Elizabeth, CW, p. 186.
39. Ibid., p. 198.
40. BL, Harley 6798, f.87.
41. Hilton, p. 304.
42. Hammer, pp. 81–82.
43. Hilton, p. 308.
44. Rose, p. 1077.
45. Ibid., p. 1081.
46. TNA SP 12/282 ff. 137r-141v.
47. Elizabeth I, CW, pp. 339–340.
48. Ibid., 341–342.
49. Plowden, A., p. 197.

Bibliography

Abbreviations
BL (British Library)
CSP (Calendar of State Papers)
CW (Collected Works)
LP (Letters and Papers)
SOR (Statues of the Realm)
TNA (The National Archives UK)

Primary Sources

Act of Uniformity, Public Act, 1 Elizabeth 1, d.2, 1559. Parliamentary Archives, HL/PO/PU/1/1558/1Eliz1n2.

Ascham, *The Scholemaster* (written 1563–68). Birmingham: 1870.

'Bird's-eye view of the Darnley murder scene, February 1567'. The National Archives, UK, MPF 1/366/1.

BL, 'Elizabeth I's manuscript draft of a speech on her marriage, 1563'. www.bl.uk/collection-items/elizabeth-is-manuscript-draft-of-a-speech-on-her-marriage-1563

BL, 'The Book of the Courtier, 1588'. www.bl.uk/collection-items/the-book-of-the-courtier-1588

Boleyn, Anne. Letters, dispatches, and chronicles, as gathered in *The Anne Boleyn Papers*. Elizabeth Norton, ed. Gloucestershire: 2013.

Camden, William. *The History of the Most Renowned and Victorious Princess Elizabeth, Late Queen of England*. London: 1675.

'Coroner's report into the death of Amy Robsart, August 1561 (translation from the original Latin)'. TNA KB 9/1073/f.80.

Digges, Dudly. *The Compleat Ambassador or Two Treaties of the Intended Marriage of Queen Elizabeth*. London: 1655.

Elizabeth I, *Collected Works*. Leah S. Marcus, Janet Mueller, and Mary Beth Rose, eds. Chicago: 2000.

Elizabeth's draft version of speech dissolving Parliament, BL MS Cotton Charter, IV.38 (2).

'Elizabeth's first speech, Hatfield, 20 November 1558'. TNA SP 12/1 f. 12.

Elizabeth I 'Tilbury Speech'. July 1588. BL Harley 6798, f. 87.

Elizabeth I to King Eric SIX of Sweden, 25 February 1560. TNA SP 70/11 f. 74.

Minutes of a second speech of the Queen to her Parliament, by the Lord Keeper, concerning her marriage and the succession to the crown, 1563. In her own handwriting. BL Lansdowne MS, 94/15.

'The Passage of our most Dread Sovereign Lady Queen Elizabeth through the city of London to Westminster the day before her coronation', 1558. mapoflondon.uvic.ca https://mapoflondon.uvic.ca/QMPS1.htm

Secondary Sources

Alford, Stephen. 'Politicians and Statesmen II: William Cecil, Lord Burghley (1520–98)', *State Papers Online 1509–1714*, Cengage Learning EMEA Ltd., 2007. www.gale.com/intl/essays/stephen-alford-politicians-statesmen-ii-william-cecil-lord-burghley

Alford, Stephen. *Burghley: William Cecil at the Court of Elizabeth I*. Yale University Press: 2008.

Bassnett, Susan. *Elizabeth I: A Feminist Perspective*. Oxford: 1997.

Bates, Catherine. 'Courtship and Courtliness: Studies in Elizabethan Courtly Language and Literature'. Balliol College, Oxford: 1988.

Bates, Catherine. *The Rhetoric of Courtship in Elizabethan Language and Literature*. Cambridge: 1992.

Bell, Ilona. *Elizabeth I: The Voice of a Monarch*. New York: 2010.

Borman, Tracy. 'Robert Dudley: Queen Elizabeth I's great love', *History Extra*, 26 June 2020. www.historyextra.com/period/elizabethan/robert-dudley-queen-elizabeth-is-great-love

Borman, Tracy. *Anne Boleyn & Elizabeth I: The Mother and Daughter Who Changed History*. London: 2023.

Borman, Tracy. *Private Lives of the Tudors*. London: reprinted 2017.

Budiansky, Stephen. *Her Majesty's Spymaster: Elizabeth I, Francis Walsingham, and the Birth of Modern Espionage*. London: 2006.

Castor, Helen. 'Elizabeth I's personality: the unfathomable queen'. *History Extra*. March 2020.

Castor, Helen. *Elizabeth I: A Study in Insecurity*. Penguin Random House UK: 2018.

Catherine Loomis, *Death of Elizabeth I: Remembering and Reconstructing the Virgin Queen*. London: 2010.

Cavendish, Richard. 'The Execution of the Earl of Essex'. *History Today*, Vol. 51, Issue 2, February 2001. www.historytoday.com/archive/months-past/execution-earl-essex

Clarke, Siobhan, and Linda Collins. *Gloriana: Elizabeth I and the Art of Queenship*. London: 2022.

Coch, Christine. 'Mother of my Contreye: Elizabeth I and Tudor Constructions of Motherhood'. *English Literary Renaissance*, Vol. 26, No. 3 Monarchs (Autumn 1996), p. 243–250.

Colthorpe, Marion E. 'The Elizabethan Court Day by Day'. Folger Shakespeare Library, 2017. https://folgerpedia.folger.edu/The_Elizabethan_Court_Day_by_Day

DeMolen, Richard L. 'Richard Mulcaster and Elizabethan Pageantry'. *Studies in English Literature, 1500–1900*, Vol. 14, No. 2, Elizabethan and Jacobean Drama (Spring 1974), p. 209–221.

Doran, Susan. 'Juno versus Diana: The Treatment of Elizabeth's I's Marriage in Plays and Entertainments, 1561–1581', *The Historical Journal*, Vol. 38, No. 2 (Jun. 1995), pp. 257–274.

Doran, Susan. *Monarchy and Matrimony: The Courtships of Elizabeth I*. London: 2002.

Doran, Susan. 'Elizabeth I and Her Favourites: The Case of Walter Ralegh'. *Elizabeth I and the 'Sovereign Arts'* (Stump, Shenk, Levin, eds). Tempe, AZ: 2011.

Doran, Susan. *Elizabeth I and Her Circle*. Oxford University Press: 2018.
Duncan, Thomas. 'The Relations of Mary Stuart with William Maitland of Lethington'. *The Scottish Historical Review*, Vol. 5, No. 18 (Jan 1908), pp. 151–160).
Dunn, Jane. *Elizabeth & Mary: Cousins, Rivals, Queens*. London: 2005.
Ellis, Jim. 'Kenilworth, King Arthur, and the Memory of Empire'. *English Literary Renaissance*, Vol. 43, No. 1 (Winter 2013), pp. 3–29.
Ellis, Sian. 'Elizabeth I slept here – a look at the Queen's summer progreses'. *British Heritage*, 21 Feb 2023. https://britishheritage.com/history/queen-elizabeth-i-slept-here
Fehrenback, R. J. 'A Letter sent by Maydens of London (1567)'. *English Literary Renaissance*, Vol. 14, No. 3, Autumn 1984, pp. 285.
Folger Shakespeare Library, 'The Elizabethan Court Day by Day – Anecdotes and Miscellaneous'. https://folgerpedia.folger.edu/mediawiki/media/images_pedia_folgerpedia_mw/0/08/ECDbD_Anecdotes_Miscellaneous.pdf
Frescoln, Katharine P. 'A Letter from Thomas Randolph to the Earl of Leicester'. *Huntingdon Library Quarterly*, Vol. 37, No. 1 (1973), pp. 83–88.
Frye, Susan. *Elizabeth I: The Competition for Representation*. Oxford: 1993
Gawronski, Sarah M. '"I Neither Omit Aught, Nor Have I Omitted Aught": Embodying a Sovereign – The Resident Ambassador in the Elizabethan Court, 1558–1560'. *All Graduate Theses and Dissertations*. (2011). https://digitalcommons.usu.edu/edt/1062
Goldring, Elizabeth. 'Gascoigne and Kenilworth: The Production, Reception, and Afterlife of The Princely Pleasures'. *English Literary Renaissance*, Vol. 44, No. 3 (Autumn 2014), pp. 363–387.
Goldring, Elizabeth. 'Princely pleasures at Kenilworth: Robert Dudley's three-week marriage proposal to Elizabeth I'. *History Extra*, 22 June 2018. www.historyextra.com/period/elizabethan/princely-pleasures-at-kenilworth-robert-dudleys-three-week-marriage-proposal-to-elizabeth-i
Gristwood, Sarah. *Elizabeth and Leicester: The Truth about the Virgin Queen and the Man She Loved*. London: 2008.
Gristwood, Sarah. *The Tudors in Love: Passion and Politics in the Age of England's Most Famous Dynasty*. London: 2021.
Hackett, Helen. 'Anne Boleyn's Legacy to Elizabeth I'. University College London. https://discovery.ucl.ac.uk/id/eprint/1569378/1/Hackett.%20Anne%20Boleyn.Book.Chapter.pdf
Hammer, Paul. 'Sex and the Virgin Queen: Aristocratic Concupiscence and the Court of Elizabeth I'. *The Sixteenth Century Journal*, Vol. 31, no. 1, Special Edition (Spring 200), pp. 77–97.
Harrington, John. *Nugae Antiquae: Being a Miscellaneous Collection of Original Papers in Prose and Verse; Written in the Reigns of Henry VIII, Queen Mary, Elizabeth, King James, etc*. London: 1779.
Harrison, Helene. *Elizabethan Rebellions*. London: 2023.
Heale, Elizabeth. 'Women and the Courtly Love Lyric: The Devonshire MS'. *The Modern Language Review*, Vol. 90, No. 2 (Apr 1995), pp. 296–313.
Heisch, Allison. 'Queen Elizabeth I: Parliamentary Rhetoric and the Exercise of Power'. *Signs*, Vol. 1, No. 1 (Autumn, 1975), pp. 31–55.
'Henry VIII, Letters to Anne Boleyn', in *Love Letters of Henry VIII to Anne Boleyn*, Fredonia Books. Amsterdam: 2006 (reprinted from 1906 edition).

Herman, Eleanor. 'Hidden Poisons of the Royal Court'. JSTOR Daily, 30 May 2018. https://daily.jstor.org/hidden-poisons-of-the-royal-court

Hibbert, Christopher. *The Virgin Queen: Elizabeth I, Genius of the Golden Age*. New York: 1991.

Hilton, Lisa. *Elizabeth: Renaissance Prince*. New York: 2014.

History of Parliament online. www.historyofparliamentonline.org/volume/1509-1558/member/heneage-thomas-1532-95

Holinshed, Raphael. *Chronicles of England, Scotland, and Ireland, Vol III, England*. London: 1808.

Hunt, Alice. *The Drama of Coronation: Medieval Ceremony in Early Modern England*. Cambridge: 2008.

Ives, Eric. *The Life and Death of Anne Boleyn*. Oxford: 2004.

James, Henry and Greg Walker. 'The Politics of Gorboduc'. *The English Historical Review*, Vol. 110, No. 435 (Feb 1995), pp. 109–121.

Jenkins, Elizabeth. *Elizabeth the Great*. New York: 1958.

Kantorowicz, Ernst. *The King's Two Bodies: A Study in Medieval Political Theology*. Princeton University Press: 1957.

Kelly, Amy. *Eleanor of Aquitaine and the Four Kings*. Harvard College: 1950.

King, John. 'Queen Elizabeth I: Representations of the Virgin Queen'. *Renaissance Quarterly*, Vol. 43, No. 1 (Spring 1990), pp. 30–74.

Levin, Carole. 'Mary I's phantom pregnancy'. *History Extra*, 12 May 2015. www.historyextra.com/period/tudor/mary-is-phantom-pregnancy

Levin, Carole. *The Reign and Life of Queen Elizabeth I*. Palgrave: 2002.

Levin, Carole. *Heart and Stomach of a King*. University of Pennsylvania Press: 1994.

Levine, Mortimer. 'A Parliamentary Title to the Crown in Tudor England'. *Huntington Library Quarterly*, Vol. 25, No. 2 (Feb 1962), pp. 121–127. www.jstor.org/stable/3816567

Lipscomb, Suzannah. 'Did Thomas Seymour sexually abuse the teenage Princess Elizabeth?' *History Extra*, 12 June 2022. www.historyextra.com/period/tudor/did-thomas-seymour-sexually-abuse-the-teenage-princess-elizabeth

Loomis, Catherine. *The Death of Elizabeth I: Remembering and Reconstructing the Virgin Queen*. Hargrave: 2010.

Elizabeth I: Collected Works. Marcus, Lea S. Janet Mueller, and Mary Beth Rose, eds. Chicago: 2000.

McLaren, Anne. 'The Quest for a King: Gender, Marriage, and Succession in Elizabethan England'. *Journal of British Studies*, Vol. 41, No. 3 (July 2002), pp. 259–290.

Meares, Hadley. 'Why Royal Guests Have Always Been a Royal Pain'. 1 April 2020. www.history.com/news/elizabeth-i-royal-progress-expense

Metraux, Julia. 'How Did Amy Robsart Die?' *JSTOR Daily*, 2 February 2023. https://daily.jstor.org/how-did-amy-robsart-die

Moore, John C. '"Courtly Love": A Problem of Terminology'. *Journal of the History of Ideas*, Vol. 40, No. 4 (Oct-Dec 1979), pp. 621–632.

Morris, Robert. 'I was never more in love with an olde howse nor never newe worke could be better bestowed'. *The Antiquaries Journal*, Vol. 89, pp. 241–305.

Mumby, Frank Arthur. *The Girlhood of Queen Elizabeth, a Narrative in Contemporary Letters*. London: 1909.

Nash, Ilana. 'A Subject without Subjection: Robert Dudley, Earl of Leicester, and The Princely Pleasures at Kenelworth Castle'. *Comitatus: A Journal of Medieval and Renaissance Studies*, Vol. 25(1), 1994, pp. 81–102.

Naunton, Robert. *Fragmenta Regalia: Memoirs of Elizabeth, Her Court and Favourites*. London: 1724 (orig. 1641).

Neale, John Ernest. *Elizabeth I and her Parliaments* (vol. 1). New York: 1958. (orig. 1900).

Neale, John Ernest. *Elizabeth I and her Parliaments* (vol. 2). New York: 1958 (orig. 1900).

Nichols, John. *Progresses and Public Processions of Queen Elizabeth* (vols. 1–3). London: 1823.

Nicolas, Harris. *Memoirs of the Life and Times of Sir Christopher Hatton*. London: 1847.

Norton, Elizabeth. *The Temptation of Elizabeth Tudor*. London: 2016.

Nortone, Thomas and Thomas Sackvyle. *The Tragedie of Gorboduc*. London: 1565.

Paranque, Estelle. *Blood, Fire, and Gold: The Story of Elizabeth I and Catherine de Medici*. London: 2022.

Paul, Joanne. 'The Dudley dynasty: the family behind the Tudors'. *History Extra*, 9 May 2022. www.historyextra.com/period/tudor/dudley-robert-edmund-dynasty-family-behind-tudors

Paul, Joanne. *The House of Dudley*. London: 2022.

Plowden, Alison. *Marriage with My Kingdom*. London: 2004.

Plowden, Edmund. *The commentaries of Reports of Edmund Plowden, of the Middle-Temple, Esq. an Apprentice of the Common Law, in Two Parts, Part 1*. London: 1816.

Princess Elizabeth to Dowager Queen Katherine Parr, c. June 1548 (SP10/2 f. 84c).

Read, Conyers. 'A Letter from Robert, Earl of Leicester, to a Lady'. *The Huntingdon Library Bulletin*, No. 9 (Apr. 1936), pp. 15–26.

'Review of Sir Christopher Hatton, Queen Elizabeth's Favorite'. *Irish Historical Studies*, Vol. 5, Issue 20, September 1947, pp. 362–363.

Ricer, Clare. *Gorboduc, or the Tragedy of Ferrex and Porrox*. Inner Temple. www.innertemple.org.uk/who-we-are/history/historical-articles/gorboduc-or-the-tragedy-of-ferrex-and-porrox

Richards, Judith M. 'Love and a Female Monarch: The Case of Elizabeth Tudor'. *Journal of British Studies*, Vol. 38, Nos. 2 (Apr 1999), pp. 133–60.

Richards, Judith M. 'Mary Tudor as "Sole Quene"?: Gendering Tudor Monarchy'. *The Historical Journal*, Vol. 40, No. 4 (Dec. 1997), 895–924.

Robinson, A. M. F. 'Queen Elizabeth and the Valois Princes'. *The English Historical Review*, Vol. 2, No. 5 (Jan. 1887), pp. 40–77.

Rose, Mary Beth. 'The Gendering of Authority in the Public Speeches of Elizabeth I'. *PML*, Vol. 115, No. 5 (Oct 2000), pp. 1077–1082.

Ross, David. 'The Essex Rebellion, 1601'. *Britain Express*. www.britainexpress.com/History/tudor/essex-rebellion.htm

Ross, Josephine. *The Men Who Would be King: The Courtships of Queen Elizabeth*. New York: 2012 (orig. 2005).

Shakespeare, William. *Much Ado About Nothing*. Published in *Mr William Shakespeare's Comedies, Histories, and Tragedies*. London: 1623.

Sharp, Janet. '"I My Self": Queen Elizabeth I's Oration at Tilbury Camp'. *Sixteenth Century Journal*, XXVII/2 (1997), pp. 421–445. www.jstor.org/stable/2543451

Sharpe, Kevin. *Selling the Tudor Monarchy: Authority and Image in Sixteenth-Century England*. London: 2009.

Solly, Meilan. 'The Royal Scandal that Rocked Elizabeth I's Teenager Years'. *Smithsonian Magazine*, 9 June 2002. www.smithsonianmag.com/history/royal-scandal-rocked-elizabeth-i-teenage-years-starz-180980199
Somerset, Anne. *Elizabeth I.* New York: 1991.
Statues of the Realm (SOR), from original records and manuscripts, reprinted London: 1963.
Taylor-Smither, Larissa J. 'Elizabeth I: A Psychological Profile'. *The Sixteenth Century Journal*, Vol. 15, No. 1 (Spring 1984), pp. 47–72.
Tinniswood, Adrian. *Behind the Throne: A Domestic History of the British Royal Household.* New York: 2018.
Waddington, Raymond B. 'Elizabeth I and the Order of the Garter'. *Sixteenth Century Journal*, Vol. 24, No. 1 (Spring, 1993). pp. 97–113.
Warnicke, Retha. 'Elizabeth I and Mary Stewart: Two British Queens Regnant: A Gender Comparison: Rational or Romantic'. *Elizabeth I and the 'Sovereign Arts'* (Stump, Shenk, Levin, eds). Tempe, AZ: 2011.
Watkins, John. 'Marriage a la Mode', in *Queens & Power in Medieval and Early Modern England*, pp. 76–97. Lincoln: 2009.
Weil, Rachel. 'Royal Flesh, Gender, and the Construction of Monarchy', in *The Body of the Queen: Gender and Rule in the Courtly World, 1500–2000*. Berghahn Books: 2006.
Whitelock, Anna. *The Queen's Bed: An Intimate History of Elizabeth's Court.* New York: 2013.
Williams, Kate. *Rival Queens: The Betrayal of Mary Queen of Scots*. London: 2018.
Williams, Penry. 'Court and Polity Under Elizabeth I'. *John Rylands University Library*, pp. 259–286. www.escholar.manchester.ac.uk/api/datastream?publicationPid=uk-ac-man-scw:1m1692&datastreamId=POST-PEER-REVIEW-PUBLISHERS-DOCUMENT.PDF
Williams, Penry. *Court and Polity Under Elizabeth I.* Manchester: 1983.
Wormald, Jenny. *Mary Queen of Scots*. London: 1988.

Index